NYSTCE
060

CST
Students with Disabilities
Teacher Certification Exam

By: Sharon Wynne, M.S.

XAMonline, INC.
Boston

To obtain permission(s) to use the material from this work for any purpose including workshops or seminars, please submit a written request to:

XAMonline, Inc.
25 First Street, Suite 106
Cambridge, MA 02141
Toll Free: 1-800-509-4128
Email: info@xamonline.com
Web: www.xamonline.com
Fax: 617-583-5552

Library of Congress Cataloging-in-Publication Data
Wynne, Sharon A.
   CST Students with Disabilities 060: Teacher Certification / Sharon A. Wynne. -3rd ed.
   ISBN 978-1-60787-157-6
   1. CST Students with Disabilities 060.   2. Study Guides.   3. NYSTCE
   4. Teachers' Certification & Licensure.   5. Careers

Disclaimer:

The opinions expressed in this publication are the sole works of XAMonline and were created independently from the National Education Association, Educational Testing Service, or any State Department of Education, National Evaluation Systems or other testing affiliates.

Between the time of publication and printing, state specific standards as well as testing formats and website information may change that is not included in part or in whole within this product. Sample test questions are developed by XAMonline and reflect similar content as on real tests; however, they are not former tests. XAMonline assembles content that aligns with state standards but makes no claims nor guarantees teacher candidates a passing score. Numerical scores are determined by testing companies such as NES or ETS and then are compared with individual state standards. A passing score varies from state to state.

Printed in the United States of America   œ-1
NYSTCE: CST Students with Disabilities 060
ISBN: 978-1-60787-157-6

Table of Contents

ACKNOWLEDGEMENTS
Special Education

Recognizing the hard work in the production of our study guides, we would like to thank those involved. The credentials and experience fulfilling the making of this study guide, aided by the professionalism and insight of those who expressed the subject mastery in specialized fields, is valued and appreciated by XAMonline. It results in a product that upholds the integrity and pride represented by modern educators who bear the name **TEACHER**.

Providers of foundational material

Founding authors 1996	Kathy Schinerman
	Roberta Ramsey
Pre-flight editorial review	Paul Sutliff
Pre-flight construction :	Brittany Good
	Harris Brooks Hughes
Authors 2006	Paul Sutliff
	Beatrice Jordan
	Marisha Tapera
	Kathy Gibson
	Twya Lavender
	Susan Wagner
Sample Test Rationale	Sidney Findley

XAMonline Editorial and Production acknowledgements

Project Manager	Sharon Wynne
Project Coordinator	Twya Lavender
Series Editor	Mary Collins
Editorial Assistant	Virginia Finnerty
Marketing Manager	John Wynne
Marketing support	Maria Ciampa
Cover design	Brian Messenger
Sales	Justin Dooley
Production Editor	David Aronson
Typist	Julian German
Manufacturing	Chris Morning/Midland Press
E-Books	Kristy Gipson/Lightningsource
Cover Administrator	Jenna Hamilton

INTRODUCTION

This one-volume study guide was designed for professionals preparing to take a teacher competency test in special education or in any field in which the principles of special education are a part of the test content. Objectives specific to the field of special education were obtained from state departments of education and federal territories and dependencies across the nation. Educators preparing to take tests in the various areas of special education should find the manual helpful, because the objectives and the scope of the discussions concerning each objective cover a wide range of the field.

The study guide offers many benefits to the person faced with the necessity of attaining a qualifying score on a competency test in special education. A large number of source materials must be covered in order to study the conceptual knowledge reflected by the objectives listed in each state study guide. These objectives encompass the major content of the special education field. These "objectives" may be called "competencies" in some states. These terms are synonymous and refer to an item of professional knowledge to be mastered.

Many prominent textbooks used by pre-service teacher training programs nationwide were researched for the content of this book. Other important resources (e.g., books, journal articles, and media) were included in the discussions about the objectives. The compilation of this research alleviates the heavy workload an individual teacher would take on attempting to research the vast body of professional material when preparing for an examination This one-volume study guide summarizes the current knowledge and accepted concepts of the field of special education, thus reducing the massive amount of material that would need to be assembled if one did not have it between a single set of covers.

The book is organized into sections by major topics. These topics often correspond to course titles and textbooks in pre-service teacher training programs. The objectives and discussions about them are the main content within each section. The discussions feature important information from textbooks in the field of special education, reported in a synthesized and summarized form. Specific references have been given for charts and quoted materials, which are included to enhance understanding of conceptual discussions. Complete reference citations can be located in the reference listings.

Finally, questions specific to the discussion of each objective have been written to help determine if the reader understands that material. Immediately following the sample test is a list of the test questions with the correct responses and a rationale for why these responses are correct. Test questions are written as teaching mechanisms and appear in the style and format of those used on tests by any state.

Though this manual is comprehensive, it in no way purports to contain all the research and applied techniques in every area of exceptionality. Research generates new applications, and continuing in-service education is a requirement for all special education professionals. This manual gives the reader a one-volume summary of the fundamentals known and practiced at the time of writing.

ABOUT THE TEST

The New York Teacher Certification Examinations are criterion-referenced and objective-based tests, developed using textbooks; New York State learning standards and curriculum guides; teacher education curricula; and certification standards. The purpose of the tests is to identify teachers who demonstrate an appropriate level of knowledge and skills that are important to teach effectively in New York State public schools.

The exam assesses the test taker's knowledge and skills of the following areas:

Subarea I. Understanding and Evaluating Students with Disabilities (Skills 1.01-5.08)
Subarea II. Promoting Student Learning and Development in a Collaborative Learning Community (Skill 6.01-13.08)
Subarea III. Working in a Collaborative Professional Environment (14.01-17.06)
Subarea IV. Promoting Student Learning and Development in a Collaborative Learning Community: Constructed-Response Assignment (objectives from Subarea II will be used to create the constructed-response assignment)

There are approximately 90 multiple-choice test questions and one constructed-response (written) assignment. The majority of the test is Subarea II (42 percent of the test). Subarea I is 27 percent of the test. Subarea III is 21 percent of the test. Subarea IV is 10 percent of the test.

Passing Score

An examinee's multiple-choice score and scores on any constructed-response assignments are added together to obtain the total test score. A score of 220 is the minimum passing score for each test. An examinee with a total test score of 220 or above passes the test.

Location, Cost, and Registration

At the time of the creation of this study guide, the cost of taking this test was $88. Registration can occur by phone, mail, or Internet. The sites and dates of testing are located on www.nystce.nesinc.com. Please refer to this site for more specific information about registration.

GREAT STUDY AND TESTING TIPS!

What to study in order to prepare for the subject assessments is the focus of this study guide, but equally important is *how* you study. You can increase your chances of truly mastering the information by taking some simple but effective steps.

1. Some foods aid the learning process. Foods such as milk, nuts, seeds, rice, and oats help your study efforts by releasing natural memory enhancers called CCKs (*cholecystokinin*) composed of *tryptopha*n, *choline*, and *phenylalanine*. All of these chemicals enhance the neurotransmitters associated with memory. Before studying, try a light, protein-rich meal of eggs, turkey, or fish. All of these foods release the memory enhancing chemicals. The better the connections, the more you comprehend.

Likewise, before you take a test, stick to a light snack of energy boosting and relaxing foods. A glass of milk, a piece of fruit, or some peanuts all release various memory-boosting chemicals and help you to relax and focus on the subject at hand.

2. Learn to take great notes. A byproduct of our modern culture is that we have grown accustomed to getting our information in short doses (i.e., TV news sound bites or USA Today-style newspaper articles).

Consequently, we've subconsciously trained ourselves to assimilate information better in neat little packages. If your notes are scrawled all over the paper, it fragments the flow of the information. Strive for clarity. Newspapers use a standard format to achieve clarity. Your notes can be much clearer through use of proper formatting. A very effective format is called the *"Cornell Method."* Take a sheet of loose-leaf lined notebook paper and draw a line all the way down the paper about 1-2" from the left-hand edge. Draw another line across the width of the paper about 1-2" up from the bottom. Repeat this process on the reverse side of the page.

Look at the result. You have ample room for notes, a left hand margin for special emphasis items or inserting supplementary data from the textbook, a large area at the bottom for a brief summary, and a little rectangular space for just about anything you want.

3. Get the concept, then the details. Too often we focus on the details and don't gain an understanding of the concept. However, if you memorize only dates, places, or names, you may well miss the whole point of the subject. A key way to understand things is to put them in your own words. If you are working from a textbook, automatically summarize each paragraph in your mind. If you are outlining text, don't simply copy the author's words. Rephrase them in your own words. You remember your own thoughts and words much better than someone else's, and subconsciously tend to associate the important details with the core concepts.

4. Ask Why? Pull apart written material paragraph by paragraph and don't forget the captions under the illustrations. Example: f the heading is "Stream Erosion," flip it around to read "Why do streams erode?" Then answer the question.

If you train your mind to think in a series of questions and answers, not only will you learn more, but you will also feel less anxiety during the test because you will be used to answering questions.

5. Read for reinforcement and future needs. Even if you only have 10 minutes, put your notes or a book in your hand. Your mind is similar to a computer; you have to input data in order to have it processed. By reading, you are creating the neural connections for future retrieval. The more times you read something, the more you reinforce the ideas you've learned. Even if you don't fully understand something on the first pass, your mind stores much of the material for later recall.

6. Relax to learn, so go into exile. Our bodies respond to an inner clock called biorhythms. Burning the midnight oil works well for some people, but not everyone. If possible, set aside a particular place to study that is free of distractions. Shut off the television, cell phone, and pager and exile your friends and family during your study period.

If you really are bothered by silence, try background music. Light classical music at a low volume has been shown to be particularly effective in aiding concentration. Music that evokes pleasant emotions without lyrics is suggested. Try just about anything by Mozart. It relaxes you.

7. Use arrows, not highlighters. At best, it's difficult to read a page full of yellow, pink, blue, and green streaks. Try staring at a neon sign for a while and you'll soon see the point—the horde of colors obscures the message. A quick note, a brief dash of color, an underline, or an arrow pointing to a particular passage is much clearer than a horde of highlighted words.

8. Budget your study time. Although you shouldn't ignore any of the material, allocate your available study time in the same ratio that topics might appear on the test.

TESTING TIPS:

1. Get smart, play dumb. *Don't read anything into the question.* Don't make an assumption that the test writer is looking for something other than what is explicitly asked. Stick to the question as written and don't read extra things into it.

2. Read the question and all the choices *twice* before answering the question. You may miss something if you don't carefully read and then re-read both the question and the answers. If you really don't have a clue as to the right answer, leave it blank on the first time through. Go on to the other questions, because they may provide a clue as to how to answer the skipped questions. If, later on, you still can't answer the skipped ones . . . ***Guess.*** The only penalty for guessing is that you *might* get it wrong. Only one thing is certain; if you don't put anything down, you will get it wrong!

3. Turn the question into a statement. Look at the way the questions are worded. The syntax of the question usually provides a clue. Does it seem more familiar as a statement than as a question? Does it sound strange? By turning a question into a statement, you may be able to spot whether an answer sounds right, and it may also trigger memories of material you have read.

4. Look for hidden clues. It's actually very difficult to compose multiple-foil (multiple-choice) questions without giving away part of the answer in the options presented. In most multiple-choice questions you can often readily eliminate one or two of the potential answers. This leaves you with only two real possibilities and automatically you have a fifty percent chance of answering the question correctly.

5. Trust your instincts. For every fact that you have read, you subconsciously retain something of that knowledge. On questions that you aren't really certain about, go with your basic instincts. **Your first impression of how to answer a question is usually correct.**

6. Mark your answers directly on the test booklet. Don't bother trying to fill in the optical scan sheet on the first pass through the test. However, be very careful not to mismark your answers when you eventually transcribe them to the scan sheet.

7. Watch the clock! You have a set amount of time to answer the questions. Don't get bogged down trying to answer a single question at the expense of ten questions you can more readily answer.

SUBAREA I.   UNDERSTANDING AND EVALUATING STUDENTS WITH DISABILITIES

COMPETENCY 0001   UNDERSTAND CHARACTERISTICS OF INDIVIDUALS WITH DISABILITIES

Skill 1.01   Identify types, etiologies, and characteristics of various disabilities

THE CAUSATION AND PREVENTION OF A DISABILITY

The characteristics and effects of learning disabilities are extremely diverse and the wide range of possibilities makes it almost impossible to pinpoint the exact cause in all cases. Listed below are some factors that can contribute to the development of a disability.

Problems in Fetal Brain Development: Depending upon when during pregnancy a disruption in brain development occurs, the result can range from a mild learning disorder to widespread disabilities or mental retardation.

Genetic Factors: Some learning disabilities (e.g., deficits in phoneme awareness, Dyslexia) do appear to have a genetic link. However, a parent's learning disability can take a slightly different form in the child. As a result, it is unlikely that specific learning disorders are directly inherited.

Tobacco, Alcohol, and Other Drug Use: Many drugs taken by the mother pass directly to the fetus during pregnancy. Research shows that a mother's usage of cigarettes, alcohol, or other drugs during pregnancy may have damaging effects on the unborn child. Mothers who smoke or drink alcohol during pregnancy are more likely to have babies with lower birth weights who are more at risk for learning disorders. Heavy alcohol use during pregnancy has been linked to fetal alcohol syndrome, a condition resulting in intellectual impairment, hyperactivity, and certain physical defects.

Problems During Pregnancy or Delivery: Complications during pregnancy can also cause learning disabilities. For example, the mother's immune system can react to the fetus and attack it as if it were an infection. This type of problem appears to cause newly-formed brain cells to settle in the wrong part of the brain. Cerebral Palsy is often the result of damage that occurs during pregnancy or delivery.

Toxins in the Environment: There are certain environmental toxins that may lead to learning disabilities. Cadmium is used in making some steel products; it can get into the soil and then into the foods we eat. Lead was once common in paint and gasoline and is still present in some water pipes.

Children with cancer who have been treated with chemotherapy or radiation at an early age can also develop learning disabilities. This is very prevalent in children with brain tumors who received radiation to the skull.

Characteristics of Emotionally Disturbed Children

Behavioral expectations vary from setting to setting; for example, it is acceptable to yell on the football field, but not when the teacher is explaining a lesson to the class. Different cultures have their own standards of behavior, further complicating the question of what constitutes a behavioral problem. Individuals also have personal opinions and standards for what is tolerable and what is not. Some behavioral problems are openly expressed; others are inwardly directed and not very obvious. As a result of these factors, the terms behavioral disorder and emotional disturbance have become almost interchangeable.

Although emotional and behavioral disorders come in many forms, studies of children with emotional and behavioral disorders indicate that children with these disorders share some general characteristics such as those listed below.

Lower academic performance: While some emotionally disturbed children have above average IQ scores, the majority are behind their peers in measures of intelligence and academic achievement. Most score in the "slow learner" or "mildly mentally retarded" range on IQ tests, averaging about 90. Many have learning problems that exacerbate or result from acting out or "giving-up" behaviors. As the child enters secondary school, the gap between the child and his or her non-disabled peers widens until he or she may be as many as two to four years behind in reading and/or math skills by high school. Children with severe degrees of impairment can be difficult to evaluate.

Social skills deficits: Children with emotional disturbances can appear uncooperative, selfish in dealing with others, unaware of what to do in social situations, or ignorant of the consequences of their actions. Difficulties with social interaction are typical of children diagnosed with emotional disabilities.

Disruptive classroom behaviors: Often, emotionally disturbed children display behavior disruptive to the classroom setting (e.g., often leaving their seat sor running around the room; hitting, fighting, or disturbing their classmates; stealing or destroying property; being defiant and noncompliant). They do not always follow directions and often do not complete assignments.

Aggressive behaviors: Aggressive children often fight or instigate their peers to strike back at them. Aggressiveness may also take the form of vandalism or destruction of property. Aggressive children also often engage in verbal abuse.

Delinquency: As children with emotional disabilities enter adolescence, they may become involved in socialized aggression (e.g., gang membership) and delinquency. Delinquency is a legal term, rather than a medical one; it describes truancy and actions that would be criminal if they were committed by adults. Not every delinquent is classified as emotionally disturbed, but children with behavioral and emotional disorders are especially at risk for becoming delinquent.

Withdrawn behaviors: Children who manifest withdrawn behaviors may consistently act in an immature fashion or prefer to play with younger children. They may daydream or complain of being sick in order to "escape." They may also cry, cling to the teacher, ignore those who attempt to interact with them, or suffer from fears or depression.

Gender factors: Many more boys than girls are identified with emotional and behavioral problems, especially hyperactivity and attention deficit disorder, autism, childhood psychosis, and problems with under-control (i.e., aggression, socialized aggression). Girls, on the other hand, have more problems with over-control (i.e., withdrawal and phobias). Boys are much more likely than girls to have problems with mental retardation and language and learning disabilities.

Age Characteristics: When they enter adolescence, girls tend to experience affective or emotional disorders such as anorexia, depression, bulimia, and anxiety at twice the rate of boys. This rate of incidence mirrors the prevalence pattern in adults.

Diagnosing Emotional and Behavioral Disorders

While almost all children at times exhibit behaviors that are aggressive, withdrawn, or otherwise inappropriate, the IDEA definition of serious emotional disturbance focuses on behaviors that persist over time, are intense, and impair a child's ability to function in society. The behaviors must not be caused by temporary stressful situations or other causes (e.g., depression over the death of a grandparent or anger over the parents' impending divorce). In order for a child to be considered seriously emotionally disturbed, he or she must exhibit one or more of the following characteristics over a *long period of time* and to a *marked degree* that *adversely affects* the child's educational performance.

- Inability to learn that cannot be explained by intellectual, sensory, or health factors
- Inability to maintain satisfactory interpersonal relationships
- Inappropriate types of behaviors
- General pervasive mood of unhappiness or depression
- Physical symptoms or fears associated with personal or school problems

Schizophrenic and psychotic children are covered under this definition. These disorders often require intensive treatment beyond the scope of the regular classroom setting.

Social maladjustment by itself does not satisfy this definition unless it is accompanied by one of the other conditions of an emotional disorder.

The diagnostic categories and definitions used to classify mental disorders come from the American Psychiatric Association's publication, *Diagnostic and Statistical Manual of Mental Disorders* (DSM-IV-TR), a handbook used by psychiatrists and psychologists. The DSM-IV-TR is a multi-axial classification system consisting of dimensions (axes) coded along with the psychiatric diagnosis. Details about this system and definitions of specific psychiatric disorders can be found at: *http://allpsych.com/disorders/dsm.html*

While the DSM-IV-TR diagnosis is one way of diagnosing serious emotional disturbance, there are other ways of classifying the various forms in which behavioral disorders manifest themselves. The following table summarizes some of these classifications.

Externalizing Behaviors	Internalizing Behaviors
Aggressive behaviors expressed outwardly toward others	Withdrawing behaviors that are directed inward
Hyperactivity, persistent aggression, irritating behaviors that are impulsive and distractible	Social withdrawal
Examples: hitting, cursing, stealing, arson, cruelty to animals, hyperactivity	Depression, fears, phobias, elective mutism, withdrawal, anorexia and bulimia

Well-known instruments used to assess children's behavior have their own categories (scales) to classify behaviors.

- The Walker Problem Identification Checklist includes measures for acting out, withdrawal, distractibility, atypical peer relations, and immaturity.
- Burks Behavior Rating Scale (BBRS) includes measures for such things as excessive self-blame and anxiety, sense of persecution, dependency and withdrawal, lack of impulse control, aggressiveness, excessive suffering, and poor sense of self or reality.
- Devereux's Behavior Rating Scale is used for adolescents and has measures similar to those of the BBRS, with the addition of sexual factors, bizarreness of speech, actions or cognition, and domineering/sadism.
- The Revised Behavior Problem Checklist has major scales and minor scales for conduct disorders, aggression, attention deficits, anxiety, withdrawal, hyperactivity, and psychotic behavior.

Disturbance may also be categorized in degrees: mild, moderate, or severe. The degree of disturbance affects the type and degree of interventions and services required by emotionally handicapped students. Degree of disturbance must also be considered when determining the least restrictive environment and the services needed for free, appropriate education for these students.

An example of a set of criteria for determining the degree of disturbance is the one developed by P. L. Newcomer (1993, p. 139):

CRITERIA	DEGREE OF DISTURBANCE		
	Mild	**Moderate**	**Severe**
Precipitating events	Highly stressful	Moderately stressful	Not stressful
Destructiveness	Not destructive	Occasionally destructive	Usually destructive
Maturational appropriateness	Behavior typical for age	Some behavior atypical for age	Behavior too young or too old
Personal functioning	Cares for own needs	Usually cares for own needs	Unable to care for own needs
Social functioning	Usually able to relate to others	Usually unable to relate to others	Unable to relate to others
Reality index	Usually sees events as they are	Occasionally sees events as they are	Little contact with reality
Insight index	Aware of behavior	Usually aware of behavior	Usually not aware of behavior
Conscious control	Usually can control behavior	Occasionally can control behavior	Little control over behavior
Social responsiveness	Usually acts appropriately	Occasionally acts appropriately	Rarely acts appropriately

Family characteristics

Having a child with an emotional or behavioral disorder does not automatically mean that the child's family is dysfunctional. However, there are family factors that can create or contribute to the development of behavioral disorders and emotional disturbance. These include:

- Abuse and neglect
- Lack of appropriate supervision
- Lax, punitive, and/or lack of discipline
- High rates of negative types of interaction among family members
- Lack of parental concern and interest
- Negative adult role models
- Lack of proper health care and/or nutrition
- Disruption in the family

Children with mild learning, intellectual, and behavioral disabilities

Some characteristics of students with mild learning and behavioral disabilities are as follows:

- Lack of interest in schoolwork
- Preference for concrete rather than abstract lessons
- Weak listening skills
- Low achievement
- Limited verbal and/or writing skills
- Better response to active rather than passive learning tasks
- Areas of talent or ability often overlooked by teachers
- Preference for special help in regular classrooms
- Higher dropout rate than regular education students
- Achievement in accordance with teacher expectations
- Requirements for modification in classroom instruction
- Easily distracted

Characteristics typical of learning disabilities:

- Hyperactivity: a rate of motor activity higher than normal
- Perceptual difficulties: visual, auditory, and perceptual problems
- Perceptual-motor impairments: poor integration of visual and motor systems, often affecting fine motor coordination
- Disorders of memory and thinking: memory deficits, trouble with problem-solving, poor concept formation and association, poor awareness of own metacognitive skills (learning strategies)
- Impulsiveness: acts before considering consequences, poor impulse control often followed by remorselessness
- Academic problems in reading, math, writing, or spelling; significant discrepancies in ability levels

Characteristics of individuals with mental retardation or intellectual disabilities:

- IQ of 70 or below
- Delayed or deficient mastery of adaptive behaviors
- Limited cognitive ability; delayed academic achievement, particularly in language-related subjects
- Deficits in memory that often relate to poor initial perception or to the inability to apply stored information to relevant situations
- Impaired formulation of learning strategies
- Difficulty in attending to relevant aspects of stimuli; slowness in reaction time or in employing alternate strategies

Characteristics of individuals with autism:

This exceptionality appears very early in childhood. Six common features of autism are:

- **Apparent sensory deficit:** The child may appear not to see, hear, or react to a stimulus, but may react in an extreme fashion to a seemingly insignificant stimulus.
- **Severe affect isolation:** The child does not respond to the usual signs of affection, such as smiles and hugs.
- **Self-stimulation:** Stereotyped behavior takes the form of repeated or ritualistic actions that make no sense to others, such as hand flapping, rocking, staring at objects, or humming the same sounds for hours at a time.
- **Tantrums and self-injurious behavior (SIB):** Autistic children may bite themselves, pull their hair, bang their heads, or hit themselves. They can throw severe tantrums and direct aggression and destructive behavior toward others.
- **Echolalia (also known as "parrot talk"):** The autistic child may repeat what he or she hears or respond to others by repeating what was said to him or her. Alternatively, the child may simply not speak at all.
- **Severe deficits in behavior and self-care skills:** Autistic children may behave like children much younger than themselves.

Skill 1.02   Demonstrating familiarity with similarities and differences among individuals with disabilities, including levels of severity and multiple disabilities

(See Skill 2.02 for IDEA definitions of specific disability terms.)
Eligibility for special education services is based on a student having one of the IDEA defined disabilities (or a combination thereof) **and** demonstrating educational need through professional evaluation.

Seldom does a student with a disability fall into only one of the categories listed in IDEA 2004. For example, a student with a hearing impairment might also have a specific learning disability, or a student on the autism spectrum might also demonstrate language impairment. In fact, language impairment is inherent in autism. Sometimes the eligibility is defined as multiple disabilities (with one listed as a primary eligibility on the IEP and the others listed as secondary). Sometimes there are overlapping needs that are not necessarily listed as a secondary disability.

Teachers of special education students should be aware of the similarities between areas of disabilities, as well as the differences.

Students with disabilities (in all areas) may demonstrate difficulties with social skills. For a student with a hearing impairment, social skills may be difficult because the student does not hear conversations. An autistic student might be unaware of the social cues given with voice, facial expression, and body language. Each of these students needs social skill instruction, but in a different way.

Students with disabilities in all areas may demonstrate difficulties in academic performance. A student with mental retardation will need special instruction across all areas of academics, while a student with a learning disability may need assistance in only one or two subject areas.

Students with disabilities may demonstrate difficulties with independence or self-help skills. A student with a visual impairment may need specific mobility training, while a student with a specific learning disability may need a checklist to help manage materials and assignments.

Special education teachers should be aware that although students across disabilities might demonstrate difficulties in similar ways, the causes could be very different and the treatment will be different as well.

Additionally, special education teachers should be aware that each area of disability has a range of involvement. Some students might have minimal disability and require no services. Others might need only a few accommodations and have a 504 plan. Some might need an IEP that outlines a specific special education program that could be implemented in an inclusion/resource program, in a self-contained program, or in a residential setting. For example, a student with ADD might be able to participate in the regular education program with a 504 plan that outlines a checklist system to keep the student organized and with additional communication between school and home. Other students with ADD might need instruction in a smaller group with fewer distractions; they might be better served in a resource room.

Because of the unique needs of each child, such programs are documented in the child's IEP (individualized education plan). Please refer to Competency 5 for more on IEP development and use.

Skill 1.03   Analyzing similarities and differences (e.g., cognitive, physical, language, social, emotional) among individuals with and without disabilities

Normality in child behavior is influenced by society's attitudes and cultural beliefs about what is normal for children. For example, the motto for the Victorian era was that "children should be seen and not heard." However, criteria for what is "normal" must involve consideration of these questions:

- **Is the behavior age appropriate?** An occasional tantrum might be expected for a toddler, but is not typical for a high school student.
- **Is the behavior pathological in itself?** Drug or alcohol use is harmful to children, regardless of how many engage in it.
- **How persistent is the problem?** A kindergarten student may be initially afraid to go to school. However, if the fear continues into the first or second grade, then the problem could be considered persistent.
- **How severe is the behavior?** Self-injurious, cruel, and extremely destructive behaviors are examples of behaviors that require intervention.
- **How often does the behavior occur?** An occasional tantrum in a young child or a brief mood of depression in an adolescent is not considered problematic. However, if the behavior occurs frequently, the behavior is not characteristic of normal child development.
- **Do several problem behaviors occur as a group?** Clusters of behaviors, especially severe behaviors that occur together, might be indicative of a serious problem, such as schizophrenia.

Certain stages of child development have their own sets of problems, and it should be kept in mind that short-term undesirable behaviors can and will occur during these stages. Child development is also a continuum, and children might manifest these problem behaviors somewhat earlier or later than their peers.

Among children between six and seventeen years of age who receive special services, the categories of specific learning disabilities and emotional disturbance are the most clearly defined. These exceptional students are very much like their peers without disabilities. The main difference is that they have intellectual, emotional, behavioral, or physical deficits that significantly interfere with their ability to benefit from education.

You may also refer to Skill 1.01 for more information about the general characteristics of students with disabilities.

Skill 1.04   Demonstrating knowledge of typical, delayed, and disordered communication patterns among individuals with disabilities

DEVELOPMENT OF LANGUAGE

Language consists of several components, each of which follows a sequence of development. Brown and colleagues were the first to describe language as a function of developmental stages rather than of age (Reid, 1988, p. 44). He developed a formula to group the mean length of utterances (sentences) into stages. Counting the number of morphemes per 100 utterances, one can calculate a mean length of utterance, MLU. Total number of morphemes/100 = MLU (e.g., 180/100 = 1.8).

The following table summarizes Brown's findings about MLU and language development:

Stage	MLU	Developmental Features
L	1.5-2.0	14 basic morphemes (e.g., in, on, articles, possessives)
LI	2.0-2.5	Beginning of pronoun use, auxiliary verbs
LII	2.5-3.0	Language forms approximate adult forms; beginning of questions and negative statements
Lv	3.0-3.5	Use of complex (embedded) sentences
V	3.5-4.0	Use of compound sentences

COMPONENTS OF LANGUAGE

Language learning includes of five components. Children progress through developmental stages in each component.

Phonology

Phonology is the system of rules about sounds and sound combinations in a language. A phoneme is the smallest unit of sound that combines with other sounds to make words. A phoneme, by itself, doesn't necessarily have meaning (exceptions would be words consisting of only one phoneme, such as 'a' and 'I'). Usually, it must be combined with other phonemes. Problems in phonology may be manifested as developmental delays, such as a delay in acquiring consonants, or as reception problems, such as misinterpreting words because a different consonant was substituted.

Morphology

Morphemes are the smallest units of language that convey meaning. Morphemes are root words or free morphemes that can stand alone (e.g., walk) and affixes (e.g., –ed, –s, –ing) that must be combined with other morphemes to make a word. Morphology refers to the system of rules for combining morphemes into words. Generally, students with problems in this area might not use inflectional endings in their words, might not be consistent in their use of certain morphemes, and might be delayed in learning certain morphemes, such as irregular past tenses.

Syntax

Syntax rules, commonly known as grammar, govern how morphemes and words are correctly combined. Wood (1976) describes six stages of syntax acquisition (Mercer, p. 347):

- **Stages 1 and 2** (birth to about 2 years): Child is learning the semantic system
- **Stage 3** (about 2 to 3 years): Simple sentences contain subject and predicate
- **Stage 4** (about 2 ½ to 4 years): Elements such as question words are added to basic sentences (e.g., where) and word order is changed to ask questions. The child begins to use "and" to combine simple sentences, and the child begins to embed words within a basic sentence.
- **Stage 5** (about 3 ½ to 7 years): The child uses complete sentences that include word classes of adult language. The child becomes aware of appropriate semantic functions of words and differences within the same grammatical class.
- **Stage 6**(about 5 to 20 years): The child begins to learn complex sentences and sentences that imply commands, requests, and promises.

A child using sentences that lack the length or complexity expected for a child of that age manifests syntactic deficits. The child might have problems understanding or creating complex sentences and embedded sentences.

Semantics

Semantics is language content: objects, actions, and relations between objects. As with syntax, Wood (1976) outlines stages of semantic development:

- **Stage 1** (birth to about 2 years): The child learns meaning while learning his or her first words. Sentences are one word, but the meaning varies according to the context. Therefore, "doggie" could mean, "This is my dog," "There is a dog," or "The dog is barking."
- **Stage 2** (about 2 to 8 years): The child progresses to two-word sentences about concrete actions. As more words are learned, the child forms longer sentences. Until about age 7, things are defined in terms of visible actions. The child begins to respond to prompts (e.g., pretty/flower), and at about age 8, the child can respond to a prompt with an opposite (e.g., pretty/ugly).
- **Stage 3** (begins at about age 8): The child's word meanings relate directly to experiences, operations, and processes. Vocabulary is defined by the child's experiences, not the adult's. At about age 12, the child begins to give "dictionary" definitions, and the semantic level approaches that of adults.

Semantic problems can take the form of: limited vocabulary; inability to understand figurative language or idioms; literal interpretations; failure to perceive multiple meanings of words and changes in word meaning from changes in context; difficulty understanding linguistic concepts (e.g., before/after), verbal analogies, and logical relationships such as possessives and spatial and temporal relationships; or misuse of transitional words such as "although" or "regardless."

Pragmatics

Commonly known as the speaker's intent, pragmatics is used to influence or control the actions or attitudes of others. Communicative competence depends on how well one understands both the rules of language and the social rules of communication, such as taking turns and using the correct tone of voice.

Pragmatic deficits are manifested by failures to respond properly to indirect requests after the age of 8 (e.g., "Can you turn down the TV?" elicits a response of "No" instead of "Yes," followed by the child turning down the volume). Children with these deficits have trouble reading cues that indicate that the listener does not understand them. Pragmatic deficits are also characterized by inappropriate social behaviors, such as interruptions or monopolizing conversations. Children may use immature speech and have trouble sticking to a topic. Problems in language development often require long-term interventions and can persist into adulthood.

Certain pragmatic deficits are associated with different grade levels:

Preschool and kindergarten

The child's speech might sound immature and the child might not be able to follow simple directions. He or she often cannot name things like the days of the week and colors. The child might not be able to distinguish between sounds and the letters associated with the sounds. The child might substitute sounds and have trouble responding accurately to certain types of questions.

Elementary school

Problems with sound discrimination persist, and the child might have problems with temporal and spatial concepts (e.g., before/after). As the child progresses through school, he or she might have problems making the transition from narrative to expository writing. Word retrieval problems might not be very evident because the child begins to devise strategies such as talking around the word he or she cannot remember or using fillers and descriptors. The child might speak more slowly, have problems sounding out words, and get confused by multiple-meaning words. Pragmatic problems show up in social situations, such as a failure to correctly interpret social cues and adjust to appropriate language, an inability to predict consequences, and an inability to formulate requests to obtain new information.

Secondary school

At this level, difficulties become more subtle. The child lacks the ability to use and understand higher-level syntax, semantics, and pragmatics. If the child has problems with auditory language, he or she may also have problems with short-term memory. Receptive and/or expressive language delays impair the child's ability to learn effectively. The child often lacks the ability to organize or categorize the information received in school. Problems associated with pragmatic deficiencies persist, but because the child is aware of them, he or she becomes inattentive, withdrawn, or frustrated.

Skill 1.05   Recognizing how social and cultural factors (e.g., beliefs, traditions, values) may affect attitudes about disabilities and the relationship among student, family, and school

Just as cultures place varying values on education and gender roles, they also hold different views of individuals with disabilities, including appropriate education, career goals, and the individual's role in society. The special educator must first become familiar with the cultural backgrounds of the students and of the community in which he or she teaches. When the special educator demonstrates respect for each individual student's culture, he or she will build the rapport necessary to work with the student, family, and community to prepare the student for future productive work, independence, and possible post-secondary education or training (IDEA 2004).

While society has "progressed," and many things are more acceptable today than they were in years past, having a disability still carries a stigma. Historically, people with disabilities have been ostracized from their communities. Up until the 1970s, a large number of people with special needs were institutionalized at birth because their relatives either did not know what to do, felt embarrassed to admit they had a child with a disability, or gave in to the cultural peer pressure to put their "problem" away. Even today, one of the most detrimental attitudes about people with disabilities is that they are unable to contribute to society.

Today, American society has move from the method of institutionalization for that of normalization. Houses in local communities are often purchased for the purpose of providing supervision and/or nursing care that allows people with disabilities to have normal social living arrangements. Congress passed laws that allow those with disabilities to access public facilities. Public facilities have widened doorways, added special bathrooms, and made other architectural adjustments. The regular education classroom teacher now learns to accept and teach students with special needs. America's media today provides education and frequent exposure to people with special needs. However, acceptance is often easier for those with physically noticeable handicaps.

At the same time, those with special needs who appear in media such as television and movies are generally those who rise above their "label" as disabled because of an extraordinary skill. Most people in the community accept the "disabled" person only once that special skill is noted. Those who continue to express revulsion or prejudice toward the person with a disability often express remorse when the special skill is noted or if peer pressure becomes too intense. This portrayal often ignores those with learning and emotional disabilities who appear normal but who often feel and suffer from the prejudices.

The most significant group any individual faces is their peers. Pressure to appear normal and not "needy" in any area remains intense from early childhood to adulthood. During teen years, when young people are beginning to express their individuality, the very experience of walking into a special education classroom often brings feelings of inadequacy and fears that peers will label the student as "special." Being considered normal is the desire of most individuals with disabilities, regardless of age or disability. People with disabilities today, like those many years ago, still measure their successes by how their achievements mask or hide their disabilities.

Please refer to Competency 14 for information on how to take the child's cultural background into account when working with students and their families. Learn more about Disability in Cross-Cultural Perspective here:
http://www.disabilityworld.org

COMPETENCY 0002   UNDERSTAND THE EFFECTS OF DISABILITIES ON HUMAN DEVELOPMENT AND LEARNING.

Skill 2.01   Demonstrating knowledge of typical patterns of human development (e.g., physical, sensory, motor, cognitive, language, social, emotional)

SOCIAL EMOTIONAL DEVELOPMENT

Social and emotional development begins even before birth, as a child learns to recognize its mother's voice. Early childhood development involves the concurrent development of trust and attachment to significant others and the development of an independent identity and personality. Social development moves from independent "parallel play" to interaction with others, both adults and peers.

Upon entering first grade, most children have begun to develop relationships outside of the family and are beginning to develop some independence socially. At this developmental level, the child will often choose to play with friends rather than engage in isolated or even parental activities. The child begins to take turns and engage in simple games with groups or pairs of children. The child shows sufficient self control to handle ordinary minor conflicts and surprises and demonstrates a willingness to try to solve problems, although this may still involve seeking an adult's assistance. Children of this age can verbalize their feelings and can label their more powerful feelings.

See Skill 1.01 for more on problems in social and emotional development, and Refer to Skill 1.04 for language development.

COGNITIVE DEVELOPMENT

Children go through patterns of learning, beginning with pre-operational thought processes, and then move to concrete operational thoughts. Eventually, they begin to acquire the mental ability to think about and solve problems in their heads because they can manipulate objects symbolically. Even when children reach a stage where they can use symbols such as words and numbers to represent objects and relations, they will still need concrete reference points for some time. It is essential that children be encouraged to use and develop the thinking skills they possess by solving problems that interest them. The content of the curriculum must be relevant, engaging, and meaningful to the students.

The teacher of special needs students must have a general knowledge of cognitive development. Although children with special needs have cognitive development rates that may be different than those of other children, a teacher needs to be aware of some of the typical activities of each stage in order to determine what should be taught and when it should be taught.

The following information about cognitive development was taken from the Cincinnati Children's Hospital Medical Center at *http://www.cincinnatichildrens.org/health/info/growth/well/cognitive.htm*

Some common features indicating a progression from more simple to more complex cognitive development include the following:

Children (Ages 6-12)

Children begin to develop the ability to think in concrete ways. Concrete operations are those performed in the presence of the object and events that are to be used. Examples include knowing how to combine (addition), separate (subtract or divide), order (alphabetize and sort/categorize), and transform objects and actions (such as changing 25 pennies to1 quarter).

Adolescents (Ages 12-18)

Adolescence marks the beginning of the development of more complex thinking skills, including abstract thinking, the ability to reason from known principles (form new ideas or questions), the ability to consider many points of view according to varying criteria (compare or debate ideas or opinions), the ability to see things from different perspectives, and the ability to think about the process of thinking.

The transition from concrete thinking to formal logical operations occurs over time. Each adolescent progresses at a different rate when developing his or her ability to think in more complex ways and develops his or her own view of the world. Some adolescents might be able to apply logical operations to schoolwork long before they are able to apply them to personal dilemmas. When emotional issues arise, they often interfere with an adolescent's ability to think in more complex ways. The ability to consider possibilities as well as facts may influence decision making in either positive or negative ways.

PHYSICAL DEVELOPMENT, INCLUDING MOTOR AND SENSORY DEVELOPMENT

It is important for the teacher to be aware of the physical stages of development and how the child's physical growth affects the child's learning. In general, a child's physical abilities develop downward, from head to toe, and outward, from the torso or central body mass to the extremities. In normal development, both gross motor skills (large body movements) and fine motor skills (small, precise body movements) develop simultaneously.

There are many lists of physical milestones available from sources such as the Merck Manual Online, the Centers for Disease Control, and almost any university website. In general, physical development involves growth in both strength and coordination of all bodily systems. It includes increased refinement of sensory abilities and the improved coordination of motor and sensory systems. Although there is a range of normalcy in reaching various developmental milestones, a child who consistently misses these milestones or is delayed in reaching them is at risk for physical or learning disabilities.

From an educational standpoint, children are generally assumed to have met the following gross motor milestones by the time they enter first grade:

- Locomotion such as hopping. running, skipping, jumping, and sliding
- Alternating or moving from one gross motor activity to another in a regular pattern
- Motor activities with an object or ball, such as kicking, throwing or catching
- Motor activities involving simple tumbling exercises, such as somersaults
- Moving to a simple rhythm or beat

Fine motor skills considered necessary for success in first grade include such things as:

- Establishment of hand dominance
- "Pincer grasp" or using finger(s) and thumb to pinch something
- Some variation of the "tripod grasp" of a pencil or writing implement
- Ability to cut out large irregular patterns in paper
- Ability to draw a reasonable representation of a circle, a square, a triangle, a person (with legs, arms, face), and a house
- Ability to use both hands jointly for a task such as unscrewing a lid or putting two Lego blocks together
- Assembling large interlocking puzzle pieces
- Clothing skills such as buttoning, unbuttoning and tying shoelaces

Problems in Physical/Sensory Development

Children with physical impairments may possess a variety of disabling conditions. Although there are significant differences among these conditions, similarities also exist. Each condition usually affects one particular system of the body: the cardiopulmonary system (i.e., blood vessels, heart, and lungs), the nervous system (i.e., spinal cord, brain, nerves), or the musculoskeletal system (i.e., bones, muscles). Some conditions develop during pregnancy, birth, or infancy due to known or unknown factors that may affect the fetus or newborn infant. Other conditions occur later due to injury (trauma), disease, or factors not fully understood.

In addition to motor disorders, individuals with physical disabilities may have multi-disabling conditions such as concomitant hearing impairments; visual impairments; perceptual disorders; speech defects; behavioral disorders; mental handicaps; or impairments in performance or emotional responsiveness.

Skill 2.02   Recognizing the implications of various disabilities for physical, sensory, motor, cognitive, language, social, and/or emotional development and functioning

IDEA DEFINITIONS OF DISABILITIES

IDEA defines a very specific list of conditions as **disabilities** and describes their impact on development and educational functioning as follows.

Autism

Autism is a developmental disability that significantly affects verbal and nonverbal communication and social interaction, which isgenerally evident before age three. Autism adversely affects a student's educational performance. Other characteristics often associated with autism are engagement in repetitive activities and stereotyped movements, resistance to environmental changes or changes in daily routines, and unusual responses to sensory experiences. The term autism does not apply if a student's educational performance is adversely affected primarily because the student has an emotional disturbance. A student who manifests the characteristics of autism after age three could be diagnosed as having autism if the criteria in this paragraph are otherwise satisfied.

In 1981, the condition of autism was moved from the exceptionality category to the seriously emotionally disturbed category, and then to the category of health impaired by virtue of a change in language in the original definitions under the Education of All Handicapped Children Act (Public Law 94-142). In 1990, IDEA created a separate exceptionality category for autism.

Deafness

Deafness is a hearing impairment so severe that the student is impaired in processing linguistic information through hearing, with or without amplification, and which adversely affects a student's educational performance.

Deaf-Blindness

Deaf-blindness is concomitant hearing and visual impairments, the combination of which causes such severe communication and other developmental and educational difficulties that these students cannot be accommodated in special education programs solely for students with deafness or for students with blindness.

Emotional Disturbance

Emotional disturbance is a condition exhibiting one or more of the following characteristics over a long period of time and to a marked degree, adversely affecting a student's educational performance:

- An inability to learn that cannot be explained by intellectual, sensory, or health factors
- An inability to build or maintain satisfactory interpersonal relationships with peers and teachers
- Inappropriate types of behavior or feelings under normal circumstances
- A generally pervasive mood of unhappiness or depression
- A tendency to develop physical symptoms or fears associated with personal or school problems.

The term emotional disturbance includes schizophrenia. The term does not apply to students who are socially maladjusted unless it is determined that they have an emotional disturbance.

Hearing Impairment

A hearing impairment is difficulty hearing,, whether permanent or fluctuating, that adversely affects a child's educational performance but is not included under the definition of *deafness* in this section, which is total hearing loss

Learning Disability

A learning disability is a disorder in one or more of the basic psychological processes involved in understanding or in using language, spoken or written, which manifests itself in an imperfect ability to listen, think, speak, read, write, spell, or do mathematical calculations. The term includes such conditions as perceptual disabilities, brain injury, minimal brain dysfunction, dyslexia, and developmental aphasia. The term does not include learning problems that are primarily the result of visual, hearing, or motor disabilities, of mental retardation, of emotional disturbance, or of environmental, cultural, or economic disadvantage.

Mental Retardation

Mental retardation is significantly sub-average general intellectual functioning, existing concurrently with deficits in adaptive behavior and manifested during the developmental period, adversely affecting a student's educational performance.

Multiple Disabilities

The term multiple disabilities means concomitant impairments (such as mental retardation-blindness, mental retardation-orthopedic impairment, etc.), the combination of which causes such severe educational needs that these students cannot be accommodated by a special education program designed solely for one of the impairments. This term does not include deaf-blindness.

Orthopedic Impairment

An orthopedic impairment is a severe orthopedic condition that adversely affects a student's educational performance. The term includes impairments caused by a congenital anomaly (e.g., clubfoot, absence of some member, etc.), impairments caused by disease (e.g., poliomyelitis, bone tuberculosis, etc.), and impairments from other causes (e.g., cerebral palsy, amputation, and fractures or burns that cause contractures).

Other Health Impairment

This term describes students that have limited strength, vitality, or alertness, including a heightened alertness to environmental stimuli that results in limited alertness with respect to the educational environment. These heath impairments can be due to chronic or acute health problems, including, but not limited to, a heart condition, tuberculosis, rheumatic fever, nephritis, asthma, sickle cell anemia, hemophilia, epilepsy, lead poisoning, leukemia, diabetes, attention deficit disorder, attention deficit hyperactivity disorder, or Tourette's syndrome. These are conditions that adversely affect a student's educational performance.

Speech or Language Impairment

A speech or language impairment is a communication disorder, such as stuttering, impaired articulation, a language impairment, or a voice impairment, which adversely affects a student's educational performance.

Traumatic Brain Injury

A traumatic brain injury is an acquired injury to the brain caused by an external physical force or by certain medical conditions such as stroke, encephalitis, aneurysm, anoxia, or brain tumors with resulting impairments that adversely affect educational performance. The term includes open or closed head injuries or brain injuries from certain medical conditions resulting in mild, moderate, or severe impairments in one or more areas, including cognition, language, memory, attention, reasoning, abstract thinking, judgment, problem solving, sensory, perceptual, and motor abilities, psychosocial behavior, physical functions, information processing, and speech. The term does not include injuries that are congenital or caused by birth trauma.

Visual Impairment Including Blindness

This is impairment in vision that, even with correction, adversely affects a student's educational performance. The term includes both partial sight and blindness.

Skill 2.03 Demonstrating familiarity with developmental issues that may affect individuals with disabilities

To effectively assess and plan for the developmental needs of individuals with disabilities, special education teachers should first be familiar with the development of the typical child (see Skill 2.01). Developmental areas of speech and language, fine and gross motor skills, cognitive abilities, emotional development, and social skills should be considered. In many cases, more than one area of development will be affected by a disability. In others, a problem that *could* be the result of a disability is actually the result of a normal factor of development. These things must be taken into consideration when interpreting a child's behavior and needs.

For example, it would be inappropriate to refer a six-year-old child who is missing her front teeth to speech therapy for mispronunciation of words with the /th/ sound, because the mispronunciation is caused by the lack of teeth, not a language disability. Without a surface on which to place the tongue, the /th/ cannot be pronounced correctly. Thus, speech therapy would not be warranted.

A second grade student may have difficulty buttoning clothing. Because this is a skill that is typically mastered around age four, this might indicate a a developmental delay in fine motor skills. It is appropriate for the special educator to request consultation and possibly formal evaluation of the child's needs.

In addition to being aware of the ages of typical developmental milestones, the special education teacher should consider the sequence in which the skills are acquired. While not all children go through every step of development (e.g., some children never seem to crawl), most follow the typical sequence. In an example of language development, children usually name objects with single words long before they form phrases or sentences.

Sometimes the disability itself will hinder or prevent a child from accomplishing a developmental task. A child with a visual-spatial difficulty may not be able to see the components of a certain letter in print. Given a handwriting program that shows the parts of a letter made with wooden pieces may provide the link to the child mastering that letter formation.

The key to understanding the role of development and the needs of the special education student is to be knowledgeable of typical development and to see such skills in a number of typically developing students. This is another benefit of the inclusion classroom. Given a foundation of developmental understanding and knowledge of the specific child's disability, the special education teacher can better assess and implement an appropriate education program to meet the unique needs of the child.

Skill 2.04 **Recognizing the possible effects of medications on student learning, developing, and functioning (e.g., cognitive, physical, social, emotional)**

Students with disabilities who take medications often experience medication side effects that can impact their behaviors and educational development. Some medications may impair concentration, which can lead to poor processing ability, lower alertness, and cause drowsiness or hyperactivity. Students who take several medications often have an increased risk of behavioral and cognitive side effects.

The students' parents should let the school know when the students are beginning or changing their medication so teachers and staff can look out for possible side effects. It is important for both the teacher and the school nurse to maintain close communication with the child's parents and report any behaviors (positive or negative) that may result from the medication.

ANTIDEPRESSANTS

There are three different classes of antidepressants that students can take. One type is called selective serotonin-reuptake inhibitors (SSRIs). The SSRIs block certain receptors in the brain from absorbing the chemical serotonin. Over time, SSRIs may cause changes in brain chemistry. The side effects of SSRIs include dry mouth, insomnia or restless sleep, increased sweating, and nausea. They can also cause mood swings in students with bipolar disorders.

A second type of antidepressant is tricyclic antidepressants. They are often effective for treating depression and obsessive-compulsive behavior. They cause similar side effects to the SSRIs, such as sedation, tremors, seizures, dry mouth, light sensitivity, and mood swings in students with bipolar disorders.

A third type of antidepressant is monoamine oxidase inhibitors (MAOIs). These are not as widely used as the other two types, because many have unpleasant and life-threatening interactions with many other drugs, including common over-the-counter medications. Students taking MAOIs must also follow a special diet because these medications interact with many foods. The list of foods to avoid includes chocolate, aged cheeses, and more.

STIMULANTS

Stimulants are often prescribed to help with attention deficit disorder and attention deficit hyperactivity disorder. These drugs can have many side effects, including agitation, restlessness, aggressive behavior, dizziness, insomnia, headache, or tremors. Nonstimulant medications can also be used to treat these disorders when stimulants are not appropriate for the child.

TRANQUILIZERS

In severe cases of anxiety, an anti-anxiety medication (tranquilizer) may be prescribed. Most tranquilizers have a potential for addiction and abuse. They tend to be sedating and can cause a variety of unpleasant side effects, including blurred vision, confusion, sleepiness, and tremors.

If educators are aware of the types of medication that their students are taking, along with the myriad of side effects, they will be able to respond more positively when some of the side effects of the medications change their students' behaviors, response rates, and attention spans.

COMPETENCY 0003 UNDERSTAND TYPES AND CHARACTERISTICS OF ASSESSMENT INSTRUMENTS AND METHODS

Skill 3.01 Recognizing basic concepts and terminology used in assessment

The following terms are frequently used in behavioral and academic testing and assessment. They represent basic terminology and not more advanced statistical concepts.

Baseline—This is also known as establishing a baseline. This procedure includes collecting data about a target behavior or performance of a skill before certain interventions or teaching procedures are implemented. Establishing a baseline enables a person to determine if the interventions are effective.

Criterion-referenced test—This is a test in which the individual's performance is measured against mastery of specific skills or knowledge (criteria) rather than against the performance of other students. Criterion-referenced tests may be commercially prepared or teacher made. Criterion referenced tests are used to determine whether a student has mastered required skills.

Curriculum-based assessment—This is a type of criterion-referenced assessment that measures an individual's performance of objectives of a particular curriculum, such as a reading or math program. The individual's performance is measured in terms of which specific objectives were mastered.

Duration recording—This is used for measuring the length of time a behavior lasts (e.g., tantrums, time out of class, crying).

Error analysis—In error analysis the mistakes on an individual's test are noted and categorized by type. For example, an error analysis of a reading test could categorize mistakes by miscues, substituting words, omitted words or phrases, and miscues that are self-corrected.

Event recording—This is the number of times a target behavior occurs during an observation period.

Formal assessment—These are assessments such as standardized tests or textbook quizzes; they are objective tests that include primarily questions for which there is only one correct, easily identifiable answer. These can be commercial or teacher made assessments, given to either groups or individuals.

Frequency—This is the number of times a behavior (e.g., out-of-seat behavior, hitting, temper tantrums) occurs in a given amount of time.

Frequency distribution—This requires plotting the scores received on a test and tallying how many individuals received those scores. A frequency distribution is used to visually determine how the group of individuals performed on a test. It illustrates extreme scores and compares the distribution to the mean or other criteria.

Informal assessment—In contrast to *formal assessments,* informal assessments have less objective measures, and may include anecdotes or observations that may or may not be quantified, interviews, informal questioning during a task, etc. There are no rigid rules or procedures for administration or scoring. Many informal assessments are teacher prepared and rely upon the knowledge and judgment of the professional. An example might be watching a student sort objects to see which attribute is most important to the student, or questioning a student to see what he or she found confusing about a task.

Intensity—This is the degree of a behavior as measured by its frequency and duration.

Interval recording—This technique involves breaking the observation period into an equal number of time intervals (e.g., 10-second intervals during a 5-minute period). At the end of each interval, the observer notes the presence or absence of the target behavior. The observer can then calculate a percentage by dividing the number of intervals in which the target behavior occurred by the total number of intervals in the observation period. This type of recording works well for behaviors that occur with high frequency or for long periods of time, such as on- or off-task behavior, pencil tapping, or stereotyped behaviors.

Latency—This is the length of time that elapses between the presentation of a stimulus (e.g., a question) and the response (e.g., the student's answer).

Mean—This is the arithmetic average of a set of scores, which is calculated by adding the set of scores and dividing the sum by the number of scores in the set. For example, if the sum of a set of 35 scores is 2935, dividing that sum by 35 (the number of scores), yields a mean of 83.9.

Median—This is the middle score of a set of scores: 50 percent of the scores are above this number, and 50 percent of the scores are below this number. In the example above, if the median (middle) score was 72, 17 students would have scored less than 72, and 17 students would have scored more than 72.

Mode—This is the score most frequently tallied in a frequency distribution. In the example above, the most frequently tallied score might be 78. It is possible for a set of scores to have more than one mode.

Momentary time sampling—This is a technique used for measuring behaviors of a group of individuals or several behaviors of the same individual. Time samples are usually brief and may be conducted at fixed or variable intervals.

The advantage of using variable intervals is increased reliability because the students will not be able to predict when the time sample will be taken.

Multiple baseline design—This may be used to test the effectiveness of an intervention in a skill performance or to determine if the intervention accounted for the observed changes in a target behavior. First, the initial baseline data is collected, followed by the data during the intervention period. To get the second baseline, the intervention is removed for a period of time, and data is collected again. The intervention is then reapplied, and data is collected on the target behavior.

Norm-referenced test—A norm-referenced test is a standardized test in which an individual's performance is compared to the group that was used to calculate the performance standards on the test. Examples include intelligence tests and many achievement tests, the CTBS, WISC-R, and Stanford-Binet.

Operational definition—This is the description of a behavior and its measurable components. In behavioral observations, the description of a behavior must be specific and measurable so that the observer knows exactly what constitutes instances and non-instances of the target behavior. Otherwise, these measurements might be unreliable.

Pinpoint—This includes specifying and describing the target behavior for change in measurable and precise terms. "On time for class" might be interpreted as arriving physically in the classroom when the tardy bell has finished ringing, it might mean being at the pencil sharpener, or it might mean being in one's seat and ready to begin work when the bell has finished ringing. Pinpointing the behavior makes it possible to accurately measure the behavior.

Profile—This is done by plotting an individual's behavioral data on a graph.

Rate—This is the frequency of a behavior over a specified time period, such as 5 talk-outs during a 30-minute period or typing 85 words per minute.

Raw score—This is the number of correct responses on a test before they have been converted to standard scores. Raw scores are not meaningful because they have no basis of comparison to the performance of other individuals or an established criterion.

Reliability—This is the consistency (stability) of a test scores over time. Reliability is commonly measured in four ways:

- <u>Test-retest method</u>—This is done when the test is administered to the same group or individuals after a short period of time, and the results are compared.

- Alternate form (equivalent form)—This measures reliability by using alternative forms of testing to measure the same skills.
- Interrater reliability—This refers to the degree of agreement between two or more trained individuals observing the same behaviors or observing the same tests. A high degree of agreement indicates higher reliability.
- Internal reliability—This is determined by statistical procedures, which usually correlate one half of the test with the other half of the test or one set of questions with another.

Standard deviation—The standard deviation is a statistical measure of the variability of the scores. The more closely the scores are clustered around the mean, the smaller the standard deviation will be.

Standard error of measurement—This statistic measures the amount of possible error in a score. If the standard error of measurement for a test is + or - 3, and the individual's score is 35, then the actual score may be 32 to 35.

Standard score—This is a derived score with a set mean (usually 100) and a standard deviation. Examples are T-scores (mean of 50 and a standard deviation of 10), Z-scores (mean of 0 and a standard deviation of 1), and scaled scores. Scaled scores may be given for age groups or grade levels. IQ scores, for instance, use a mean of 100 and a standard deviation of 15. (See Skill 4.04 for more on interpreting these scores.)

Standardized tests—These are formal tests that are administered to either groups or individuals in a specifically prescribed manner, with strict rules to keep administration procedures, scoring, and interpretation of results uniform in all cases. Such tests have been normed in very specific and uniform ways that allow comparisons to be made across populations, ages or grades, or over time for a particular student. Intelligence tests, achievement tests, and most diagnostic tests are standardized tests.

Task analysis—This is done by breaking an academic or behavioral task down into its sequence of steps or prerequisite skills. Task analysis is necessary when preparing criterion-referenced tests and performing error analysis. It is a critical part of functional and vocational skills training as well. A task analysis for a student learning to do laundry might include:

- Sort the clothes by type (white, permanent press, delicate).
- Choose a type, and select the correct water temperature and setting.
- If doing a partial load, adjust the water level.
- Measure the detergent.
- Turn on the machine.
- Load the clothes.
- Add bleach and fabric softener at the correct times.
- Wait for the machine to stop spinning completely before opening it.

- Remove the clothes from the machine and place them in the dryer.

A task analysis could be done for drying and folding as well.

Validity—This is the degree to which a test measures what it claims to measure, such as reading readiness, self-concept, or math achievement. A test may be highly reliable, but it will be useless if it is not valid. There are several types of validity to consider when selecting or constructing an assessment instrument.

- <u>Content validity</u> examines the question of whether the types of tasks in the test cover or measure the skill or characteristic that the test claims to measure.
- <u>Criterion–referenced validity</u> involves comparing the test results with another valid criterion of the same skill or characteristic that the test claims to measure. There are two types of criterion-referenced validity:
  - <u>Predictive validity</u> refers to how well a test will relate to a future criterion level, such as the ability of a reading test administered to a first-grader to predict that student's performance in third or fifth grade.
  - <u>Concurrent validity</u> refers to how well the test relates to an independent criterion measure given at the same time.
- <u>Construct validity</u> refers to the ability of the test to measure a theoretical construct, such as intelligence, self-concept, and other non-observable behaviors. This is a much more abstract form of validity, and requires a complex review of related research.

Please refer to Skill 4.04 for more on interpreting and using measures of validity in the educational setting.

Skill 3.02   Identify types, characteristics, and methods of formal and informal assessment

Assessment types can be categorized in a number of ways, most commonly in terms of *what* is being assessed or *how* the assessment is constructed, and these distinctions often dictate how the test is to be used. It is important to understand these differences to be able to correctly interpret assessment results.

FORMAL VS. INFORMAL

This variable focuses on *how* the assessment is constructed or scored. As noted in Skill 3.01, **formal assessments** can include standardized criterion-referenced instruments, norm-referenced instruments, and commercially or teacher-prepared inventories. They are objective and quantifiable. **Informal assessments** include non-standardized instruments, such as checklists, developmental rating scales, observations, error analysis, interviews, teacher reports, and performance-based assessments.

Formal assessments, such as standardized tests, are useful for comparing a student's performance to that of other students or to an established standard, and their objectivity makes them useful for establishing eligibility and demonstrating mastery of skills, as well as diagnosis of specific deficits.

Informal evaluation strategies are an integral part of both diagnosis and instructional design. An advantage of using informal assessments is the ease of design and administration as well as the usefulness of the information the teacher can gain about the student's strength and weaknesses. The flexible administration and content of informal assessments allows the assessment to be individualized to suit the needs of the student and provide very specific information for designing instruction to meet the student's needs.

Some instruments can be both formal and informal tools. For example, observation may incorporate structured observation instruments as well as other informal observation procedures, including professional judgment. When evaluating a child's developmental level, a professional may use a formal adaptive rating scale while simultaneously using professional judgment to assess the child's motivation and behavior during the evaluation process.

NORM REFERENCED VS. CRITERION REFERENCED

This distinction is based on the standard to which the student's performance is being compared. As described in Skill 3.01, **Norm referenced tests** establish a ranking and compare the student's performance to an established norm. *What* the student knows is less important than *how similar* the student's performance is to a specific group. Norm Referenced tests are, by definition, standardized. Because the student's performance is compared to an established "norm," these tests are often used in determining eligibility for special needs services.

Criterion referenced tests measure a student's knowledge of specific content, usually related to classroom instruction. On these tests, *what* the student knows is more important than how he or she compares with other students. Examples include math quizzes at the end of a chapter, or some state-mandated tests of specific content. Because these tests measure what a student can or cannot do, results are especially useful for identifying goals and objectives for IEPs and lesson plans.

GROUP VS. INDIVIDUAL ASSESSMENTS

This variable refers to the manner of presentation: whether the assessment is given to a group of students or on a one-to-one basis. Group assessments can be formal or informal, standardized or not, and criterion or norm referenced. Individual assessments can be found in all these types as well.

ALTERNATIVE ASSESSMENTS

See Skill 3.05.

RATING SCALES AND CHECKLISTS

These are generally self-appraisal instruments completed by the student or observation-based instruments completed by the teacher or parents. The focus is frequently on behavior or affective areas such as interest, motivation, attention or depression. These tests can be formal or informal and some can be standardized and norm referenced. Examples of norm-referenced tests of this type would be ADHD rating scales or the Behavior Assessment System for Children.

Skill 3.03   Demonstrating familiarity with principles and procedures for selecting, evaluating, and using educational and adaptive behavior assessment instruments and methods

It is important for teachers to understand basic principles applicable to making decisions about what type of instruments to use or design. Several authors have identified principles useful in selecting, designing, and interpreting assessments in the classroom.

PRINCIPLES OF ASSESSMENT

Linn and Gronlund (1995) identify five principles of assessment:

1. Clearly specifying what is to be assessed has priority in the assessment process.
2. An assessment procedure should be selected because of its relevance to the characteristics or performance to be measured.
3. Comprehensive assessment requires a variety of procedures.
4. Proper use of assessment procedures requires an awareness of their limitations.
5. Assessment is a means to an end, not an end in itself.

Drummond lists six critical questions to ask about possible assessments when making a choice among them:

1. What specific assessment judgments and decisions have to be made?
2. What information is needed to make the best decisions?
3. What information is already available?
4. What assessment methods and instruments will provide the needed information?
5. How should appropriate instruments be located?
6. What criteria should be used in selecting and evaluating assessment instruments?

Stiggins (1997) adds to these the principle that assessment is both a teaching and a learning tool, not just something done to provide grades and placements. In addition to these general principles, special education teachers must also consider modifications and adaptations of the assessment instruments and processes to accommodate students with special needs. (Please refer to Skill 5.03 for more about accommodations in assessments.)

Please refer to Skill 3.04 for more information on the importance of selecting an assessment based upon the intended purpose or use of the test

SPECIAL ISSUES IN USING ADAPTIVE BEHAVIOR ASSESSMENTS

Adaptive behaviors commonly include communication and social skills, daily living skills, personal care skills, and other skills that are needed to function at home, at school, and in the community. An adaptive behavior measure is a comprehensive assessment of an individual's independent living skills relative to the skills of the individual's age peers. It is a significant tool in eligibility consideration for students with mental handicaps and in the development of effective educational interventions.

Measurements of adaptive behavior should take into account the student's behavior and skills in a number of settings, including the classroom, school, home, and community. In order to get an accurate assessment, the adaptive behavior should be measured by a variety of different people in different settings.

The primary method of measuring adaptive behavior is through structured interviews with teachers and parents. A professional trained to administer an adaptive behavior rating scale, such as a school counselor, interviews the student's parents and teachers. Parental input is a critical part of the adaptive behavior assessment process because there are many daily living skills that are observed primarily at home.

Additional methods of measuring adaptive behavior include analyzing the student's records from schools, watching the student in specific circumstances, and testing the student's skills by giving him or her specific tasks to complete. The rating scales are created to address areas such as communication, self-care, home-living, social skills, community use, self-direction, health and safety, functional academics, leisure, and work.

Some of the most common adaptive behavior instruments include the following:

Measure	Format	Useful Derived Information
American Association of Intellectual and Developmental Disabilities (2010)	Rating scale or interview	Factor scores of personal, social, and community, plus two maladaptive domains
Adaptive Behavior Assessment System: school, parent, and adult forms (Harrison & Oakland, 2003)	Multiple formats including rating scale, interview, and self report for adults; multiple formats encouraged	Composite, plus scores in ten adaptive skills areas
Comprehensive Test of Adaptive Behavior (Adams, 2000)	Rating scale with behavioral composite plus tests that are used if the behavior has not been observed	Seven domains: self-help, home, independence, social, sensory, motor, and language/academic
SIB-R: Scales of Independent Behavior—Revised (Bruininks et al, 1996)	Highly structured interview conducted by professional or paraprofessional	Composite plus motor, social interaction and communication, personal living, and community living; maladaptive behaviors included
Vineland Adaptive Behavior Scales (Balla, Cicchetti, & Sparrow, 2005)	Semi-structured interview requiring well-trained professional; school form uses a rating scale format	Composite plus communication, daily living, motor (0-6 yrs), and socialization; no maladaptive behavior content

Learn more about Behavioral Assessments here:
http://www.specialednews.com/behavior/behavnews/CECbehavassess021900.html

Skill 3.04   Recognizing appropriate purposes, uses, and limitations of various types of assessment instruments

Please refer to the previous skills in this section for detailed descriptions of types of assessments.

PURPOSES FOR ASSESSMENT

In the education of students with disabilities, assessment is used to make decisions about the following:

- Screening and initial identification of children who might need services
- Diagnosis of specific learning disabilities and areas of strength and weakness
- Selection and evaluation of teaching strategies and programs (formative assessment)
- Determination of the child's present level of academic performance
- Classification and program placement
- Development of goals, objectives, and evaluation for the IEP
- Eligibility for a program
- Continuation of a program
- Effectiveness of instructional programs and strategies
- Effectiveness of behavioral interventions
- Accommodations needed for mandated or classroom testing
- Progress toward mastery of specific learning objectives (summative assessment)
- Readiness and prerequisite skills
- Interest and attitude assessments to identify areas of high interest for motivational purposes

Matching Purpose to Specific Assessment Decisions

Before choosing an assessment, it is critical to determine the purpose of the assessment—that is, the manner in which it is to be used. Most of the above uses fall into three broad categories: screening, eligibility, diagnosis and placement; designing goals, objectives and accommodations for IEP development; making instructional decisions; and monitoring progress.

Screening, Diagnosis, Eligibility and Placement

Norm-referenced assessments are critical to these decisions because eligibility is based in large part on the degree to which a student is successful in school compared to age and grade peers. The existence of a disability alone does not qualify a student for special services; the disability must be preventing the student from functioning on the same level as the peer group.

Intelligence tests are often used as part of these processes. These tests are standardized and norm referenced. Examples are the *Wechsler Intelligence Scale for Children-Fourth Edition (WISC-IV), Stanford-Binet IV*, and *Kaufman Assessment Battery for Children-Second Edition (KACB-II)*. Some intelligence tests are designed for use with groups, and are used for screening and identification purposes, while individual tests are used for classification and program placement. Because intelligence is a quality that is difficult to define precisely, results of intelligence tests alone should not be used to discriminate or define an individual's potential.

Modern intelligence tests often include measures of multiple intelligences (Gardner, 1999), and these tests can further refine placement decisions for students with special needs. In many cases, a significant discrepancy between scores on different intelligences helps to identify or diagnose specific learning disabilities. Such measures also help show how a disability impacts performance in different areas of the curriculum.

There are many standardized achievement and educational skills tests, including state mandated testing, that are also used by school systems to help determine eligibility and placement.

IEP DEVELOPMENT

Skill 4.04 discusses the use of various assessments in the development of an IEP. Part of the IEP, of course, includes an overview of all testing results and their implications for diagnosis, eligibility, and placement, as described above. In addition, description of current levels of performance as well as goals and objectives will depend upon assessment. In these areas, non-standardized assessments and informal assessments may be used as part of the decision process.

Making Instructional Decisions Based on Assessment Results

Assessment is key to providing differentiated and appropriate instruction to all students and to monitoring progress toward objectives. These are the areas in which teachers will most often use assessment. Teachers should use a variety of assessment techniques to determine the existing knowledge, skills, and needs of each student. Depending on the age of the student and the subject matter under consideration, diagnosis of readiness can be accomplished through pretests, checklists, teacher observation, or student self-reports. Diagnosis serves two related purposes—to identify those students who are not ready for the new instruction and to identify what prerequisite knowledge is lacking for each student.

Some standardized test scores will be useful for instructional planning. Intelligence tests that include multiple intelligences, as mentioned above, and criterion-referenced educational achievement tests can often pinpoint specific skill deficits that require instruction. They can also provide information on learning styles that will help the teacher design instruction suitable to each student's needs. Some standardized tests also have lists of accommodations that can be used for students with special needs, and these must be carefully recorded and rules about their use strictly followed.

Informal classroom assessments can also help the teacher with instructional planning. For example, a student who can answer multiple choice questions correctly, but cannot put that information into writing, may have encoding problems or even a form of Dysgraphia. Assessment of what the child *can* do is as important as assessment of what he *cannot* do, because it helps pinpoint the locus of a problem or disability. A child who can correctly compute an entire math worksheet quickly but cannot do a simple word problem does not have math problem; he has a language or reading problem. This student would need strategies for relating the vocabulary and language of math to the concrete facts he already knows. (See Skills 4.05 and 4.08 for more details on using assessment to design instruction.)

LIMITATIONS OF VARIOUS TYPES OF ASSESSMENT

Validity

Teachers must make careful and informed decisions when selecting and interpreting assessments if the assessments are to be useful for individual students. For example, many standardized tests have published measures of validity. However, teachers need to remember that the test is only valid for their class if it measures what *they* want to measure. A test can be valid in one setting, for a particular set of measurements, and invalid in another setting because the teacher wants to measure something else. An expert's statement that a test is valid is only relevant if the assessment tests what the teacher wants to test, is appropriate for *that* teacher's students, and meets any special needs of the student population.

When using norm-referenced assessments, teachers must be informed about the student group on which the test was normed and whether their student(s) fit in that normative group. If the test was normed on inner city students 20 years ago, it might not be appropriate for a classroom full of modern students in a rural community.

Bias

Testing bias can severely limit the usefulness of any type of assessment and teachers must be alert for such bias in any assessment they use. Bias in testing occurs when the information within the test or the information required to respond to a multiple choice question or constructed response (essay question) on the test is information that is not available to some test takers who come from a different cultural, ethnic, linguistic or socio-economic background than the majority of the test takers (or the group on which the test was normed). Because they have not had the same prior linguistic, social, or cultural experiences, these test takers are at a disadvantage when taking the test, and no matter what their actual mastery of the material taught by the teacher, cannot address the "biased" questions. Generally, other "non-biased" questions are substituted, and eventually the biased questions are removed from the examination.

An example of such bias would be reading comprehension questions about the well-known fairy tale of the gingerbread boy. These questions might be simple and accessible for most children born in the United States. However, children who are recent arrivals from a different culture (e.g., the Dominican Republic) in which the story of the gingerbread boy is not known would be at a serious disadvantage. In that situation, alternative questions consistent with the students' background would need to be constructed.

Of particular importance to teachers in special education is the bias that occurs when the test purports to measure one skill, but the manner in which it measures that skill depends on *another* skill that is limited in children with certain disabilities. For example, an open response question requiring written output to demonstrate comprehension of an inference about cause and effect is biased against students with writing disabilities. These students might fully understand the inferential cause and effect relationship but be unable to write well enough to demonstrate that comprehension. This test question would therefore be invalid for that population. See Skill 4.03 for more about testing accommodations for such students.

It is important to note that bias is not simply a matter of a question or a test being unfair. The results are simply not useful to the teacher because they stem from a bias rather than from whatever skill the test is intended to measure.

Skill 3.05   Demonstrating knowledge of alternative assessments (e.g., authentic assessment, portfolio assessment)

Special education teachers must be familiar with the various methods of alternative assessments in order to properly evaluate the goals and objectives of students who cannot be adequately assessed by standardized tests utilizing paper and pencil methods.

Naturalistic (authentic) assessments are designed to be as close to real life as possible. They can be formal or informal, depending upon how they are constructed. An example of an authentic test item would be calculating a 20 percent sales discount on a popular clothing item after the student has studied math percentages.

These assessments are particularly effective in addressing the functional skills that enhance a student's independence and social interactions in a variety of settings (e.g., school, home, community). Functional skills best addressed by this method include vocational skills such as following directions, socially acceptable behavior, and measurable work ethics. Naturalistic assessments require planning for instruction to occur in various settings. The advantages of this method include a "real world setting" that allows for culturally appropriate materials. The disadvantages of this method include the requirements for long-range planning and reduced efficiency in both teaching and assessing the skill that is to be measured.

Performance-based assessments use a form of evaluation that examines a skill necessary to complete a project. An example of this method would be evaluating the math skill "order of operations" by evaluating how a student solved an algebraic expression. Another example would be observing how the skill of buttoning a shirt is progressing when having a student complete the task of putting a shirt on.

Portfolio assessments are a mode of evaluation that are a good way to document the beginning, middle, and end of a student's yearly progress. This method utilizes samples of work compiled throughout a given period of time. Portfolio assessments are often used to track academic growth and progress in writing within regular education classrooms. The portfolio assessment also provides the teacher with a way to explain a student's present levels to parents.

There are many forms of portfolio assessment. The purpose, nature, and policies of portfolio assessment vary greatly from one setting to another. Generally, however, portfolios are aligned with curriculum goals or standards for a particular child. Qualitative changes over time can be readily apparent from work samples. Such changes are difficult to establish with strictly quantitative records typical of the scores recorded in the teacher's grade book

Dynamic assessments are tailor-made evaluation tools that look at how a student learns as well as possible impediments to a student's successful achievement of a goal. Dynamic assessments look first at what must be taught and how it is taught. Next, possible impediments to the student's success in this goal are examined to provide possible insight into a student's success/failure to meet a goal. When the impediments have been examined, it is then possible to look at the goal and distinguish between performance and ability. For this reason, it is an ideal method to use when evaluating student progress that may have been inhibited by a cultural norm. Identifying impediments allows for the evaluator to assess if a different teaching strategy might be more effective for students to attain the objectives and goals in their IEPs.

Anecdotal records are notes recorded by the teacher concerning an area of interest in or concern about a particular student. These records should focus on observable behaviors and should be descriptive in nature. They should not include assumptions or speculations regarding affective areas such as motivation or interest. These records are usually compiled over a period of several days to several weeks.

Questioning is one of the most frequent and useful forms of assessment in the classroom. As the teacher questions the students, he or she collects a great deal of information about the degree of student learning and potential sources of student confusion. Although questioning is often viewed as a component of instructional methodology, it is also a powerful assessment tool if the teacher is skilled in its use.

Learn more about raising achievement through alternative assessments: *http://www.ed.gov/ policy/elsec/guid/raising/alt-assess.html* and learn more about how to ensure equity when giving alternative Assessments: *http://www.ncrel.org/sdrs/areas/issues/methods/assment/as800.html*

Recommended Reading: Notari-Syverson & Losardo (2001).

Skill 3.06 Demonstrating familiarity with strategies for collaborating with families and with other professionals in the assessment process

The assessment process is an essential part of developing an individualized program for students and it is also critical for designing instruction that is responsive to each student's needs. Since it is necessary to address all of the needs of each child, information should be gathered from a variety of sources.

In addition to the general education teacher, parent participation is a vital part of the assessment process. The parent can provide needed background information on the child, such as a brief medical, physical, and developmental history. Paraprofessionals, doctors, and other professionals are also very helpful in providing necessary information about the child.

It is sometimes necessary to help parents and other professional understand the ongoing purpose of assessment as something more than a way to put grades on a report card. Helping parents understand how assessments are used to help individualize instruction for their child can go a long way toward eliciting parental help in the process. It is important to remember that consulting with anyone other than the parents (e.g., pediatrician, counselor) about the child will require signed parental permission.

METHODS OF GATHERING INFORMATION

Interviews: Interviews can be in person, by phone, or on paper. The related parties can be invited to a meeting to conduct the interview; if a parent does not respond after several attempts, the paper interview may be sent or mailed home.

Questionnaires and ratings or checklists (see Skill 3.01): Some questionnaires may consist of open-ended questions, and some may contain several questions that are to be answered using a rating scale. The answerer circles ratings ranging from 1 to 5 or 1 to 7 (Strongly Disagree to Strongly Agree).

Conferences/Meetings: With parents' permission, it might be useful to conduct a meeting either one-on-one or in a group setting to gather information about the child. Everyone involved who may be able to offer information about the child's academic progress, physical development, social skills, behavior, medical history, and/or needs should be invited to attend.

Observation: Sometimes observing a child in the family situation or in a situation that has presented problems can be helpful. Use of rubrics and observational samples and checklists (see Skill 3.01) can help make the information obtained more objective and useful.

Skill 3.07	Demonstrating an understanding of legal provisions, regulations, guidelines, and ethical concerns related to assessment, including preserving confidentiality

The wording in federal law is very explicit about the manner in which evaluations must be conducted and about the existence of due process procedures that protect against bias and discrimination. Provisions in the law include the following:

- Testing children in their native or primary language unless it is clearly not feasible to do so. IDEA legislation requires that assessment be not only in a language but also in a form that will give the most accurate picture of a child's abilities or disabilities. Beyond the obvious implications for ESL students, the requirement that it be in the most appropriate form is also significant. Because students with disabilities are often limited in one or another mode of expression or reception of information, a form of response that is fully accessible to the child must also be found.
- The use of evaluation procedures selected and administered to prevent cultural or ethnic discrimination (see Skill 3.04 for examples)
- The use of assessment tools validated for the purpose for which they are being used (e.g., achievement levels, IQ scores, adaptive skills)

- Assessment by a multidisciplinary team utilizing several pieces of information to formulate a placement decision. IDEA legislation specifically requires that no single assessment or measurement tool may be used to determine eligibility or placement. This is a critical assessment principle and one that is often overlooked. It is easy to look at the results of one assessment and jump to conclusions about a student's abilities or needs. To get an accurate picture of a child's needs, however, it is necessary to use a variety of measures, and the law requires that educators do so.

Furthermore, parental involvement must be part of the development of the child's educational program. According to the law, parents must:

1. Be notified before their child's initial evaluation or any change in placement by a written notice in their primary language describing the proposed school action, the reasons for it, and the available educational opportunities
2. Consent, in writing, before the child is initially evaluated

Parents may:

1. Request an independent educational evaluation if they feel the school's evaluation is inappropriate
2. Request an evaluation at public expense if a due process hearing decision is that the public agency's evaluation was inappropriate
3. Participate on the committee that considers the evaluation, placement, and programming of the student

All students referred for evaluation for special education should have the results of a relatively current vision and hearing screening on file. This will determine the adequacy of sensory acuity and ensure that learning problems are not due to a vision and/or hearing problem.

Finally, as in all educational endeavors, confidentiality is a critical requirement. The Family Educational Rights and Privacy Act of 1974 states that all assessment and discussion of assessment is to be considered strictly confidential and shared only with those immediately involved in decision making and delivery of services to students. Parents have the right to review any and all assessments and their written approval is needed before assessment information can be shared with anyone else (e.g., counselors, outside medical or treatment sources, etc.).

All portions of the special education process, from assessment to placement, are strictly confidential to parties outside of the people who will directly be servicing the student. Under no circumstances should information be shared outside of the realm of parent/guardian and those providing related services without the consent of the parent/guardian. Teachers should be vigilant about confidentiality in the workplace as well. Casual conversations, even with other teachers, would violate confidentiality unless the other teachers play a role in providing services to the child.

Please refer to Skill 4.07 for New York State legal requirements regarding minority student identification.

Skill 3.08   Understanding the implications of limited English proficiency in the assessment of students with disabilities

The No Child Left Behind legislation includes students with limited English proficiency and students with disabilities in the accountability system. It judges them by the same standard used for all other students. In the past, students with limited English proficiency (LEP) were often excluded from high-stakes, large-scale assessments because educators believed it was not in the best interest of students to take the tests.

Students who have LEP **and** a disability have an even greater chance of not having their educational needs met. In many cases, educators will have to assess whether a student's problem in the classroom can be attributed to the student's language difficulties, a disability, or a combination of both. Whenever possible, reference should be made to any previous testing or scoring done in the student's native language. If a child new to this country is struggling with reading, for example, it is important to know whether reading problems existed when the child was attending classes in her native language. A child who was making good progress in reading in her native language will have reading skills and concepts that can help bridge the gap to reading in English. Such a child may still struggle in reading, but it would not be due to a reading disability.

Conversely, a child who had already been struggling to read in his native language will probably have even more trouble learning to read in English. Not only are the concepts and skills applicable to reading in his native language unable to form a bridge to English, such a history may be indicative of a reading disability that transcends mere LEP.

The NCLB legislation was designed to make sure that students in subgroups in which low percentages of students meet standards would receive attention in schools. Educators are concerned that excluding students from testing could be detrimental to students because it allows their needs to remain unknown. Including them in the assessments, when practical, ensures that the needs of these students are not ignored.

The policy for LEP students and students with disabilities under the No Child Left Behind legislation was changed in February 2004. One change was that schools were no longer required to give students with limited English proficiency their state's reading test if the students had been enrolled in a U.S. school for less than a year. Schools are still required to give these students the state's math test, but they may substitute an English-proficiency test for the reading test during the first year of enrollment.

As was the case before this change, states have a one-year grace period before they must include the scores of students with limited English proficiency in the calculations for adequate yearly progress. The second rule change permits states to count students who have become proficient in English within the past two years in their calculations of adequate yearly progress.

Please refer to Skill 5.07 for information on assessing and designing instruction for LEP students with disabilities in the classroom.

Learn more about LEP theory and practice in special education:
http://www.specialednews.com/behavior/behavnews/CECbehavassess021900.html

COMPETENCY 0004   UNDERSTAND PURPOSES, METHODS, AND PROCEDURES FOR IDENTIFYING STUDENTS WITH DISABILITIES AND EVALUATING THEIR PROGRESS

Skill 4.01   Identify procedures used for screening, prereferral, referral, classification, and declassification

PREREFERRAL

According to New York State Education Law and the Commissioner's Regulations, as cited at the state website (*www.emsc.nysed.gov/specialed/lawsregs*), school districts are required to design intervention plans to assist at-risk students prior to referral for full scale special education evaluation. These pre-referral interventions can take many forms (e.g., classroom and instructional accommodations made by the general education teacher, school-wide intervention programs) and should be individualized for the student in question. The purpose of these interventions is to meet the needs of as many students as possible in the general education classroom *without* referring them to special education. Only after appropriate attempts have been made and have failed is the referral process begun.

REFERRAL

Referral is the process through which a teacher, parent, or some other person formally requests an evaluation of a student to determine eligibility for special education services. In New York, if the prereferral interventions were not successful, the student suspected of having a disability is referred to a multidisciplinary team called the Committee on Special Education (CSE) or the Committee on Preschool Special Education (CPSE). With the parents' written consent, the CSE arranges for an evaluation of the student. This request for referral must include a description of all the prereferral interventions, the degree to which these were or were not successful, and information on why they were not successful. If no prereferral intervention occurred, the reason for this omission must be carefully documented.

Please refer to Skill 4.07 for state law regarding referral and classification of minority students.

EVALUATION

Evaluation is comprehensive and includes norm- and criterion-referenced tests (e.g., IQ and diagnostic tests), curriculum-based assessment, systematic teacher observation (e.g., behavior frequency checklist), samples of student work, and parent interviews. The purpose of the evaluation is twofold: to determine eligibility for special education services and to identify a student's strengths and weaknesses in order to plan an individual education program (IEP).

According to the rules of the New York Commissioner of Education (8 NY ADC 200.4 [b]), an initial evaluation to determine the student's weaknesses must *also* include:

- A physical examination
- A psychological evaluation (if determined appropriate for school-age students, but mandatory for pre-school children)
- A social history
- Observation of the child in his or her current educational setting
- Other tests or assessments that are appropriate for the child (such as a speech and language assessment or a functional behavioral assessment)
- Vocational assessments (required at age 12)

See Skill 3.04 for more information on the types of assessments that might be used, and Skill 3.07 for more information on legal issues regarding these assessments.

ELIGIBILITY

Eligibility is based on criteria defined in federal law. It is important to remember that, for the purposes of special education, the presence of a disability in and of itself does not qualify a child for special services. The disability must negatively impact the child's educational performance in ways that can be documented by the CSE. Specifically, IDEA defines **Student with a Disability** as an individual with a disability who has not attained the age of 21 prior to September 1st; who is entitled to attend public schools; who, because of mental, physical or emotional reasons, has been identified as having a disability; and who requires special services and programs approved by the department.

In general, results of evaluation assessments need to show a significant deficit in at least one area of educational performance that results from a disability, and/or a significant discrepancy between potential and performance. If considered eligible for special education services, the child's disability should be documented in a written report stating specific reasons for the decision.

A meeting must be held with the CSE committee in which the parent and other professionals take part to discuss the results. If the child qualifies, three-year re-evaluations for the purpose of determining the progress toward goals and the changing needs of the student will be required. During the re-evaluation, continued eligibility for services in special education must be assessed using a range of evaluation tools similar to those used during the initial evaluation. Please refer to Skill 3.07 for details on legal and due process principles relevant to this process.

IEP DEVELOPMENT

The CSE committee convenes to discuss the child's current functional level along with assessment results and information the committee has gathered. From that information, the committee agrees on the goals the child should be working toward. The committee then discusses the supports, services, and modifications that the child needs to reach those goals. Finally, the committee determines where those special education services will be provided (location and placement). The location where services will be provided and the student's placement must be in the student's least restrictive environment. Please refer to Skill 4.03 for information on placement and Skill 5.02 for IEP development.

DECLASSIFICATION

IDEA law requires three-year re-evaluations of students eligibility for special education services. If it is determined that a student no longer has a disability, that the disability no longer adversely affects the student's educational performance, or that the student's needs can be served without special education services, declassification is recommended. Accommodations and modifications in the general education setting could remain in place. These recommendations should be documented on the student's final IEP. Please refer to Skill 3.07 for the legal ramifications of declassification.

Skill 4.02   Identifying appropriate assessment instruments and methods, including alternative assessment, for monitoring the progress of individuals with disabilities

The three year evaluations required by IDEA and described in Skill 4.01 will usually use a broad range of standardized assessments similar to those used for the original eligibility evaluation. Comparison of scores with those of the original evaluation can be used to document student progress.

This might include achievement tests, which can be used as diagnostic and progress monitoring tools because the strengths and weaknesses in skill development are defined. Typically, when used as a diagnostic or progress monitoring tool, an achievement test measures one basic skill and its related components. For example, a reading test could measure reading recognition, reading comprehension, reading fluency, decoding skills, and sound discrimination. Each skill measured is reported in sub-classifications. In order to render pertinent information, achievement tests must reflect the content of the curriculum and the IEP goals and objectives. Such assessment can document major steps in student progress.

Many of the assessments used to document progress in three year evaluations are constructed and normed in such a way that they can be administered only every one to three years, so teachers need to monitor student progress on a much more frequent basis through other means. Such progress monitoring does not always require full-scale standardized assessment. Many of the more informal and teacher-made assessments described in Skills 3.02, 3.03, and 3.04 can be used for this purpose. The teacher will need to align her chosen forms of assessment with individual student needs and IEP goals, as well as with the required curriculum. In many cases the alternative assessments described in Skill 3.05 will be useful for monitoring progress.

Please refer to Skill 4.05 for more about using assessment to monitor progress and design individualized instruction. Refer to Skill 9.03 for assessments specifically related to monitoring reading progress.

Skill 4.03 Recognizing the importance of assessment in placement and accommodation decisions

IDEA law requires that each child receiving special education services be placed in his or her least restrictive environment. This means that the placement of the student depends on his or her current functional level; however, the best location for the child is as close to full time in the general education class as possible while still providing for the student's weaknesses. Assessment information (see Skills 3.02 through 3.05) will help determine the child's least restrictive environment and give key information to assist with accommodation decisions. (For more information on accommodations, see Skill 5.03.)

It must be remembered that the choice of a specific type of assessment will depend upon the unique needs of each child and the environments in which the disabilities are most troublesome. A student who demonstrates difficulty interacting with peers and acts impulsively might not be effectively evaluated with a portfolio. Anecdotal records, questioning, and certain checklists could give a better picture of the extent to which such peer interactions are detrimental to the student's (and others') wellbeing and success. Conversely, a student who displays academic difficulty is better assessed with samples of work (like a portfolio) and carefully chosen formal tests.

Special education services occur at a variety of levels, some more restrictive than others. The largest number of students (i.e., those with mild disabilities) are served in settings closest to normal educational placements. Service delivery in more restrictive settings is limited to students with severe or profound disabilities, who comprise a smaller population within special education, or to students whose disabilities require specialized instructional techniques not suitable for the larger general education class. The exception is correctional facilities, which serve a limited and restricted populace.

Deno (1970) refers to a "cascade of services" like the one shown below. The multidisciplinary team must be able to match the needs of the student with an appropriate placement in such a cascade system of services.

Cascade System of Special Education Services

Level 1	Regular classroom, including students with disabilities who are able to learn with regular class accommodations, with or without medical and counseling services
Level 2	Regular classroom with supportive services (e.g., consultation, inclusion)
Level 3	Regular classroom with part-time special classroom (e.g., itinerant services, resource room)
Level 4	Full-time special classroom (e.g., self-contained)
Level 5	Special stations (e.g., special schools)
Level 6	Homebound
Level 7	Residential (e.g., hospital, institution)

According to Polloway, et al. (1994), two assumptions are made when students are placed using the cascade of services as a guide. First, a child should be placed in an educational setting as close to the regular classroom as possible and placed only as far away from this least restrictive environment as necessary to provide appropriate education.

Second, program exit should be a goal. A student's placement might change when the team obtains data suggesting the advisability of an alternative educational setting. As adaptive, social, cognitive, motor, and language skills are developed, the student may be placed in a lesser restrictive environment. The multidisciplinary team is responsible for monitoring and recommending placement changes when appropriate.

The law also identifies related services that might be required if special education is to be effective, and these services must be in place regardless of the placement of the student on such a cascade of services.

Skill 4.04 **Interpreting and applying formal and informal assessment data (e.g., standard scores, percentile ranks, stanines, grade equivalent scores, age equivalent scores, environmental inventories, rubrics) to develop an individualized instructional program**

The knowledge of how to interpret and apply formal and informal assessment data is very important to the development of IEPs. An IEP is designed around the child's strengths and weaknesses, so correctly interpreting the implications of assessment data is critical in determining those strengths and weaknesses.

METHODS OF ASSESSING DATA

The use of informal assessments is addressed in Skills 3.02 through 3.04. Because many informal assessments are teacher-designed or modified to suit very specific assessment purposes, their interpretation is fairly straightforward. Formal, standardized testing, however, might be more difficult to interpret.

Results of formal, standardized assessments are given in derived scores, which compare the student's raw score to the performance of a specified group of subjects. Criteria for the selection of the group may be based on characteristics of age, sex, or geographic area. The test results of formal assessments must always be interpreted in light of which type of tasks the individual was required to perform and the "norm" group to which he or she is being compared (see Skills 3.01 and 3.02 for more). The most commonly used derived scores are as follows.

Age and Grade Equivalents

Age and grade equivalents are considered developmental scores because they attempt to convert the student's raw score into an average performance of a particular age or grade group.

Age equivalents are expressed in years and months (e.g., 7-3 would mean 7 years and 3 months old). In the standardization procedure, a mean is calculated for all individuals of that particular age who took the test. If the mean or median number of correct responses for children 7 years and 3 months was 80, then an individual whose raw score was 80 would be assigned an age equivalent of 7 years and 3 months (7-3). Grade equivalents are a type of age equivalent score based on years and months in school (e.g., 6.2 would read sixth grade, second month). Grade equivalents are calculated on the average performance of a group at that point in the school year.

Age and grade equivalents often seem practical and easy to understand, particularly when talking to parents. Use of such scores is widespread in the field of education, in large part because the concept of a grade equivalent is intuitively comfortable to those without testing expertise, such as parents and students. However, these scores are so often misinterpreted by parents and teachers alike that the International Reading Association (IRA) has issued a statement (1981) strongly urging teachers and schools **not** to use them. If they are used, the teacher must be very careful to explain what they do and do not mean. (See Skill 14.06 for more about how to help parents understand such scores.)

In addition, Venn (2004) points out additional difficulties with these scores. Research shows that the accuracy and reliability of age and grade equivalencies decrease as the students age. Finally the units in which age and grade equivalents are expressed are not consistent among tests,, so a child's grade equivalency on one test cannot be compared to his or her grade score on another. Venn also notes that in 1999 the American Psychological Association advocated the elimination of age and grade scores completely for all these reasons.

Quartiles, Deciles, and Percentiles

These measurements indicate the percentage of scores that fall below the individual's raw score. Quartiles divide the score into four equal parts; the first quartile is the point at which 25 percent of the scores fall below the full score. Deciles divide the distribution into ten equal parts; the seventh decile marks the point below which 70 percent of the scores fall. Percentiles are the most frequently used measure. A percentile rank of 45 would indicate that the individual's raw score was at the point below which 45 percent of the other scores fell.

Standard Scores (see also Skill 3.01)

Standard scores are raw scores with the same mean (average) and standard deviation (variability of asset of scores). In the standardization of a test, about 68 percent of the scores will fall above or below 1 standard deviation of the mean of 100. About 96 percent of the scores will fall within the range of 2 standard deviations above or below the mean. A standard deviation of 20, for example, means that 68 percent of the scores fall between 80 and 120, with 100 as the mean. Standard scores are useful because they allow for the direct comparison of raw scores from different individuals. When interpreting scores, it is important to note what type of standard score is being used.

Most standardized test manuals will explain how to interpret results so the team does not make errors and assume that a test result means something it does not. For example, it is important to understand that a percentile score of 45 means something very different from a score of 45% correct on a quiz. The 45% correct would probably be a failing grade, but the 45th percentile score is well within the normal range of performance.

Not only must the scores be interpreted in terms of the norm, but comparison of performance among subtests, such as the Verbal and Performance IQ scores of the WISC-IV, must be considered. IEP goals and objectives will be written for skills that are significantly below the norm or significantly below the student's typical skill level on other subtests.

The test manual will also contain information about how the results can be used (e.g., using the K-ABC-II to identify gifted children) and how they are not to be used (e.g., assuming that a 3rd grade student who gets a score comparable to a

5th grader on a 3rd grade test is ready to do 5th grade work, an assumption that would not be correct). Information on use with special populations, such as ESL students, students with visual impairments, physical impairments, or learning disabilities will also be covered in the manual.

Particular care must be taken in interpreting some tests. Intelligence test scores, for example, should be interpreted in terms of performance and not in terms of the test taker's potential.

In terms of IEP development, the most useful results of any type of testing are those that pinpoint specific strengths and weaknesses and specific learning styles and needs of the student. Global IQ scores or overall achievement scores are less useful than the measure of specific skills such as visual integration, working memory, or decoding skills.

Rubrics

Rubrics can be very useful in assessing components of critical skills and pinpointing areas to be included in IEP goals and objectives. A rubric simply lists a very specific set of behaviors or responses required for a particular level of performance. Using a rubric as a checklist can provide detailed information on elements of a skill that need special attention.

Environmental or Ecological Inventories

These are designed to collect information about a specific individual's natural environment so instruction can be planned that will allow that individual to be as independent as possible in that chosen environment. Such an inventory is a list of very specific skills necessary for an individual to live successfully in a particular environment. It might be the skills necessary for getting from class to class on time in high school; the skills necessary to do or even *get to* a specific job; the skills necessary to cook or do laundry, and so on. The inventory is highly individualized and is based on task analyses. These analyses will enable educators to design IEP goals and objectives and the instruction necessary to help the student meet those goals. They are important in planning adaptive behavior curricula throughout a child's educational life, but are particularly relevant as transition to adult life is being planned.

Skill 4.05 **Identifying strategies for using assessment data and information from general education teachers, other professionals, individuals with disabilities, and parents to make instructional decisions and modify learning environments**

Please refer to Skill 3.04 about assessments used for instructional decisions, and Skill 6.01 about modifying learning environments.

HOW TO USE ASSESSMENT DATA

In order to effectively use assessment to drive instruction, a teacher must be able to use assessments to diagnose problems and progress in student ability. Interpretation of test results for purposes of diagnosis goes beyond normative and criterion assessments. It is not enough to know how a student compares to age or grade peers (normative assessments), nor is it enough to know whether a child has mastered a particular set of criteria (criterion-referenced assessment). In the field of special education, the teacher already knows that the student doesn't perform at grade level and hasn't met grade level criteria; this is why the student has been referred for special education help. What the teacher needs to know is **why** the student has these problems, and **what to do about it**. The teacher needs to be able to interpret assessment results to determine as closely as possible the exact nature of the student's problem and the best strategy for helping the student to overcome the problem.

Generally, this means the teacher will be using a combination of assessment sources, including standardized testing done by the school or outside agencies, classroom quizzes and assessments, informal observations and works samples, and even parental input. Some of this information will already be available in the student's IEP or, possibly, 504 document. The teacher will need to be able to interpret and apply this information, as well as his or her own observations.

Standardized intelligence testing can provide clues to the locus of, say, a reading problem. For the teacher, the overall composite intelligence measures are less useful than the subtests. A student might have an overall intelligence rating that is well within normal ranges, or even above normal, but have serious deficiencies in one or more subtests. It is these specific subtests that the teacher needs for diagnosis and design of instructional methods.

For example, testing may show that a student has adequate processing speed but a very limited working memory. Such a combination might lead to problems that mirror attention difficulties, but which have their roots elsewhere. This child is processing information quickly, but can't hold enough pieces of information in working memory long enough to make correct decisions. This student needs to be taught strategies for expanding working memory, for "chunking" information so more will fit in the limited working memory, and for carrying the pieces along the way to a decision. This might include note taking and graphic organizers or other mnemonic devices.

Testing might show another child to have adequate working memory, logic, and long term memory, but a very slow processing speed. This child needs a very different set of strategies to learn well. Extra time for assignments, avoiding the repetition of verbal instructions (which interrupts his processing), and written or visually based instructions could be more efficient learning strategies for this child.

Standardized educational testing done by the school can also provide diagnostic clues to problems and possible treatments in the classroom. Educational testing will often have subtests of individual skills, such as word recognition, fluency, literal or inferential comprehension, writing composition and mechanics, and so on. Closely examining these areas can help a teacher diagnose problems and design remedies.

For example, if the educational testing shows a child has adequate sight word recognition skills in isolation, but cannot read connected text fluently, it might be a good idea to go back and look at the student's phoneme segmentation and blending skills. Does the student have a basic problem blending at the phoneme level? Combined with the text reading problem this may indicate more than just a phoneme awareness issue; it could be more of an overall problem with putting pieces of information together. Further diagnostic information might be found by looking at the student's ability to handle simple physical puzzles and recognize a whole from parts of a picture. A student with a disability based here will need instruction that helps him or her learn how to put information together. This might start at the most basic physical level with puzzles and progress to the use of word prediction software to help the child generalize this skill to a reading context.

APPLYING ASSESSMENT DATA TO THE LEARNING ENVIRONMENT

The assessment information gathered from various sources can also be used to manage various aspects of the learning environment, such as the following.

Classroom Organization: The teacher can vary grouping arrangements (e.g., large group, small group, peer tutoring, or learning centers) and methods of instruction (teacher directed, student directed).

Classroom Management: The teacher can vary grading systems, vary reinforcement systems, and vary the rules (differentiate for some students).

Methods of Presentation:

- Content: amount to be learned, time to learn, and concept level
- General structure: advance organizers, immediate feedback, memory devices, and active involvement of students
- Type of presentation: verbal or written, transparencies, audiovisual

Methods of Practice:

- General structure: amount to be practiced; time to finish; group, individual, or teacher-directed; and varied level of difficulty
- Level of response: copying, recognition, or recall; with and without cues
- Types of materials: worksheets, audiovisual, texts

Methods of Testing:

- Type: verbal, written, oral, or demonstration
- General structure: time or amount, group or individual
- Level of response: multiple choice, essay, recall of facts

Skill 4.06   Recognizing the importance to the decision making process of background information regarding academic, medical, and family history and cultural background

Relevant background information regarding the student's academic, medical, and family histories should be used to identify students with disabilities and evaluate their progress. It is also critical for collaborating with both families and the students themselves (see Skills 14.01-14.04 for details).

An evaluation report should include the summary of a comprehensive diagnostic interview by a qualified evaluator. A combination of candidate self-report interviews (with families and others) and historical documentation (such as transcripts and standardized test scores) is recommended.

The evaluator should use professional judgment as to which areas are relevant in determining a student's eligibility for accommodations due to disabilities. The evaluation should include developmental history; relevant medical history, including the presence or absence of a medical diagnosis for the present symptoms; academic history, including results of prior standardized testing; reports of classroom performance; relevant family history, including the primary language of the home and the student's (and parents') current level of fluency of English; relevant psychosocial history; a discussion of dual diagnosis, alternative or co-existing mood, behavioral, neurological, and/or personality disorders, along with any history of relevant medication use that may affect the individual's learning; and exploration of possible alternatives that could mimic a learning disability.

By utilizing all possible background information in the assessment, the team can rule out alternative explanations for academic problems, such as poor education, poor motivation and study skills, emotional problems, or cultural and language differences. If the student's entire background and history is not taken into account, it is not always possible to institute the most appropriate educational program for the student with disabilities.

Refer to Skill 14.04 for information on the relevance of cultural background.

Skill 4.07   Demonstrating knowledge of the implications of diversity with regard to assessment, eligibility, programming, and placement

IDEA regulations (Indicator #9) specifically target the over-representation of minority students and students from diverse language and cultural backgrounds among those diagnosed with disabilities and referred for special education services.

The New York State Department of Education (NYSED) monitors the proportion of students from diverse populations who are referred for special education in each school in the state. Any school found to have a disproportionate number of minority students referred for special education must conduct a self review according to strict state guidelines. The purpose of the self review is to determine whether the disproportionate representation is the result of improper assessment and identification. Results are reported to NYSED. The specific protocol for this review was revised in April 2010, and details can be found at NYSED / P-12: EMSC / Special Education / State Performance Plan / Indicator 9 / Self-Review Monitoring Protocol–Disproportionate Identification of Racial and Ethnic Groups.

Please refer to Skill 3.04 for information on the limitations of assessments used with students from diverse backgrounds, and to Skill 3.07 for legal issues regarding assessment of such students.

FAIR ASSESSMENT PRACTICES

The issue of fair assessment for individuals from minority groups has a long history in law, philosophy, and education. Slavia and Ysseldyke (1995) point out three aspects of this issue that are particularly relevant to the assessment of students.

1. **Representation**
   Individuals from diverse backgrounds need to be represented in assessment materials. It is essential that persons from different cultures be represented fairly. Of equal importance is the presentation of individuals from differing genders in non-stereotypical roles and situations.

2. **Acculturation**
   It is important that individuals from different backgrounds receive opportunities to acquire the tested skills, information, and values. When students are tested with standardization instruments, they are compared to a set of norms in order to gain an index of their relative standing and to make comparisons (in special education, usually for eligibility or placement decisions). The test assumes that all the students tested have a comparable acculturation; that is, educational, socioeconomic, and experiential background, rather than simply race

or ethnicity. (Slavia & Ysseldyke, 1991). Differences in experiential background should therefore be accounted for when administering tests (see Skill 3.04).

3. **Language**
   The language and concepts that comprise test items should be unbiased. Students should be familiar with the terminology and references used on tests, especially when test results will be used for decision-making purposes.

Skill 4.08   Use ongoing assessment to evaluate and modify instruction

Please refer to Skill 4.05 for more on using various assessments to design and modify instruction, to Skill 4.02 for using assessment to monitor progress toward goals, and to Skill 7.02 for differentiated instruction.

Assessment skills should be an integral part of teacher training, where teachers are able to monitor students learning using pre- and post-assessments of content areas; analyze assessment data in terms of individualized support for students and instructional practice for teachers; and design lesson plans that have measurable outcomes and definitive learning standards. Assessment information should be used to provide performance-based criteria and academic expectations for all students when evaluating whether students have learned the expected skills and content of the subject area.

For example, in an Algebra I class, teachers can use assessments to see whether students have learned the prerequisite knowledge for success in the class. If the teacher provides students with a pre-assessment on algebraic expression and ascertains that the lesson plan should be modified to include a pre-algebraic expression lesson refresher unit, the teacher can create quantifiable data to support the need for additional resources to support student learning. Once the teacher has taught the unit on algebraic expression, a post-assessment test can be used to test student learning and a mastery exam can be used to test how well students understand and can apply the knowledge to the next unit of math content.

The teacher must be concerned not only with the student's readiness for a particular lesson, but also with the degree to which the specific teaching approach is compatible with individual student learning styles and disabilities. Initial assessments of student learning styles and self knowledge concerning the teacher's own preferred style can be helpful in designing the most appropriate lessons for students. (Please refer to Skill 7.02 for more on differentiated lesson design.)

COMPETENCY 0005   UNDERSTAND PROCEDURES FOR DEVELOPING, IMPLEMENTING, AND AMENDING INDIVIDUALIZED EDUCATION PROGRAMS (IEPS) FOR STUDENTS WITH DISABILITIES

Skill 5.01   **Recognizing the rights, roles, and functions of IEP team members (e.g., special education teacher, student, parents/guardians, general education teacher, speech language therapist, occupational therapist, school administrator)**

According to IDEA 2004, the IEP team includes the parents of a child with a disability; not less than one regular education teacher of said child (if the child is, or may be, participating in the regular education environment); not less than one special education teacher, or where appropriate, not less than one special education provider of said child; a representative of the local educational agency; an individual who can interpret the instructional implications of evaluation results; at the discretion of the parent of the agency, other individuals who have knowledge or special expertise regarding the child, including related services personnel as appropriate; and, whenever appropriate, the child with a disability.

The role of the representative of the local education agency is to provide or supervise the provision of specifically-designed instruction to meet the unique needs of the child. This is usually the school principal if this is the first time the child has been evaluated. If the representative is not an expert on evaluations, then one of the people who participated in the actual testing of the child must be present.

The role of the teacher is to identify the short- and long-term goals for the student and to report on the student's current progress including strengths and weaknesses.

The school must allow any other individual the parents want to invite to attend the meeting. This might be a caseworker involved with the student's family, people involved with the day-to-day care of the student, or any person the parent feels can contribute vital information to the meeting.

The parents or guardians can also bring someone to help them understand the IEP or the IEP process, such as a parent advocate or a lawyer experienced in educational advocacy.

There are lists of related services that may be considered during a CSE meeting. These include developmental, corrective, and other supportive services that are required to help a child with special needs benefit from special education. These related services can include speech and language therapy, audiology services, psychological services, physical and occupational therapy, recreation and extracurricular activities, counseling services, and medical services for diagnostic or evaluation purposes.

The IEP should specify the services to be provided, the extent to which they are necessary, and who will provide the services. If a specialist such as a speech teacher or occupational therapist will provide specific services, they should be included in the CSE team. This way, they can give input on the types of services required, what is available, and what may be beneficial to the student in question. In this case, information on how the student is doing in particular specialist areas should also be included with the evaluation regarding speech therapy and occupational therapy.

Skill 5.02 **Identifying information that must be specified in an IEP (e.g., present levels of performance, achievable goals, measurable objectives, benchmarks, types of assistive technology that students may need, extent of participation in the general education curriculum)**

It is important to understand how much the law affects the required components of the IEP. Educators must keep themselves apprised of the changes and amendments to laws (such as IDEA) as well as the required manner in which they must be implemented. Teachers should be aware that IDEA's new Indicator 13 is changing the way IEPs are written. The federal government is requiring changes in IEPs to create an easier way to collect statistics on student success at reaching post-school goals. While many of the requirements have been used for years, compliance is now mandated and must be documented. Indicator 13 requirements (I-13) are noted in the following list of the elements required in an IEP:

1. The student's present level of academic performance and functional performance. Beginning with IDEA 97, the Present Levels of Educational Performance (PLEP) was changed to require a statement of how the child's disability affects his or her involvement and progress in the general curriculum. IDEA 97 also established that there must be a connection between the special education and general education curriculum. For this reason, the PLEP was required to include an explanation of the extent to which the student will *not* be participating with non-disabled children in the general education class, extracurricular events, and non-academic activities.
   I-13: Student voice must now be included in each Present Level of Performance. This means that Academic, Social, Physical, Management, etc. must include one student voice statement either in the strengths, needs, or both. For example, "John reads fluently on a 3rd grade level. He is able to add and subtract two digit numbers. He has difficulty with grouping and multiplying. *John states that he would rather read than do math.*" Student voice can express the student's strengths, preferences,

and/or interests. When the child begins to do vocational assessments, student voice should be related to transition to the post-school activities of his or her choice.

2. A statement of how the disability affects the student's involvement and progress in the general education curriculum. Preschool children must have a statement explaining how the disability affects the child's participation in appropriate activities.

3. A statement of annual goals or realistically anticipated attainments
   I-13: All goals must be directly correlated to student needs. This means that if a need is stated in the present levels, it must have a goal. These goals should, when possible, have benchmarks denoting possible levels of achievement

4. Short-term objectives are no longer required on every IEP. Students with severe disabilities or those taking an alternate assessment might need short-term objectives to lead to the obtainment of annual goals.

5. A statement of when the parents will be notified of their child's progress, which must be at least as often as the regular education student's parents are notified

6. Modifications or accommodations for participation in statewide or citywide assessments; or, if it is determined that the child cannot participate, why the assessment is inappropriate for the child and how the child will be assessed. The IEP team determines how the student will participate. Alternate assessments need to be aligned with the general curriculum standards set for all students and should not be assumed appropriate only for those students with significant cognitive impairments.

7. Specific educational services, assistive technology, and related services to be provided, as well as those who will provide them
   I-13: The intended special education program, such as a substantially separate classroom or a resource room pull-out, must be on the IEP. The stated program must align with the needs of the student given in the Present Levels of Performance. The Needs in the Present Levels of Performance must justify both the program and services (e.g., a speech/language service must be justified by a statement of needs in that area).

8. Evaluation of criteria and timelines for determining whether instructional objectives have been achieved

9. Projected dates for initiating services with their anticipated frequency, location, and duration

10. The extent to which the child will not participate in the regular education program and the rationale for this (see I-13 under #7)

11. Transition information. Beginning when a student is 14, and annually thereafter, the student's IEP must contain a statement of his or her transition service needs under the various components of his or her IEP. This relates to the components that focus on the student's courses of study (e.g., vocational education or advanced placement); when appropriate, it also includes interagency responsibilities and links for

possible future assistance. Beginning at least one year before the student reaches the age of maturity under state law, the IEP must contain a statement that the student has been informed of the rights under the law that will transfer to him or her upon reaching the age of maturity. 20 U.S.C. 1414 (d)(1)(A)(i)

I-13: IEPs now must include a statement of post-school activities and goals including:

- Instruction
- Related services
- Community experiences
- The development of employment and other post adult living objectives, when appropriate
- Acquisition of daily living skills
- Functional vocational evaluation

Post-secondary goals must be measurable. This means that they must be stated using the word "will."

Wrong: Bill *wants* to become a doctor. Correct: Bill *will* become a doctor.

All six areas must be addressed on the IEP. However, the IEP can include a statement that "the student has no needs in a particular area *at this time.*"

Skill 5.03   Demonstrating knowledge of supports and accommodations needed for integrating students with disabilities into various program placements

Please refer also to differentiated instruction techniques in Skill 7.02.

The specific supports and accommodations needed will depend upon each student's specific needs, so no comprehensive list can be made. Depending upon a child's specific needs, accommodations such as these are typically found in IEPs:

- Subject-specific word banks available for all written assignments
- Repeat, not rephrase instructions, or simplify and rephrase instructions (depending upon the specific disability)
- Visual/ verbal cues
- Task breakdown
- Multisensory approach strategies for word retrieval
- Information chunking strategies and aids/mnemonic devices
- Graphic organizers and writing templates
- Study guides
- Extra time to respond orally

- Minimize recall tasks on quizzes and tests and allow alternate methods of demonstrating knowledge (e.g., rather than defining the word "product" on a math test, have the student circle the product in the number sentence: 5 x 15 = 75).
- Step-by-step math templates
- Calculator
- Reduced work load
- Frequent breaks or "fidget" objects

MODIFICATION OF MATERIALS

One area in which modification or accommodation will often be needed involves content area texts. Modifying reading materials is often necessary when including special education students in the general education classroom. The goal of text modification is to present the material in a manner that the student can better understand while preserving the basic ideas and content.

Many of the adaptations and modifications helpful to students with disabilities can be seen in terms of Cummins' (1994) analysis of the cognitive demands of comprehending the text. Such adaptations can either lighten the cognitive burden or make it easier for the student to carry that burden. Cummins' work with students with limited English proficiency (LEP) led him to analyze tasks in terms of two variables: amount of context and cognitive demand. Text that has a lot of context for a student will be easier than text with little or no context. Cognitive demand is a measure of how much information must be processed quickly. A cognitively demanding text presents a lot of information at one time or in rapid succession and is more difficult to understand. Less cognitively demanding text presents only single pieces of information or concepts to process, and separates it into discrete, small steps. When modifying text to accommodate students with special needs, focus on changes that will provide more context and simplify the wording and concepts.

Simplifying Texts

- Use a highlighter to mark key terms, main ideas, and concepts. In some cases, a marker may be used to delete nonessential content.
- Cut and paste: the main ideas and specific content are cut and pasted on separate sheets of paper. Additional headings or other graphic aids can be inserted to help the student understand and organize material.
- Supplement with graphic aids or tables.
- Supplement with study guides, questions, and directed preview.
- Use self-correcting materials.
- Allow additional time or break content material into smaller, more manageable units.

Rewriting Content Material

In some cases, it might be necessary to simply rewrite the content material to make it accessible to students with reading disabilities. The most common specific learning disabilities involve reading difficulties, so one of the most common requirements will be finding or revising text for learners who cannot read at grade level or who have difficulty comprehending what they read in content areas such as science and social studies.

In order for such students to have equal access to the grade level curriculum in content areas, it is often necessary to revise printed material so students can access it at their reading level. Whether selecting published materials or revising them for the students, these guidelines should be followed in order to increase context, reduce cognitive demand, and provide content material that students with learning disabilities can access.

- Avoid complex sentences with many relative clauses.
- Avoid the passive tense.
- Try to make the topic sentence the first sentence in a paragraph.
- Make sure paragraphs have a concluding sentence that restates the topic sentence in another way.
- Use simple, declarative sentences that present only one main idea or concept at a time.
- Use simple, single syllable, concrete words rather than more complex words (e.g., "an arduous journey" should be "a hard trip").
- Eliminate nonessential information in favor of the main concepts necessary to teach.
- Try to use only one tense in all the sentences.
- Add diagrams and illustrations whenever possible and deliver information through labels rather than complete sentences.
- Whenever possible, include multisensory elements and multimodalities in the presentation.
- Avoid unfamiliar names and terms that will "tie up" the student's cognitive efforts (e.g., while the student is trying to figure out how to read the name "Aloicious" he or she will miss the point of the sentence; change the name to "Al").

Taped Textbooks

Textbooks can be taped by the teacher or aide for students to follow along. In some cases, the students might qualify for recordings of textbooks from agencies such as Recordings for the Blind.

Parallel Curriculum

Projects such as Parallel Alternative Curriculum (PAC) or Parallel Alternative Strategies for Students (PASS) present the content at a lower grade reading level and come with tests, study guides, vocabulary activities, and tests.

Supplementary Texts

Book publishers such as Steck-Vaughn publish a series of content-area texts that have been modified for reading level, amount of content presented on pages, highlighted key items, and visual aids.

ACCOMMODATIONS IN TEST-TAKING SITUATIONS

Teachers of students with special needs will frequently find it necessary to modify their assessment techniques and procedures in order to accurately assess the students' knowledge and skills. Because certain disabilities can interfere with performance on an assessment, it is often necessary for the task to be broken down and each part tested separately.

Many of the common accommodations and modifications in testing are designed to separate the specific skill or knowledge being tested from some other ability or skill impacted by a disability. For example, when testing a student with dyslexia on retention of a concept in science, it would be inappropriate to use a reading/writing assessment. The student's response to a written test would be confounded by the inability to read the test or to compose readable written responses. In such cases an oral exam might more accurately assess the student's science knowledge.

In general, Accommodations or modifications in assessment usually fall into the following categories:

Setting: Changes in the location of the testing, such as separate seating or room, special lighting or noise buffers, adaptive furniture, small group or one to one testing

Timing and scheduling: Changes in the duration or time of the test such as allowing extra time or an absence of time limits, frequent breaks, or scheduling the test at a time of day when a student functions best (has had specific medication, etc.)

Presentation of test: Changes in how the test is given to a student, such as oral testing, large print or Braille, sign language, colored overlays or special paper, etc. This would also include technology that changes printed text to electronic text that can be modified, enhanced, programmed, linked, and searched, or allowing the teacher to clarify directions or read the test to the student.

Student responses: Changes in how the student is allowed to respond to the test, such as allowing oral responses, multiple choice rather than essay, cloze procedures to provide scaffolding, dictating open responses, use of assistive devices such as computer keyboards, spell checkers, writing software, etc.

Skill 5.04   Analyzing issues related to the preparation and amendment of an IEP

Please refer to Skill 4.01 for issues regarding referral and eligibility, to Skill 5.01 for information on IEP team members and contributors, and to Skill 5.02 for information on mandated contents of an IEP.

It is important to remember that preparation of an IEP is a joint task carried out by the IEP *team* and is not the work of only one party or contributor. Teachers may come to the meeting with suggested goals and objectives, but the body of collected assessment and the appropriateness of placement and goals will be discussed by all members. Due process rights (see Skill 3.07) protect parent interests if a disagreement arises, but it is best for the student if individuals at the meeting can act as a team, jointly planning what is most appropriate for the child. Confrontational and adversarial attitudes and remarks will be detrimental to the IEP process.

One of the most important things for teachers to remember about an IEP is that it is a *legally binding document*. Teachers, administrators and schools are all parties who are bound by law to abide by the requirements of the IEP. This means, for example, that general education teachers, special education teachers, administrators, and *all* staff are required to provide the accommodations listed in the IEP. Recent court cases have held both schools and individual teachers culpable when IEP accommodations were not provided, and significant fines have been levied against both schools and individual teachers in such cases. Once it is signed by all parties, an IEP carries the weight of law and must be followed. An IEP must be signed by the parent/guardian of the child and by the school district's representative before it can be put into effect.

In addition to sections mentioned in earlier skills, the team must also make decisions about a variety of practical issues:

Extended school year is considered for each student and determination is made based on whether or not the student will have difficulty regaining skills that might be lost during the summer months if extended school year is not attended. Evidence of this probable regression must be documented.

Transportation is considered for the student, including the need for special transportation and any special equipment or personnel that might be needed.

Overall percentage of time in special/regular education is determined, as well as the rationale of why other percentages of time (greater or lesser) were not chosen.

Parental consent and notification of a CSE meeting is required. Parents should be notified in writing ten days prior to a CSE meeting. A total of three contacts should be made with the parent prior to the meeting. Recent court cases have ruled that messages left on a phone answering machine or with a non-parent/guardian are not considered adequate contact. Written notification is preferred, though documented person-to-person phone contact will sometimes suffice. Parents should also be provided with a document outlining their rights in the special education process. The CSE meeting may be held without a parent if the parent consents. Although parental consent is required for initial testing, subsequent consent is not needed unless a change in placement is being considered.

Reconvening (amendment) might be requested by school personnel or parents at any time that the program is considered not to be meeting the needs of the student. However, according to the IDEA 2004, changes may be made in the IEP as deemed necessary by the CPSE (Committee on Pre-school Special Education) or CSE (Committee on Special Education); as with regular IEP meetings, parent participation is not mandatory, but parent consent is.

Multi-year CSE meetings are now being used in some school districts when the existing program seems appropriate for the student. This is an effort to minimize paperwork and meeting times.

Three-Year Reevaluation Meetings determine the appropriateness of the student's program and the possible need for additional testing.

Skill 5.05   Demonstrating knowledge of characteristics and purposes of various CSE meetings (e.g., annual review, triennial review)

Although New York State conforms to IDEA and its revisions, it is essential that all special education teachers become aware of the New York State regulations on special education, found in the New York Administrative Code. Part 200 (8 NYADC 200) defines the characteristics and purposes of the CSE meetings; it is revised almost every five years. Part 201 (8 NYADC 201) covers the disciplinary procedures and protocols for students receiving special education services. For the purposes of preparing for the NYSTCE Content Specialty Exam on Special Education, the following information will take much of its content directly from both Part 200 and Part 201.

PURPOSES FOR CSE MEETINGS

There are six defined reasons for a CSE to take place:

Initial: The initial CSE is the first CSE held. It is due to a referral on the part of school personnel or parents/guardians. Preschool children, like those who are school age, may be evaluated for in order to determine whether or not a child's disability can be deemed to adversely affect his or her ability to learn.

Annual review: Once a year, reviews of IEPs are given at a CSE. The purpose of these meetings is to determine if progress is being made and if the student's program remains appropriate. For these purposes, *program* means the student's placement (i.e., inclusion, 12:1:1, 8:1:1), test modifications, and the necessary academic and instructional interventions to aide a student's learning ability.

Triennials (three year reviews): This type of CSE is similar to an initial CSE meeting. Like the annual reviews, the triennials are also reviews, but they are more extensive and may require additional testing to provide verification that the student's current placement continues to be appropriate or needs to be changed. The intent in making the third-year review is to provide a point at which the whole child must be looked at, rather than providing a basic review of present levels of performance.

Amendments (change of program/placement): It is not unusual for teachers, parents, and administrators to note possible ways to best assist a student to achieve his or her learning potential. Amendment CSEs are convened by the request of a parent or teacher and look at specific needs for change in the "immediate future." For this reason, expedited requests for CSEs are recorded as Amendment CSEs. An example would be a mother's request to add the test modification of a scribe for her son to be put in place before his Regents Exam in three months.

Manifestation Determination: This is a CSE held when a student has been removed from his or her academic environment for a period of more than 10 consecutive days (usually for disciplinary reasons), or if the student has received a series of suspensions that add up to more than 10 school days a year. School districts often make this policy stricter by requiring a Manifestation Determination CSE when a student reaches a series of suspensions that add up to eight academic days within a school year. This insures compliance with Part 201.

The purpose of this CSE is to determine if the behavior that resulted in a suspension was a result of the student's disability. One example would be a student with special needs who swears at a teacher and is suspended as a result; the CSE must determine whether the student's behavior is a manifestation of the student's disability (in this case, Tourette's Syndrome).

Post-school transition: The last CSE before a student leaves the school district "umbrella" of special education services can be the one that provides lasting opportunities for the student. Since the student was 14 years old, transitional evaluations and statements have been important. It is here that students and their parents should be given what can be considered "lasting resources and supports" that will grow as the young adult with special needs steps out into society. One of the most basic of resources that teachers need to think of is the test modifications for their students. Test modifications can follow students through life, providing several occupational opportunities.

Skill 5.06 **Demonstrating understanding of the purposes and components of transition planning, including the coordination of members of various disciplines and agencies to ensure the systematic transition at all levels (birth to adulthood) of students with disabilities**

Transition planning is necessary whenever a student transitions or changes from one program or setting to another throughout life.

TRANSITIONING TO AND THROUGHOUT SCHOOL

Federal, State and local requirements for transition planning services are broken down for the Individualized Family Service Plan (IFSP) and Individualized Education Program (IEP). The IFSP provides early intervention services planning and documentation for an infant or toddler with a disability from birth to three years of age and his or her family. It also prepares all parties for the IEP process, which provides special education services planning and documentation for school-aged students with exceptionalities aged three to twenty-one years.

The IFSP and the IEP should address the needs of students as they move from preschool to school, from grade to grade, and (in some cases) from program to program within the school setting. The participants in the transition process include children and their families, service coordinators, early intervention practitioners involved in a child's future/pending/current IFSP program, IFSP teams and preschool teachers, early childhood special educators, related services practitioners, administrators, and future/pending/current IEP teams. In order to facilitate transition success among these diverse groups of participants, skilled cross-agency communication with achievement based collaboration is required. Communication and collaboration are frequently quoted as the most significant challenges from people involved in the transition process.

According to the National Early Childhood Transition Center (NECTC), individuals with disabilities experience the same difficulties with transitions as individuals who develop typically, but often to an even higher degree. Goals should be written that will support important aspects in proactive transitioning from one program of development to another for the individuals and their families. In addition to the overall purpose of reducing stress and helping all parties experience success in the new setting, the following are important transition principles:

- Services should be uninterrupted; appropriate services, equipment, and trained staff should be available in new settings
- Transition should avoid any duplication in assessment and goal planning.
- Transition should be marked by ongoing communication and collaborative partnerships.
- Transition should be viewed as a process.
- Transition should meet legal requirements and make decisions in a timely manner.
- Transition should model non-confrontational and effective advocacy that families can emulate throughout their children's lives.

The NECTC scrutinizes and authenticates strategies involved in both early and later childhood transitioning and has made the following suggestions to improve transition at all levels:

- A regular routine/schedule will help promote successful transitioning and will provide the child with a sense of predictability and routine.
- Broad community support results in the highest quality of services for ongoing education and transitioning of children.
- Visiting the new setting in advance and meeting peers and staff improves success.
- Staff from sending and receiving programs must communicate with and, if possible, visit one another and the child's family.
- Transition strategies should be tailored to meet individual needs rather than a generic procedure designed to fit all students.

TRANSITIONING TO POST-SECONDARY LIFE

Transition planning is mandated in the Individuals with Disabilities Education Act (IDEA) and the specific legal requirements for the IEP are outlined in Skill 5.02. This section will cover practical aspects of the process and an overview of transition services. The above comments about transitioning within the school setting are also applicable to transitioning out of school and into the adult world.

Transition planning and services focus on a coordinated set of *student-centered* activities designed to facilitate progression from school to post-school activities. Others involved in post-school transition planning include parents, secondary personnel, post-secondary personnel, counselors, and any relevant community personnel, organizations, company representatives, vocational education instructors, and job coaches; all may be members of the transition team. Transition planning should be flexible and focus on the developmental and educational requirements of each individual student.

It is important that the student play a key role in transition planning. This entails asking the student to identify preferences and interests and to attend meetings on transition planning. The degree of success experienced by the student in post-secondary educational settings depends on the student's degree of motivation, independence, self-direction, self-advocacy, and academic abilities developed in high school (see Skill 6.05).

In order to contribute to the transition planning process, the student should:

- Understand his or her disability and the impact it has on learning and work; implement achievable goals
- Present a positive self-image by emphasizing strengths while understanding the impact of the disability
- Know how and when to discuss and ask for needed accommodations
- Seek instructors and learning environments that are supportive
- Establish an ongoing personal file that consists of school and medical records, an individualized education program (IEP), a resume, and samples of academic work

The primary role of parents during transition planning is to encourage and assist students in planning and achieving their educational goals. Parents should also encourage students to cultivate independent decision-making and self-advocacy skills.

Please refer to Skill 11.07 for more on transition planning for post-school life.

Skill 5.07   Use assessment data and information to plan appropriate individual programs for all students with disabilities, including those from culturally and/or linguistically diverse backgrounds

Previous skill sections have covered many of the issues that must be considered in the use of assessment data and other information to plan appropriate individual programs for students with disabilities. Skills in Competency 0004 cover the use of many forms of assessment for placement, instructional design, and classroom modifications. Skill 4.07 specifically covers issues relevant to cultural and linguistic diversity. Earlier skills in this section (Competency 0005) detail IEP design, and Skill 5.03 lists the types of accommodations that might be needed for various students.

In summary, assessment data and information are critical resources for the special educators using the IEP to design day-to-day instructional programs for a particular student (see Skill7.02 for more information). This data can provide information on the student's current level of functioning in social skills, speech, language, academics, cognitive skills, and fine and gross motor skills. (It is important to note that the student's classroom performance should also be taken into account when writing current level of performance.)

Assessment data can also reveal specific deficits that affect the teacher's choice of instructional methods for a particular student (see Skill 4.05 for more information). For example, a student who has tested as having a deficit in rote memory skills might have an IEP objective to rote count to 25 or to recite the alphabet. A student who demonstrates a reading delay of two years might have IEP goals and objectives that reflect that he or she will demonstrate comprehension skills with material at that grade level.

The need for programming in specific therapies could also be the result of formal assessment. Such therapies might include speech and language therapy, physical therapy, occupational therapy, vision therapy, or music therapy. Formal assessment and school behaviors might result in a functional behavioral plan as a part of the IEP.

The special education student with a culturally or linguistically diverse background will need additional considerations. Although a student does not qualify for special education services simply due to diversity in cultural or linguistic background, some students who come from a diverse background certainly qualify for special education services. The individual student's cultural background should be considered when designing appropriate instruction and intervention.

STUDENTS WITH DISABILITIES AND LIMITED ENGLISH PROFICIENCY (LEP)

When planning programs for students who have both a disability and LEP, assessment of the student's level of English proficiency will be critical to success. It is important that the teacher understand how to interpret the development of *different kinds* of English proficiency.

Jim Cummins (1994 and 1999) describes the stages of second language learning and how they impact academic learning in English. He describes two levels of English language acquisition: BICS and CALP.

BICS (Basic Interpersonal Communication Skills) are the conversational English skills that are learned first. Conversational English is highly contextualized; that is, it is supported by facial expressions, body language, gestures, and other supports found in face-to-face communication. It is also relatively undemanding cognitively. In students without disabilities, BICS takes about 2 years to fully master.

CALP (Cognitive Academic Language Proficiency) refers to the language level needed to learn academic subjects taught in that language. This form of language proficiency depends heavily on linguistic cues alone, has very little context, and is far more formal and difficult to learn. This is the form of English that is used in classrooms and textbooks. Research shows that for students without disabilities average time to proficiency varies with the student's age of arrival in the U.S.:

- Age 8-11 at arrival: 4-5 years to proficiency
- Age 5-7 at arrival: 5-8 years to proficiency
- Age 12+ at arrival: Longer, and probably will not reach this level by high school graduation

In teaching LEP students with disabilities, it is important to remember that BICS fluency—that is, fluency with everyday conversation—is **not** the same as CALP fluency—that is, the fluency needed to learn to read and read to learn in English as a second language—**and** that students with disabilities might take much longer to reach these levels of English fluency in both BICS and CALP.

When designing a program for these students, materials and activities must be at the student's developmental level and English language level and must, as needed, parallel skills in the child's first language and then in English. The special education teacher must also remember to foster an appreciation and respect for the student's cultural and linguistic background.

Skill 5.08   Demonstrating understanding of requirements for creating and maintaining records and preserving confidentiality

One of the most important professional practices a teacher must maintain is student confidentiality. This extends far beyond paper records and goes into the realm of oral discussions. Teachers are expected not to mention the names of students or their diagnoses and problems in conversations with those who are not directly involved with them, both inside and outside of school. (See Skill 14.07 for statement of the law on privacy).

In the school environment, teacher record-keeping comes in three main formats with specific confidentiality rules. All of the records stated below should be kept in a locked place within the classroom or in an office within the school:

1. **Teacher's personal notes on a student**
   When a teacher takes notes on a student's actions, including behaviors and/or grade performances that are not intended to be placed in a school recorded format (such as a report card or an IEP progress report), the teacher may keep this information private and confidential to his or her own files. Teachers may elect to either share this information or not.

2. **Teacher's daily recorded grades and attendance of the student**
   A teacher's grade books and attendance records are to be open to the parent/guardian of the child. Only that child's information may be shared—not that of other children. However, this information must be kept confidential from public view.

3. **Teacher notations on records that appear in the student's cumulative file**

There are specific rules regarding the sharing of the cumulative records of students:

- Cumulative files will follow a student who transfers within the school district, from school to school.
- All information placed in a cumulative file may be examined by the parent at any time it is requested. If parents show up to review their child's cumulative file, the file should be shown as it is in its current state. IEPs are typically **not** kept in cumulative files, but are maintained in a confidential location. However, they, too, are available upon demand to parents.
- When information from a cumulative file is requested by another person/entity other than the parent/guardian, the information may not be released without the express written consent of the parent/guardian. The parental consent must specify which records may be shared with the other party of interest.
- A school in which a student intends to enroll may receive the student's educational record without parental consent. However, the school sending that information must make a reasonable attempt to notify the parent/guardian of the request (FERPA).

Today's world is quickly becoming a digital environment. Teachers now communicate with email and keep records in digital formats, often within a district-mandated program. Teachers should keep in mind that emails and other electronic formats can be forwarded and are as indelible as permanent ink. In addition, since email is not generally a fully secure form of communication, many school systems do **not** allow the use of email for communicating confidential information. Under no circumstances should confidential information about students be placed on a Web site, whether the site is school generated or not. If teachers do use email for material that does not need to be kept confidential, they should maintain a professional decorum, just as when they are writing their own records that will be seen outside of their personal notations.

Learn more about confidentiality and the law at:
http://www.wrightslaw.com/info/ferpa.index.htm

SUBAREA II.   PROMOTING STUDENT LEARNING AND DEVELOPMENT IN A COLLABORATIVE LEARNING COMMUNITY

COMPETENCY 0006   UNDERSTAND METHODS OF PLANNING AND MANAGING TEACHING AND LEARNING ENVIRONMENTS FOR INDIVIDUALS WITH DISABILITIES

Skill 6.01   Demonstrating knowledge of basic principles of classroom management and research-based best practices for managing learning environments for students with disabilities

CLASSROOM MANAGEMENT TECHNIQUES

Classroom management plans should be in place when the school year begins. Developing a management plan takes a proactive approach—that is, deciding which behaviors will be expected of the class as a whole, anticipating possible problems, and teaching these behaviors early in the school year. When students with disabilities are involved, the teacher should consider the impact each child's disability could have on behavior and possible problems that might arise, and also be proactive in planning to prevent these problems.

For example, if a teacher knows that a student has ADHD and his IEP calls for alternate positions for working (e.g., standing, lying down, and movement), the teacher should take this into consideration when setting up the classroom and when designing the behavior management plan.

Behavior management techniques should focus on positive procedures that can be used at home as well as at school. Involving the students (including those with disabilities) in the development of the classroom rules lets the students know the rationale for the rules and allows them to assume responsibility for them. Once the rules are established, enforcement and reinforcement for following the rules should begin immediately and should be consistent.

Consequences, both positive and negative, should be introduced when the rules are introduced; these should be clearly stated and understood by all of the students. The nature of the consequence should match the nature of the behavior in question. For example, free time activities are good rewards for students who work hard and finish their work on time. Removal from a group and "time out" is a reasonable negative consequence for a student who is misbehaving in a way that disturbs others. The teacher must apply the consequence consistently and fairly so the students will know what to expect.

About four to six classroom rules should be posted where students can easily see and read them. These rules should be stated positively and describe specific behaviors so they are easy to understand. Certain rules may also be tailored to meet the target goals and the IEP requirements of individual students (for example, a new student who has had problems with leaving the classroom might need an individual behavior contract to assist him or her with adjusting to the class rule about remaining in the assigned area).

As the students demonstrate the behaviors, the teacher should provide reinforcement and corrective feedback. Periodic "refresher" practice can be done as needed; for example, it can be done after a long holiday or if students begin to "slack off." A copy of the classroom plan should be readily available for substitute teacher use, and the classroom aide should also be familiar with the plan and procedures.

The teacher should clarify and model the expected behavior for the students. In addition to the classroom management plan, a management plan should be developed for special situations, (e.g., fire drills) and transitions (e.g., going to and from the cafeteria). Periodic review of the rules, modeling of the rules, and practice may be conducted as needed.

When students with disabilities are involved, there might need to be differentiation in some rules. For example, a classroom rule that students work quietly and do not talk might need to be revised for a student whose IEP states that he needs to "self coach" and talk himself through tasks, or for a student with Tourette's Syndrome who cannot help small verbalizations. The teacher will need to arrange the classroom so that these behaviors to not disturb others and will need to help students understand that everyone learns differently.

Motivation

Before the teacher begins instruction, he or she should choose activities that are meaningful, relevant, and at the appropriate level of student difficulty. This is particularly true for students with disabilities, who are more likely to act out when demands are beyond their ability to meet. Teacher behaviors that motivate students include:

- Maintaining success expectations through teaching, goal setting, establishing connections between effort and outcome, and self-appraisal and reinforcement
- Having a supply of intrinsic incentives such as rewards, appropriate competition between students, and the value of the academic activities
- Focusing on students' intrinsic motivation through adapting the tasks to students' interests, providing opportunities for active response, using a variety of tasks, providing rapid feedback, incorporating games into the lesson, and allowing students the opportunity to make choices, create, and interact with peers

- For some students with disabilities, extrinsic rewards and token systems (prize charts, etc.) might be necessary. Often the student's IEP will specify use of such tools.
- Stimulating students' learning by modeling positive expectations and attributions. Project enthusiasm, and personalize abstract concepts. Students will be more motivated if they know what they will be learning. The teacher should also model problem-solving and task-related thinking so students can see how the process is done.

For adolescents, motivation strategies are usually aimed at getting the student actively involved in the learning process. Because the adolescent has the opportunity to get involved in a wider range of activities outside the classroom (e.g., job, car, being with friends), stimulating motivation may be the focus even more than academics.

Motivation can be improved by allowing the student a degree of choice in what is being taught or how it will be taught. The teacher will, if possible, obtain a commitment either through a verbal or written contract with the student. Adolescents also respond well to regular feedback, especially when that feedback shows that they are making progress.

Classroom Interventions

Classroom interventions anticipate student disruptions and nullify potential discipline problems. Every student is different and each situation is unique; therefore, the specific intervention chosen will depend upon the student and the situation. Good classroom management requires the ability to select appropriate intervention strategies from an array of alternatives. The following nonverbal and verbal interventions are explained in Henley, Ramsey, and Algonzzine (1993).

1. **Nonverbal interventions:** The use of nonverbal interventions allows classroom activities to proceed without interruption. These interventions also enable teachers to avoid "power struggles" with students. A simple tap on the desk or a prearranged signal can be used.
2. **Body language:** Teachers can convey authority and command respect through body language. Posture, eye contact, facial expressions, and gestures are examples of body components that signal leadership to students.
3. **Planned ignoring:** Many minor classroom disturbances are best handled through planned ignoring. When teachers ignore attention-seeking behaviors, students often do likewise.
4. **Signal interference:** There are numerous nonverbal signals that teachers can use to quiet a class. Some of these are making eye contact, snapping fingers, frowning, shaking the head, or making a quieting gesture with the hand. A few teachers present signs like flicking the lights, putting a finger over the lips, or winking at a selected student.

5. **Proximity control:** Teachers who move around the room often merely need to stand near a student or small group of students, or gently place a hand on a student's shoulder, to stop a disturbing behavior. Teachers who stand or sit as if rooted are compelled to issue verbal directions in order to deal with student disruptions.

6. **Removal of seductive objects:** Some students become distracted by certain objects. Removing seductive objects eliminates the need some students have to handle, grab, or touch objects that distract their attention. One of the best ways to accomplish this is to "fall in love" with the object and express a concern to place it somewhere safe, like on your desk. It should be noted that some students with disabilities may actually *need* such fiddle objects to improve their attention and help them be still. Such accommodations will often be in the student's IEP.

7. **Verbal interventions:** Because nonverbal interventions are the least intrusive, they are generally preferred. Verbal Interventions are useful after it is clear that nonverbal interventions have been unsuccessful in preventing or stopping disruptive behavior.

8. **Humor:** Some teachers have been successful in dispelling discipline problems with a quip or an easy comment that produces smiles or gentle laughter from students. This does not include sarcasm, cynicism, or teasing, which increase tension and often create resentment.

9. **Sane messages**: Sane messages are descriptive and model appropriate behavior. They help students understand how their behavior affects others. "Karol, when you talk during silent reading, you disturb everyone in your group," is an example of a sane message.

10. **Restructuring**: When confronted with student disinterest, the teacher may make the decision to change activities. The teacher can use this type of restructuring to regenerate student interest.

11. **Hypodermic affection**: Sometimes students get frustrated, discouraged, and anxious in school. Hypodermic affection lets students know they are valued. Saying a kind word, giving a smile, or just showing interest in a child may give the encouragement that is needed.

12. **Praise and encouragement**: Effective praise is directed at the student behavior rather than at the student personally. "Catching a child being good" is an example of an effective use of praise that reinforces positive classroom behavior. Comments like "You are really trying hard" encourage student effort. To be effective, praise should be specific and truthful.

13. **Alerting**: Making abrupt changes from one activity to another can bring on behavior problems, particularly for students with certain disabilities. Alerting helps students to make smooth transitions by giving them time to make emotional adjustments to change.

14. **Accepting student feelings**: Providing opportunities for students to express their feelings, even those that are distressful, helps them to learn to do so in appropriate ways. Role playing, class meetings or discussions, life space interviews, journal writings, and other creative modes help students to channel difficult feelings into constructive outlets.

Transfer between classes and subjects are of particular importance for many students with disabilities. Effective teachers use class time efficiently. This results in more time on task. When the teacher shifts from one activity to another in a systemic, academically oriented way, students are more engaged and better retain subject matter. One way teachers can use class time efficiently is through a smooth transition from one activity to another; this activity is also known as "management transition."

One factor that contributes to efficient management transition is the teacher's management of instructional material. Effective teachers gather their materials during the planning stage of instruction. By doing this, a teacher avoids flipping through things looking for the items necessary for the current lesson. (Momentum is lost and student concentration is broken when this type of interruption occurs.)

Additionally, teachers who keep students informed of the sequencing of instructional activities maintain systematic transitions, because the students are prepared to move on to the next activity. For example, the teacher may say, "When we finish with this guided practice together, we will turn to page 23, and each student will do the exercises. I will then circulate throughout the classroom, helping on an individual basis. Okay, let's begin." Following an example such as this will lead to systematic, smooth transitions between activities because the students will be turning to page 23 when the class finishes the practice without a break in concentration.

When students with disabilities are involved, even more concrete methods might help. Many students with disabilities benefit from a visible, individually designed schedule for the day, specifying what happens when. Use of picture icons for various subjects and activities can be useful and the teacher can use an auditory or visual signal such as a bell, a picture on a stick, or any other symbol to prepare students for the next activity.

Another method that leads to smooth transitions is to move students in groups and clusters rather than seating them one by one. This is called "group fragmentation." For example, if some students do seat work while other students gather for a reading group, the teacher moves the students in predetermined groups. Instead of calling the individual names of the students in the reading group, which would be time consuming and laborious, the teacher simply says, "Will the blue reading group please assemble at the reading station. The red and yellow groups will quietly do the vocabulary assignment I am now passing out." As a result of this activity, the classroom is ready to move on in a matter of seconds rather than minutes.

Additionally, the teacher may employ academic transition signals, which are defined as teacher utterances that indicate movement of the lesson from one topic or activity to another by indicating where the lesson is and where it is going. For example, the teacher may say, "That completes our description of clouds;

now we will examine weather fronts." Like the sequencing of instructional materials, this keeps the students informed about what is coming next so they will move to the next activity with little or no break in concentration.

Early in the year, the teacher should pinpoint the transition periods in the day and anticipate possible behavior problems, such as students habitually returning late from lunch. After identifying possible problems with the environment or the schedule, the teacher should plan proactive strategies to minimize or eliminate those problems. Proactive planning also gives the teacher the advantage of being prepared, addressing behaviors before they become problems, and incorporating strategies into the classroom management plan right away. Transition plans can be developed for each type of transition, and the expected behaviors for each situation can be taught directly to the students.

For helpful hints on classroom interventions, see:
http://www.behavioradvisor.com/RememberYourGoal.html

Skill 6.02 **Demonstrating an understanding of the roles of the special educator, general educator, and other professionals in creating a learning environment that promotes students' achievement of goals and objectives**

THE TEAM APPROACH TO SPECIAL EDUCATION

The special educator is trained to work in a team approach. This occurs from the initial identification of students who appear to deviate from what is considered the normal performance or behavior for particular age- and grade-level students. The special education teacher is a part of the student support team. If the student is referred, the special education teacher may be asked to collect assessment data for the forthcoming comprehensive evaluation. This professional then generally serves on the multidisciplinary eligibility, IEP, and placement committees. If the student is placed in a special education setting, the special educator continues to coordinate and collaborate with regular classroom teachers and support personnel at the school-based level.

Support professionals are available at both the district- and school-based levels and they contribute valuable services and expertise in their respective areas. A team approach incorporating district ancillary services and local school-based staff is essential if students are to achieve their goals.

1. **School psychologist:** The school psychologist participates in the referral, identification, and program planning processes. He or she contributes to the multidisciplinary team by adding important observations, data, and inferences about the student's performance. As he or she conducts an evaluation, the psychologist observes the student in the classroom environment, takes a case history, and administers a battery of formal and

informal individual tests. The psychologist is involved as a member of a professional team throughout the stages of referral, assessment, placement, and program planning.

2. **Physical therapist:** A physical therapist works with disorders of bones, joints, muscles, and nerves following medical assessment. Under the prescription of a physician and as specified in the IEP, the therapist helps to prevent further disability or deformity and/or to help the student improve physical skills important to educational success. This therapy may include the use of adaptive equipment and prosthetic and orthotic devices to facilitate independent movement.

3. **Occupational therapist:** This specialist is trained in helping students develop self-help skills (e.g., self-care and motor, perceptual, and vocational skills). The students are actively involved in the treatment process to quicken recovery and rehabilitation. An occupational therapist may also help students with disabilities that affect writing skills.

4. **Speech and language pathologist:** This specialist assists in the identification and diagnosis of children with speech or language disorders. In addition, he or she makes referrals for medical or rehabilitation needs, counsels family members and teachers, and works on the prevention of communicative disorders. The speech and language therapist concentrates on rehabilitative service delivery and continuing diagnosis.

5. **Administrators**: Building principals and special education directors (or coordinators) provide logistical as well as emotional support. Principals implement building policy procedures and control designation of facilities, equipment, and materials. Their support is crucial to the success of the program within the parameters of the base school. Administrators are particularly important in supporting the sometimes complex scheduling procedures that help members of the child's team consult and provide services in an efficient and nonintrusive manner. Special education directors provide information about federal, state, and local policies, which is vital to the operation of a special education unit. In some districts, the special education director might actually control certain services and materials. Role clarification, preferably in writing, should be accomplished to ensure effectiveness of program services.

6. **Guidance counselors, psychometrists, and diagnosticians**: These specialists often lead individual and group counseling sessions and are trained in assessment, diagnostic, and observation skills, as well as personality development and functioning abilities. They can apply knowledge and skills to multidisciplinary teams and assist in the assessment, diagnosis, placement, and program planning process.

7. **School nurse**: The school nurse offers valuable information about diagnostic and treatment services. He or she is knowledgeable about diets, medications, therapeutic services, health-related services, and care needed for specific medical conditions. Reports of communicable diseases are filed with the health department, to which a health professional like the school nurse has access. A medical professional can

sometimes obtain cooperation from the families of children with disabilities in ways that are difficult for the special education teacher.

8. **Regular teachers and subject matter specialists:** These professionals are trained in general and specific instructional areas, teaching techniques, and overall child growth and development. They serve as a vital component of the referral process as well as in the subsequent treatment program if the student is determined eligible. They work with the students with special needs for the majority of the school day and function as a link to the children's special education and medical programs.

9. **Paraprofessional:** This staff member assists the special educator and often works in the classroom with the special needs students. He or she helps prepare specialized materials, tutor individual students, lead small groups, and provide feedback to students about their work. The paraprofessional's observations can be very helpful when designing instruction.

Learn more about specific support roles for those working with children who have special needs here:
www.cec.sped.org/Content/NavigationMenu/ProfessionalDevelopment/CareerCe nter/JobProfiles/

Skill 6.03   Applying techniques of collaborative planning with general educators and other professionals

COLLABORATIVE PARTNERSHIPS IN A CLIMATE OF ACCOUNTABILITY

The National Association of Special Education Teachers (NASET), 2006, states that the growth of the standards-based curriculum, combined with NCLB's requirement that students with disabilities participate in state- and district-wide testing, has resulted in a profound need for improved collaborative partnerships between general education and special education teachers. While such collaboration has always been desirable, now that both general education and special education teachers are held accountable for student success it has become even more critical that they work together to help the student achieve that success.

NASET's review of recent research indicates that there are many very effective models of collaboration available to teachers, such as the "Applied Collaboration" model used by the Minnesota Department of Children, Families, and Learning, Division of Special Education (see *www.appliedcollaboration.net*), which research has shown to be particularly effective. However, collaboration often fails because teachers do not have adequate training in how and when to use such models, nor do they have the administrative support necessary to collaborate successfully.

NASET further states that "Special educators must become more adept in content knowledge and curriculum development, and general educators must understand their role in implementing IEP goals and objectives—that is, how to accommodate students with disabilities within the general education classroom" (page 3).

NASET advocates creating a "curriculum base" that would provide specific training and examples for general educators about how to include students with special needs, how to handle accommodations, and so forth—in other words, more practical teacher training in the area of special education. NASET also suggests that curriculum standards be written as "preferred curriculum" that has greater flexibility to allow adjusting entry-level goals and objectives within the curriculum for students with special needs.

According to NASET's review of research, one of the most powerful factors in the successful collaboration of general and special educators is level of knowledge and support of the local administration. They consider administrative support to be a critical factor for successful collaboration. This is because the "real problem," according to NASET, is the level of organization and commitment necessary to set things up so educators can meet, communicate and collaborate.

COLLABORATION STRATEGIES

Whatever model of collaboration teachers use, research highlights a number of characteristics important for success. Reinhiller (1996, p 46) suggests that any collaboration efforts begin with consideration of the following questions:

- Why do we want to co-teach?
- How will we know whether our goals are met?
- How will we communicate and document our collaboration?
- How will we share responsibility for instruction of all students?
- How will we gain support from others?

Mastropieri and Scruggs (2000) list the following practices as critical to successful collaboration:

- Include as much co-planning time as possible before starting
- Determine goals and objectives
- Inform parents and solicit help
- Build in common planning time (it is here that administrative support is so important)
- Develop systematic measures to evaluate effects of teaching
- Assess student and teacher attitudes toward co-teaching beforehand
- Document how responsibilities are to be shared
- Establish shared goals
- Use effective communication techniques
  - Active listening

- o Depersonalize situations
- o Brainstorm possible solutions
- Summarize goals and solutions in writing

Teachers need diversity in their instructional toolkits, and research has shown that educators who collaborate become more diversified and effective in their implementation of curriculum and assessment of effective instructional practices. Teachers who team-teach or have daily networking opportunities can create a portfolio of available instructional methods and techniques that can be used to individualize instruction for students.

Skill 6.04   Demonstrating familiarity with factors involved in creating a learning environment that is safe, positive, and supportive, in which diversity is celebrated, and that encourages active participation by learners in a variety of individual and group settings

One thing teachers can do to help students with and without disabilities is to arrange the physical environment and the routine organization and classroom procedures in a way that meets the needs of the students and enhances learning. Although the specific elements of any given classroom organization will depend upon the needs of the students, some general principles need to be considered when arranging the class. In order to help individualize the classroom, teachers can review cumulative records, IEPs, and 504 documents for information about student needs, and can also get information about the student preferences through direct interviews or Likert-style checklists in which students rate their preferences.

PHYSICAL SETTINGS

Noise

Students vary in the degree of quiet that they need and the amount of background noise or talking that they can tolerate without getting distracted or frustrated. Students with attention deficit issues might need a quiet, undecorated corner, whereas some students respond well to bright, colorful surroundings.

Temperature and Lighting

Students also vary in their preference for lighter or darker areas of the room, tolerance for coolness or heat, and ability to see the chalkboard, screen, or other areas of the room. Students with disabilities such as Irlen Syndrome might need shielded light rather than the common florescent light. Allowing a student to wear a cap with a bill can be helpful if alternative lighting is not available.

Spatial Arrangements

This refers to the student's needs for his or her workspace and preference for the type of work area, such as desk, table, or learning center. Some students work better standing up at a counter or even lying down with a clipboard. Proximity factors such as closeness to the other students, the teacher, or high-traffic areas such as doorways or pencil sharpeners might help the student to feel secure and stay on task, or might serve as distractions, depending on the individual. Students with physical disabilities might need wider aisles, space to turn around, etc.

INSTRUCTIONAL GROUPS AND ARRANGEMENTS

In addition to the overall physical organization of the room, classroom groupings can be modified for a variety of needs and purposes. Five basic types of grouping arrangements are typically used in the classroom.

Large Group with Teacher

Examples of appropriate activities for this arrangement include show and tell, discussions, watching plays or movies, brainstorming ideas, and playing games. Science, social studies, and most other subjects, except for reading and math, are often taught in large groups. The advantage of large group instruction is that it is time-efficient and prepares students for higher levels of secondary and post-secondary education settings. However, in large groups instruction cannot be as easily tailored to the needs of students with disabilities, who may become bored or frustrated. Mercer and Mercer (1985) recommend the following guidelines for effective large-group instruction:

- Keep instructions short, ranging from 5 to 15 minutes for first grade through seventh grade and 5 to 40 minutes for grades 8 through 12.
- Use questions to involve all students, use lecture-pause routines, and encourage active participation among the lower-performing students.
- Incorporate visual aids to promote understanding and to maintain a lively pace.
- Break up the presentation with different rates of speaking, giving students a "stretch break", varying voice volume, etc.
- Establish rules of conduct for large groups and praise students who follow the rules.

Small Group Instruction

Small group instruction usually includes 5 to 7 students and is recommended for teaching basic academic skills such as math facts or reading. This model is especially effective for students with learning problems. Composition of the groups should be flexible to accommodate different rates of progress through instruction. The advantages of teaching in small groups is that the teacher is better able to provide individualized instruction, give more frequent feedback, and monitor student progress more closely.

One Student with Teacher

One-to-one tutorial teaching can be used to provide extra assistance to individual students. Such tutoring may be scheduled at set times during the day or provided as the need arises. The tutoring model is typically found more in elementary and resource classrooms than in secondary settings and is often an essential part of special education.

Peer Tutoring

In an effective peer tutoring arrangement, the teacher trains the peer tutors and matches them with students who need extra practice and assistance. In addition to academic skills, the arrangement can help both students work on social skills such as cooperation and self-esteem. Both students could be working on the same material, or the tutee could be working to strengthen areas of weakness. The teacher determines the target goals, selects the material, sets up the guidelines, trains the student tutors in the rules and methods of the sessions, and monitors and evaluates the sessions. Care must be taken, however, to avoid the appearance that some students are smarter than others and that the "smarter" students have more work because of the "slower" students. It can be very helpful if the teacher can find something that allows the tutee in one situation to act as tutor in another.

Cooperative Learning

Cooperative learning differs from peer tutoring in that students are grouped in teams or small groups and the methods are based on teamwork, individual accountability, and team reward. Individual students are responsible for their own learning and share of the work as well as the group's success. As with peer tutoring, the goals, target skills, materials, and guidelines are developed by the teacher. In addition, teamwork skills might need to be taught. By focusing on team goals, all members of the team are encouraged to help each other as well as to improve their individual performance.

Finally, teachers should be familiar with building safety routines (fire drills, intruder and emergency codes and procedures) and ensure that substitute teachers, paraprofessionals, and all adults who work with the students are also familiar with these procedures.

Skill 6.05   Recognizing instructional management techniques that encourage self-advocacy and increased independence

Self-advocacy involves the ability to effectively communicate one's own rights, needs, and desires and to take responsibility for making decisions that impact one's life. Learning about oneself involves the identification of learning styles, strengths and weakness, interests, and preferences. For students with mild disabilities, developing an awareness of the accommodations they need will help them ask for necessary accommodations on a job and in post-secondary education. Students can also help identify alternative ways they can learn.

TEACHING SELF-ADVOCACY

Although self-advocacy involves understanding one's limitations as well as strengths and being able to verbalize needs, it does not mean that the students should ask for help on everything and always rely on others for assistance. Appropriate levels of independence must also be taught. Good self-advocates know how to ask questions, emphasize their own strengths, find creative ways to accomplish goals in spite of their disabilities, and even get help from other people when necessary. They do not let other people do everything for them.

Instruction in independence and self-advocacy should begin as soon as the child enters the classroom. Teachers should listen to the student's problems and ask the student for input on possible changes that he or she might need. The teacher should talk with the student about possible solutions, soliciting student ideas and discussing the pros and cons of various options. A student who self-advocates should feel supported and encouraged, so the teacher might need to let the students implement some of their own ideas and help them evaluate the results rather than handing out all the answers and solutions ready-made for the student to use.

The student should also be encouraged to verbalize specific needs or preferences when appropriate. A student with ADHD, for instance, might be taught to raise a hand and tell the teacher that he would prefer to do his desk work on the floor with a clipboard or standing at a counter. A student with an obsessive-compulsive disorder that involves picking up, mouthing, and fiddling with inappropriate items (pebbles from the playground, beads off of clothing, etc.) might be taught to ask for more appropriate fiddle and oral objects (e.g., small mints or tiny edibles chosen for this purpose) when she feels the compulsion arise. Goals such as these might be written into a child's IEP.

Learning to be more independent takes practice at many levels and occurs gradually. The key thing for the teacher to remember is that in order to become more independent, the student *must experience success at being independent.* The teacher must design step-by-step procedures that allow students to practice greater and greater independence in ways they can handle successfully. This might mean something as simple as a goal that the student will complete three problems or work independently for 10 minutes. Often such goals are written into the IEP. Teachers can also have students role play various situations, such as setting up a class schedule, moving out of the home, and asking for accommodations needed for a task (e.g., "OK, Johnny, what do **you** think you will need to get this done?").

One important way to foster independence and self-advocacy is simply to communicate high expectations to all students, including those with disabilities, and to communicate confidence that each student can meet those expectations. The teacher should establish a classroom understanding that there is more than one way to accomplish a task and that each student may work differently toward shared or individual goals. The emphasis should be on helping students develop the confidence that they can figure out a way to accomplish a task or meet a goal even if they do not all do so in the same way. This sets the stage for learning how to obtain the accommodations some students will need.

SELF-ADVOCACY DURING THE TRANSITION PROCESS

There are many elements of developing self-advocacy skills in students who are involved in the transition process. Helping the student to identify future goals or desired outcomes in transition planning areas is a good place to start. Self-knowledge is critical for the student in determining the direction that transition planning will take. The student should be an active member of the transition team as well as the focus of all activities. Students should be encouraged to express their opinions throughout the transition process. They need to learn how to express themselves so that others listen and take them seriously. See Skill 5.06 for more on the transition process.

To learn more about how to teach self-advocacy, see:
http://www.pacer.org/parent/php/PHP-c95.pdf

Skill 6.06   Demonstrating an understanding of effective collaboration among teachers and other professionals to design and manage daily routines, including transition time that promote students' success in a variety of instructional settings

Please see Skill 6.03 for details on collaboration and planning among teachers and other professionals.

Depending on a student's disability and on the school setting, special education teachers need to work with speech pathologists, school psychologists, occupational therapists, social workers, general education teachers, and community workers to plan the optimal education program for each student. Special education teachers might work in inclusive settings, co-teach, or team-teach with general education teachers. In many cases, this means that the student transitions from one location to another throughout the day, or that various teachers or specialists enter the child's classroom periodically throughout the day. In some cases, the student might be involved in a small group activity while other students are in parallel groups.

Collaboration among all involved parties is necessary to ensure that these transitions occur smoothly and that the student's time on task is maximized. Using techniques discussed in Skill 6.03, collaborators can focus on designing transition routines that are consistent throughout the day and in all settings. If, for example, a student needs a specific alert signal for transitions, then all those who work with the student should use the same signal.

As mentioned in Skill 6.03, the scheduling of these transitions is critical to success, and this will involve collaborating with administrators who set up the schedule as well as other service providers.

Teachers who value collaboration, sharing, and peer-oriented learning usually attempt to create similar communities in their classes, and this can help the student manage transitions throughout the building and the day.
To learn more how to collaborate effectively with the general education teacher, see: *http://www.teachervision.fen.com/teaching-methods/resource/2941.html*

Skill 6.07 Demonstrating familiarity with techniques for supporting the functional integration of students with disabilities in various settings, including general education settings

REVIEW OF STUDENT NEEDS WITH INCLUSION TEACHER AND SUPPORT STAFF

It may be determined at a student's IEP meeting that some time in the general education setting is appropriate. The activities and classes listed for inclusion may be field trips, lunch, recess, physical education, music, library, art, computers, math, science, social studies, spelling, reading, and/or English. The IEP will specify which classes and activities are involved as well as the amount of time that the student will be with general education peers. The IEP will also list any modifications or accommodations that will be needed.

The specific modifications and accommodations that are needed for the general education classroom will vary depending upon the individual child's needs, but might include such things as the amount of work or type of task required, (e.g., a reduced number of spelling words or writing the vocabulary word that goes with a given definition instead of writing the definition that goes with a given word), or changes to the school environment, or the use of necessary equipment to overcome a disability (e.g., use of an FM system or providing printed notes). See Skill 5.03 for typical accommodations and modifications and their implications for the general education classroom.

Teacher attitudes toward inclusion are among the most powerful factors that determine its success. Prior to the student starting in a general education placement, the general education teacher and support staff (if any) should be in-serviced on the student's disability and his or her needs according to the IEP. Sometimes this in-servicing happens as the student's IEP is developed. At other times it is done at a later date.

STUDENT EXPECTATIONS IN THE INCLUSION SETTING

The student with a disability should be well aware of his or her responsibilities in the general education setting ahead of time. These expectations should be a combination of behavior and task performance. Although the student should be aware of needed accommodations and modifications, and should be a self-advocate for these, the student should not use his or her disability as an excuse for not fulfilling the expectations.

Students might benefit from previewing material, using a checklist to keep track of materials and assignments, keeping an assignment notebook, reviewing materials after the lesson, and using study aids such as flashcards. Sometimes a behavior tracking chart may also be used.

MONITORING STUDENT PROGRESS IN THE INCLUSION SETTING

Once the student is in the general education setting for the time and activities listed on the IEP, the special education teacher will need to monitor student progress. This can be done through verbal follow-up with the general education teacher or by asking the general education teacher to periodically complete a progress form. Of course, grades, the student's ability to restate learned information, and the student's ability to answer questions are also indicators of student progress.

EVALUATION OF STUDENT'S FUTURE PLACEMENT IN THE INCLUSION SETTING

If the student is successful in the general education activities and classes listed on the IEP, the special education teacher may consider recommending that the IEP team ease back on modifications and accommodations on the next IEP or increase the student's participation in general education.
If the student has difficulty, the IEP team may consider adding more modifications or accommodations on the next IEP. If the student has significant difficulty, he or she might need to receive more services in the special education classroom.

Skill 6.08   Recognizing appropriate collaborative techniques for ensuring the positive and effective functioning of classroom paraprofessionals, aides, and volunteers

Please also refer to Skill 6.03.

This section specifically addresses the working relationship teachers should have with those they encounter in the classroom environment. There are six basic steps to having a rewarding collaborative working relationship, whether the coworkers are paraprofessionals, aides, or volunteers. While it is understood that there are many titles for those who may be assisting in your room, this section will summarize their titles as "classroom assistants."

1. **Get to know each other**
   The best way to start a relationship with anyone is to find time alone to get to know each other. Give your new classroom assistant the utmost respect and look at this as an opportunity to share your talents and learn those of your coworker. Share what your strengths and weaknesses are, and listen to his or hers. This knowledge could create one of the best working relationships you have ever had.

2. **Remember that communication is a two-way street**
   Communication is especially important with your classroom assistant. Let the assistant see you listening. Encourage him or her to ask for more information. Also remember that asking your classroom assistant for details and insights might help you further meet the needs of your students. It is also your responsibility to remove and prevent communication barriers in your working relationship. You are the professional! You must be the one to avoid negative criticism or put-downs. Do not "read" motivations into the actions of your classroom assistant. Learn about him or her by communicating openly.

3. **Establish clear roles and responsibilities**
   The Access Center for Improving Outcomes of All Students K-8 has defined these roles in a graph available at
   http://www.k8accesscenter.org/training_resources/documents/Tchr-ParaCollaboration.pdf.

   Note that while the graph can be a useful starting place, it is often helpful to write out what roles and expectations you have for your classroom assistant together in a contract-type fashion.

4. **Plan together**
   Planning together lets your classroom assistant know that you consider him or her valuable; it also provides a timeline of expectations that will aid both of you in your classroom delivery to the students and gives the

impression to your students that you both know what is going to happen next.

5. **Show a united front**

   It is essential to let your students know that both adults in the room deserve the same amount of respect. Have a plan in place on how you should address negative behaviors both individually and together. **Do not** make a statement in front of your students that your classroom assistant is wrong. Take time to address issues you may have regarding class time privately, never in front of the class.

6. **Reevaluate your relationship**

   Feedback is wonderful! Stop every now and then and discuss how you are working as a team. Be willing to listen to suggestions. Taking this time gives you an opportunity to improve your working relationship.

To learn more about creating a classroom team, see: *http://www.aft.org/pubs-reports/psrp/classroom_team.pdf*

COMPETENCY 0007 UNDERSTAND PRINCIPLES OF CURRICULUM DEVELOPMENT AND INSTRUCTIONAL PLANNING FOR STUDENTS WITH DISABILITIES

Skill 7.01 Demonstrating knowledge of instructional planning for a variety of inclusive models (e.g., co-teaching, push-in, consultant teaching [CT])

According to IDEA 2004, students with disabilities are to participate in the general education program to the extent that it is beneficial to them. As these students are included in a variety of general education activities and classes the need for collaboration among teachers grows.

CO-TEACHING

One model for collaboration that is used for general education and special education teachers is co-teaching. In this model, both teachers actively teach in the general education classroom. Perhaps both teachers will conduct a small science experiment group at the same time, switching groups at some point in the lesson. Perhaps, in a social studies lesson, one teacher will lecture while the other teacher writes notes on the board or points out information on a map. In the co-teaching model, the general education teacher and special educator often alternate roles within a class period or at the end of a chapter or unit.

PUSH-IN TEACHING

In the push-in teaching model, the special educator teaches parallel material in the general education classroom. When the regular education teacher teaches word problems in math, for example, the special educator might be working with some students on setting up the initial problems and having them complete the computation. Another example would be in science: while the general education teacher asks review questions for a test, the special educator works with a student who has a review study sheet to show the answer from among a group of choices.

In the push-in teaching model, it may appear that two versions of the same lesson are being taught or that two types of student responses and activities are being monitored on the same material. The push-in teaching model is considered one type of differentiated instruction in which two teachers are teaching simultaneously.

CONSULTANT TEACHING

In the consultant teaching model, the general education teacher conducts the class after planning with the special educator how to differentiate activities so that the needs of the student with a disability are met.

For example, in a social studies classroom using the consultant teaching model, both teachers might discuss what the expectations will be for a student with a learning disability and fine motor difficulty when the class does reports on states. They may decide that doing a state report is appropriate for the student; however, the student could use a computer to write the report so that he or she can utilize the spell check feature and so that the work is legible.

RESOURCE ROOM OR PARTIAL PULL-OUT

The resource room is a specialized instructional setting where students go for short periods of special work in order to learn specific skills and behaviors in which the students are deficient. The students spend the remainder of the day in the regular classroom. Generally, the resource room is inside the school environment where the child goes to be taught by a teacher who is certified in the area of disability. The accommodations and services provided in the resource room are designed to provide the student access to an equal education in spite of his or her disability, and to help the student catch up and perform with peers in the regular classroom. In this case, the student returns to the regular classroom for other subjects because this is the Least Restrictive Environment (LRE). The resource room is usually a bridge to mainstreaming.

Resource room time should be scheduled so that the student does not miss academic instruction in his or her classroom or miss desirable nonacademic activities. For maximum effectiveness, the general education teacher and the special education teacher (in the resource room) collaborate on differentiating the student's activities so the activities can be integrated into the mainstream classroom.

SUBSTANTIALLY SEPARATE CLASSROOMS

In some cases, a child's disability makes it impossible for the student to succeed in a mainstream classroom. Some students might need very specialized forms of instruction not available in the general education class, or might have emotional, attention, or medical difficulties that prevent them from accessing the curriculum in a large group. For these students, a separate classroom where they receive their academic instruction is required. Special education teachers and, often, additional aides staff these classes and deliver specialized services.

Even in such a separate classroom, however, instructional collaboration between general education and special education teachers is very important. Children in these classrooms typically spend at least part of the day—lunch, recess, enrichment and social activities, etc.—with a general education class. In order for transitions to move smoothly, teachers must coordinate times and activities. Often the general education teacher will include the special education students in special projects where their work can be displayed with that of their grade peers. For example, when an entire grade level is doing display boards on dinosaurs or states, the special education teacher might modify the lesson so the students in the separate classroom produce a display as well.

Skill 7.02   Demonstrating knowledge of instructional methods, techniques, and curricula, including assistive and instructional technologies, used with students to accommodate specific disabilities

Please refer to Skill 8.06 for information on the use of assistive and instructional technologies.

No two students are the same, so it follows that no students *learn* in the same way. To apply a one-dimensional instructional approach is to impose learning limits on students. A teacher must acknowledge the variety of learning styles and abilities among students and apply multiple instructional methods to ensure that every child has appropriate opportunities to master the subject matter, to demonstrate such mastery, and to improve learning skills with each lesson.

Students' attitudes and perceptions about learning are powerful factors influencing academic focus and success. When instructional objectives center on students' interests and are relevant to their lives, effective learning is more likely to occur. If a student thinks a task is unimportant, he or she will not put much effort into it. If students think they lack the ability or resources to successfully complete tasks, even attempting the tasks becomes too great a risk. Not only must teachers understand the students' abilities and interests, they must also help students develop positive attitudes and perceptions about tasks and learning.

DIFFERENTIATED INSTRUCTION

In recent years, increasing emphasis has been put on incorporating at least some principles of *differentiated instruction* into classrooms with students of mixed ability. Tomlinson (2001) states that teachers must first determine where the students are with reference to an objective, and then tailor specific lesson plans and learning activities to help each student learn as much as possible about that objective. The effective teacher seeks to connect all students to the subject matter through multiple techniques with the goal that each student will relate to one or more techniques and excel in the learning process. This is particularly relevant to the instruction of students with disabilities. Differentiated instruction encompasses modifying curriculum in several areas.

Content

What is the teacher going to teach? In other words, what does the teacher want the students to learn? Differentiating content means that students have access to aspects of the content that pique their interest, with a complexity that provides an appropriate challenge to their intellectual development but does not go beyond their frustration level. When students with special needs are included in a classroom, this often means modifying a lesson plan so that it has several levels. One common way to structure such levels is the following:

A **basic level** might address the content of the objective at a cognitively less demanding level (e.g., knowledge, the lowest level on Bloom's taxonomy). Example: The student or student group matches names to planets on a diagram or correctly defines key vocabulary words.

A **moderate level** could address the content at a higher level than basic, a level that gets closer to the standard but is still less demanding (e.g., comprehension). Example: After learning that the Earth orbits the sun due to the Sun's greater gravity, challenge the student or student group to give other examples of objects orbiting other objects and explain why this happens in their own words.

A **mastery level** might address the objective at the level most students should reach given state standards (e.g., analysis). Example: The student or student group compares two planets based on a set of variables.

An **advanced level** would address the objective at a higher level aimed at gifted students who can go beyond the required curriculum (e.g., the highest level on Bloom's taxonomy, evaluation). Example: The student or student group is given a real or fictional theory of planetary movement and asked to evaluate its accuracy in light of the facts they have learned in the unit.

Process

The process of differentiated instruction is the classroom management techniques that maximize instructional organization and delivery for the diverse student group. These techniques should include dynamic, flexible grouping activities, in which instruction and learning occur as whole-class, teacher-led activities as well as in a variety of small group settings, such as teacher-guided small group, peer learning and teaching (while the teacher observes and coaches), or independent centers or pairs. Such techniques should also include strategies for anchor activities and smooth transitions from activity to activity.

Product

The product of differentiate instruction is the expectations and requirements placed on students to demonstrate their knowledge or understanding. The type of product expected from each student should reflect that student's own capabilities. When working with students with special needs, each student's IEP will provide guidelines on the best way to assess the student's progress and any testing accommodations that must be made. Please refer to Skill 3.05 for information on alternative assessments.

Skill 7.03   Demonstrating understanding of the connection between curriculum and IEP goals and objectives

The No Child Left Behind Act, PL 107-110 2002 addresses accountability of school personnel for student achievement, with the expectation that every child will demonstrate proficiency in reading, math, and science. For example, all students should know how to read by grade three.

General education curriculum should reflect state learning standards. Because special educators are responsible for teaching students to a level of proficiency comparable to that of their non-disabled peers, this curriculum should also be followed closely in the special education program and be reflected in the relevant IEP goals and objectives.

Naturally, certain modifications and accommodations will be necessary to meet learning standards. IEP goals and objectives are based on the unique needs of the child with a disability in meeting the curriculum expectations of the school (and the state/nation). Consider some of the following cases:

- Teachers in grades k-3 are mandated to teach reading to all students using scientifically-based methods with measurable outcomes. Some students (including those with disabilities) will not learn to read successfully unless taught with a phonics approach. Such a student's IEP should have a reading/decoding goal and a set of objectives related to teaching the phonics the child needs in order to learn to read. It is then the responsibility of the general education teacher and special education teacher to incorporate phonics into reading instruction according to the state curriculum standards. This might mean, for example, finding phonics-based reading material that covers a curriculum area such as recognizing similes and metaphors.
- Students are expected to understand place value when learning mathematics. While some students will quickly grasp the mathematical concept of groupings of tens (and the further skills of adding and subtracting large numbers), others will need additional practice. Research shows that many students with disabilities need a hands-on approach. For example, the students will need additional instruction and practice could use snap-together cubes to grasp the grouping-by-tens concept. The IEPs for such children might have a goal and a set of objectives for learning to master the material first when using manipulatives, later for drawing or illustrating the problem, and finally for doing the problem without manipulatives.

Skill 7.04   Demonstrating an understanding of effective collaboration among teachers and other professionals to develop and implement appropriate curricula for students with disabilities

Please refer also to Skills 6.02, 6.03, and 6.06. The techniques described in those sections can be applied to collaboration in curriculum development by treating the various professional parties as one unified transdisciplinary team.

Every member of a collaborative team has precise knowledge of his or her discipline, and transdisciplinary teams integrate these areas. For example, an ESL teacher can provide knowledge regarding the development of language skills and language instruction methodology. Counselors and psychologists can impart knowledge as human development specialists and use their expertise by conducting small-group counseling and large-group interventions. School staff and instructors can benefit from what mainstream teachers add in the area of performance information and knowledge of measures and benchmarks. Special education teachers can provide insight into designing and implementing behavior management programs and strategies for effective instruction to students with special needs. Speech pathologists can contribute their knowledge of speech and language development and provide insight into the identification of learning disabilities in language-minority students.

Transdisciplinary teaming requires team members to build on the strengths and the needs of their particular populations. Therefore, each professional can contribute when it comes to developing and implementing appropriate curricular needs.

Skill 7.05   Demonstrate familiarity with strategies for integrating affective, social, and career/vocational skills with academic curricula

A major focus of special education is to prepare students to become working, independent members of society. IDEA 2004 (Individuals with Disabilities Education Act) also includes preparing students for further education. Certain skills beyond academics are needed to attain either level of functioning.

AFFECTIVE AND SOCIAL SKILLS

These skills are necessary in all areas of life. When an individual is unable to acquire information about the expectations and reactions of others, or when those cues are misinterpreted, he or she is missing an important element needed for success as an adult in the workplace and in the community.

Special education should incorporate a level of instruction in the affective/social area because many students will not develop these skills without instruction, modeling, practice, and feedback. Skills in Competency 12 discuss specific techniques and programs for teaching social competence. In general, however, whatever social skills are taught, and whatever program of instruction is used, these skills will be found throughout the academic curriculum. In many cases, the specific skills, as well as the context in which they will be taught and used, will be prescribed by goals and objectives in the student's IEP. Affective and social skills taught throughout the school setting might include: social greetings; eye contact with a speaker; interpretation of facial expressions, body language, and personal space; ability to put feelings and questions into words; and use of words to acquire additional information, as needed.

INTEGRATING CAREER AND VOCATIONAL SKILLS

Skills in Competency 11 discuss specific issues related to instruction for career and vocational skills. Much of career education may occur outside the classroom; however, like social skills, career and vocational skills will be rooted in IEP goals and objectives and will be addressed throughout the academic curriculum as well. The term **Community-Referenced Instruction (CRI)** refers to classroom instruction that is specifically designed to meet the student's needs in the community setting. CRI involves analyzing specific skills necessary for daily life or work in the community, and then teaching and practicing these skills in a school setting. For example, if it is determined that a particular student will need to use public transportation to get to work, lesson plans designed to teach such skills as reading a bus map, recognizing bus signs and bus route labels, waiting in line for a bus, getting on a bus, notifying the driver of the desired stop, etc., would be implemented first in the classroom, or in riding the bus to and from school.

To be effective, classroom CRI conditions should mirror "natural" real-world conditions as closely as possible. In the above example, actual bus maps should be used, perhaps along with photos of bus stops and of buildings along a habitual route so that the student can practice recognizing when to get off the bus, etc. The more closely school experiences match the real world, the better able the student will be to generalize those skills learned in school to the outside community.

Career and vocational skills that focus on responsibility for actions, a good work ethic, and independence should also be incorporated into the academic setting. If students can regulate their school work habits, they are more likely to be able to carry over those skills into the workforce. The special education teacher may assess the student's level of career and vocational readiness by using the following list:

- Being prepared by showing responsibility for materials/school tools, such as books, assignments, study packets, pencils, pens, and assignment notebooks

- Knowing expectations by keeping an assignment notebook and asking questions when unsure of the expectations
- Use of additional checklists as needed
- Use of needed assistive devices
- Completing assignments on time to the best of his or her ability

An additional responsibility of the special educator when teaching career and vocational skills is the recognition of the variety of vocations and skills that are present in the community. For example, if academics are not an area in which students excel, other exploratory or training opportunities should be provided. Such opportunities might include art, music, culinary arts, childcare, technical trades, or building instruction. These skills can often be included within the academic setting. For example, a student with a strong vocational interest in art could be asked to create a poster to show information learned in a science or social studies unit. By addressing a career or vocational interest and skill this way the teacher is also able to establish a program of differentiated instruction.

Skill 7.06   Recognizing strategies and techniques for ensuring the efficient and effective use of instructional time

SCHEDULE DEVELOPMENT

Schedule development depends on the type of class (elementary or secondary) and the setting (regular classroom or resource room). There are, however, general rules of thumb that apply to both types and settings:

1. Allow time for transitions, planning, and setups. Transitions can be particularly difficult for some students with disabilities. It can help to have observable visual or auditory signals to serve as warnings about upcoming changes and transitions, as well as clearly posted schedules and routines. This is especially important for students with disabilities.
2. Aim for maximum instructional time by pacing the instruction and allotting time for practicing the new skills.
3. Proceed from short assignments to long ones, breaking up long lessons or complex tasks into short sessions or step-by-step instruction. Again, many students with disabilities will have such accommodations written into their IEPs.
4. Follow a less preferred academic subject or activity with a highly preferred academic subject or activity.
5. In settings where students are working on individualized plans, do not schedule all the students at once in activities that require a great deal of teacher assistance. Arrange for anchor activities that allow independent work.
6. Break up a longer segment into several smaller segments with a variety of activities.

Special Considerations for Elementary Classes

1. Determine the amount of time that is needed for activities such as P.E., lunch, and recess. Be sure to include transition time in your schedule.
2. Allow about 15 to 20 minutes each for opening and closing exercises. Spend this time on "housekeeping" activities such as collecting lunch money, going over the schedule, cleaning up, reviewing the day's activities, and getting ready to go home.
3. Schedule academics for periods when the students are most alert and motivated, usually in the morning. Take into consideration the affect regular medication for conditions such as ADHD could have on your students.
4. Build in time for slower students to finish their work; during this time, others may work at learning centers or on other activities of interest. Allowing extra time gives the teacher time to give more attention where it is needed, conduct assessments, and for students to complete or correct work.

Special Considerations for Secondary Classes

Secondary school days are usually divided into five, six, or seven periods of about 50 minutes each, with time for homeroom and lunch. Students cannot stay behind and finish their work because they have to leave for a different room. Resource room time should be scheduled so that the student does not miss academic instruction in his or her classroom or miss desirable nonacademic activities. In schools where ESE teachers also co-teach or work with students in the regular classroom, the regular teacher will have to coordinate lesson plans with those of the special education teacher. Consultation time will also have to be budgeted into the schedule.

Please see Skill 6.01 for more time and transition management strategies.

Skill 7.07   Demonstrating knowledge of methods for preparing and organizing materials to implement daily lesson plans

In their book on research-based teaching strategies, Saphier et al (2008) present research showing that the amount of time actually spent on "instruction is directly tied to classroom organization and management skills" (p. 52). If the teacher must delay or interrupt instruction to locate materials, boot up an assistive technology device, copy an extra worksheet, etc., then it is the *teacher* not the student, who is "off-task."

This goes beyond simply having commonly used supplies (e.g., pencils, paper, and textbooks) available to students in accessible locations. It is essential that the teacher actually plan for the set up and organization of materials and that this organization reflect the nature of the lesson and the specific needs of the students with disabilities. The teacher might, for example, have a table with each lesson's supplies set up in a specific spot. The arrangement will differ depending upon the type of lesson. A reading discussion might require a small group seated at a horseshoe table near a table holding a variety of phonics materials, while an interactive science lesson might need experimental materials, recording sheets, and so forth set up near a sink.

When teaching students with disabilities it might help to have visual pictures of the materials *they* are to bring or get out for each lesson (e.g., a picture of pencil, phonics folder, dry erase marker and board under the heading "Phonics Practice," or math book, pencil, paper and manipulatives under the "Math" heading). All assistive technology devices and computer support or instructional equipment (see Skill 8.06 for more) should be on, booted up, and already set to the lesson's program or place. Any additional accommodations prescribed by individual students' IEPs should also be at hand (e.g., if Bobby needs a fiddle object, or Pat needs a magnifying glass or window card for tracking, these should be *right there* when class begins).

Any instructions or lists of written information that need to be displayed during a lesson should already be written down and available at a glance. The teacher might, for example, use a sheet of chart paper with such information written for each lesson ahead of time and keep the paper turned backwards until it is time to turn it around for display during a lesson. Alternatively, chalkboard notes could be under a pull-down map that can be rolled up when the notes are needed.

Skill 7.08 Demonstrating understanding of language diversity and various communication styles and modes in planning effective instruction for students with disabilities

The average classroom today is composed of several different cultures. The teacher's understanding of students' actions and the manner in which the teacher communicates with them require foresight into what cultural background students bring with them to the classroom. Knowledge of this background will help special education teachers to serve both as advocates and as interpreters for the student who may appear "odd," even though he or she is simply doing what is expected in his or her culture. This is especially true for those who are new to the country or are in the elementary level.

For example, imagine a teacher who considers all her Vietnamese students to be polite, but slow learners who refuse to participate in class. This impression probably occurs because her Vietnamese students are quiet and do not take part in classroom discussions. This impression would be different if this same teacher had learned that children in Vietnam believe their teachers are never wrong, they are taught through rote memorization, and classroom discussion/open participation is a foreign concept to them.

Unfortunately, some teachers might think that students of a certain culture learn more slowly in one area, misunderstanding the fact that they may simply learn differently. Therefore, it is often a good idea to learn as much as possible about the learning styles of the students, even complementing instruction with peer tutoring, and allowing for a sharing of different cultural strengths as a way to build a unique opportunity for understanding.

Please refer to Skill 5.07 for more on language diversity.

COMPETENCY 0008   UNDERSTAND PRINCIPLES AND METHODS INVOLVED IN INDIVIDUALIZING INSTRUCTION FOR STUDENTS WITH DISABILITIES

Skill 8.01   Demonstrating an understanding of effective collaboration among teachers and other professionals to individualize instruction in a variety of inclusive models (e.g., co-teaching, push-in, consultant teaching [CT])

Skills 6.02, 6.03, 6.06, and 6.08 cover many aspects of collaboration, and Skills 7.01 and 7.04 cover collaboration for curriculum design in a variety of settings.

Key to the sort of collaboration necessary for individualized instruction using any of the models of inclusion is the need for all parties involved to understand the goals, objectives, and accommodations in each child's IEP, as well as the overall principles of Differentiated Instruction (see Skill 7.02). This, combined with the principles of collaboration discussed the above skills, will enable educators to work together to individualize instruction.

Skill 8.02   Applying techniques for planning, adapting, and sequencing instruction to meet IEP goals and objectives

The teacher of students with disabilities is faced with the task of not only teaching the standards-based curriculum, but also with designing instruction to meet the (often varied) goals and objectives of the students' IEPs. A significant part of designing instruction to meet IEP goals and objectives is determining how to align that instruction with the standards-based curriculum.

INCORPORATING IEP GOALS AND OBJECTIVES INTO DAILY CURRICULA

The teacher will be teaching a wide variety of subjects (e.g., reading, writing, math, science, social studies) throughout the day and will need to carefully plan which IEP objectives will be addressed in which subject lessons. This decision will depend upon the specific objectives, but some general guidelines will help.

Some IEP objectives (e.g., social and behavioral objectives) can best be addressed throughout the day in virtually all subject areas. If a child's IEP specifies learning to raise his hand before speaking or using words to describe his feelings rather than striking out, these would be relevant objectives throughout the day. An objective for increasing independent work time to, say, 10 minutes would be worked into any lesson throughout the day that included desk work.

Other IEP goals and objectives will be more easily addressed in some lessons than in others, and the teacher will need to plan accordingly. For example, a goal for the student to write a short summary of chronological events would be more suitable to a reading lesson involving fiction than either a science lesson or a math lesson. The sequence of tasks designed for this goal might involve highlighting events in the text with numbered sticky arrows, followed by listing events on a graphic organizer of the Story Marker type, and then writing a summary based on that organizer.

Alternatively, a goal about learning to list the main idea and several supporting details about a topic might better be addressed in a science or nonfiction reading. This sequence might involve first highlighting the main idea and details in different colors, then writing them onto a graphic organizer, and so forth. The teacher will need to spend time carefully choosing when and where to address each and every objective of each child's IEP.

USING DIFFERENTIATED INSTRUCTION TO ADAPT LESSONS FOR IEP GOALS

In order to use Differentiated Instruction (Skill 7.02) to address goals and objectives for students with disabilities, it will be necessary to make modifications. Although the specific modifications will depend on each individual child's needs, remember that skills are building blocks when organizing and sequencing objectives. A taxonomy of educational objectives, such as that provided by Bloom (1956), can be helpful in constructing and organizing objectives. Simple, factual knowledge of material is low on this cognitive taxonomy, and should be addressed early in the sequence. Some examples of using factual knowledge are matching, memorizing definitions, and memorizing famous quotes. Eventually, objectives should be developed to include higher-level thinking such as comprehension (i.e., being able to use a definition); application (i.e., being able to apply the definition to other situations); synthesis (i.e., being able to add other information); and evaluation (i.e., being able to judge the value of something). Such a taxonomy can be used with the Differentiated Instructional practices discussed in Skill 7.02 to find entry points for each standard and align the goal not only with the standard, but also with the child's current level of performance.

For example, suppose a learning standard asks the students to apply word analysis and vocabulary skills to comprehend selections, and a particular student's IEP objective is to demonstrate the ability to use knowledge of common root words and affixes to define unfamiliar words. Using the Differentiated Instruction approach discussed in Skill 7.02, a sequence of differently leveled lesson objectives might read:

- **Basic level:** Student will differentiate root words and common affixes by circling or highlighting the root word.
- **Moderate level:** Student will differentiate root words from affixes, then select the correct meaning for the affix from a group of 4 possible meanings.

- **Mastery level:** Student will differentiate root words from common affixes, state the meaning of the root word, and state how each affix changes the meaning of the root word.

Further examples of this procedure for designing appropriate instruction can be found in Skill sections for language arts (Competency 0009) and mathematics (Competency 0010).

LESSON PLAN DEVELOPMENT

Lesson plans are important for guiding instruction in the classroom because they outline the steps of teacher implementation and assessment of the teacher's instructional effectiveness and student learning success. Teachers should be able to objectify and quantify learning goals and targets in terms of effective performance-based assessments and projected criteria for identifying when a student has learned the material presented. Where applicable, these should reflect IEP objectives.

Although the teacher need not type a formal lesson plan for every activity, the components of such a lesson plan should always be present. These are the steps that need to be followed to ensure that the lesson plan achieves the teacher's purpose. A typical format for a written lesson plan would include the following items:

1. **Unit description:** Describes the learning and classroom environment
   a. **Classroom characteristics**: Describes the physical arrangements of the classroom and the student grouping patterns for the lesson being taught
   b. **Student characteristics**: Demographics of the classroom that include the number, gender, and cultural and ethnic backgrounds of the students, as well as students with IEPs

2. **Learning goals, targets, and objectives**: What are the expectations of the lesson? Are the learning goals appropriate to the state learning standards and district academic goals? Are they tied to individual students' IEP objectives? Are the targets appropriate for the grade level and subject content area and inclusive of a multicultural perspective and global viewpoint?

3. **Learning experiences for students**: How will student learning be supported by the learning objectives? What prior knowledge do the students need, and how will the lesson be modified for those with special needs? How will multicultural variables be incorporated? What will be done to motivate and engage students?

4. **Rationales for learning experiences**: Provide information on how the lesson plan addresses student learning goals and objectives and address whether the lesson provides accommodations for students with IEPs and support for marginalized students in the classroom.

5. **Assessments**: Construct pre and post assessments that evaluate student learning as it relates to the learning goals and objectives. Do the assessments include a cultural integration that addresses the cultural needs and inclusion of students? Do assessments incorporate accommodations needed by students with special needs?

Skill 8.03   Demonstrating knowledge of instructional and remedial methods, techniques, and materials used to address individual students' learning styles, strengths, and needs

Please refer to Skill 7.02 to read about differentiated instructional techniques. Skill 4.05 may also be a helpful skill to review.

Many of the instructional techniques useful to students with disabilities might be described as "just good teaching practice—but more if it." Students with disabilities might need a reduced rate of presentation or presentation in smaller units. Students with disabilities might need much more review (see section on overlearning, below). New vocabulary and symbols should be introduced one at a time, and the relationships of the components to the whole should be stressed. Students with disabilities might need concrete or multimedia presentation and illustration of concepts. Students' background information should be recalled to connect new information to the old. Students with disabilities may need that background to be created for them. Finally, teach strategies or algorithms first and then move on to tasks that are more difficult. Students with disabilities might need templates and problem solving lists to help them learn new material and retain it.

ADDRESSING STUDENTS' NEEDS

There are a number of procedures teachers can use to address the varying needs of the students. Some of the more common procedures include:

Varied assignments: A variety of assignments on the same content allows students to match learning styles and preferences with the assignment. This variety also enhances the Differentiated Instruction techniques described in Skill 7.02.

Multi-modal presentations: Many students with disabilities benefit from concrete presentations that utilize more than one approach. Presenting information in a variety of concrete, often multisensory ways can help students grasp and retain information.

Cooperative learning: Cooperative learning activities allow students to share ideas, expertise, and insight in a non-threatening setting. The focus tends to remain on positive learning rather than competition.

Structured environment: Some students benefit from clear, visual structure that defines the expectations and goals of the teacher. This might be a written or pictorial list of main points or steps in the lesson.

Clearly stated assignments: Assignments should be clearly stated, along with the expectation and criteria for completion. Written rubrics and samples are good ways to provide support.

Overlearning: As a principle of effective teaching, overlearning recommends that students continue to study and review after they have achieved initial mastery. The use of repetition in the context of varied assignments offers the means to help students pursue and achieve overlearning. This is particularly effective for students with disabilities.

Visualization: Many students with disabilities have weak visualization skills. Using art concepts such as visual imagery to help students process the concepts of reading, math, and science creates a mental mind mapping of learning for students processing new information. It can be helpful to provide explicit instruction and practice in visualizing information, problems, and possible solutions. This skill can be generalized to many curriculum areas.

SELECTING AND MODIFYING MATERIALS TO MEET STUDENT NEEDS

In attempting to evaluate the instructional level of teaching materials, several questions should be asked by the teacher.

- **Does the publisher state the readability level of the material, and does the readability level remain consistent throughout?** If not, the teacher might need to determine readability level and select texts that are appropriate for each student.
- **Is there more than one book or story lesson for each level?** Students with disabilities might need much more practice at each level than students without disabilities. The teacher might need to find additional texts to provide this additional practice.
- **Is there an attempt to control the use of content-specific vocabulary?** Is the interest level appropriate for the content, illustrations, and age of the students who will use the material? This is very important, because many students with disabilities have the *interests* of their age peers, but much lower reading or cognitive levels. In addition, it is customary to provide grade level curriculum topics in content areas (e.g., Solar System in third grade, or the Constitution in fourth grade), so it is important to find content materials that are presented in a form that students with disabilities can

access. Please refer to Skill 5.03 for techniques for modifying content area text.

A great amount of time and research has been devoted to developing criteria for selecting instructional materials that meet the needs of students with disabilities. Most researchers (e.g., Henley, Ramsey, & Algozzine [1996]; Morsink [1984]; Brown [1983]; Hammill & Bartel [1986]; Smith [1983]) suggest evaluating materials in terms of their **relevance** or **utility**.

Relevance

Materials selected for use with exceptional students should be pertinent to their needs, so the teacher will need to consider the relevancy of the materials for use with his or her special needs students in relation to the academic, behavioral, developmental, and physical needs of students; their learning styles; and the behavioral objectives specified in their IEPs. Hammill and Bartel (1986) recommend an examination of the following factors when evaluating relevance:

- Are the skills and concepts required of the students present?
- Is there a history of success or failure with use of certain methods?
- Are there characteristics that imply needs (e.g., orthopedic restrictions, family problems, ethnic or cultural diversity)?
- What range of student difference does the material encompass?
- Are there readiness behaviors specified that are prerequisites for the students?
- Has any effort been made to assess or control the complexity of the language, either receptively or expressively?
- Is the material obviously intended for younger children, or has it been adapted for use with older students (e.g., high interest, low vocabulary)?
- What are the target populations for whom the materials were developed? Are they identified?

Utility

Usefulness or practicality is another criterion essential for evaluating instructional materials to be used with special needs students. When considering utility, Brown (cited in Smith [1983]) suggests that questions similar to the following be asked:

- What is the comprehensiveness or breadth of the program?
- Is the material sequenced so that mastery can be achieved before progressing to the next step, or are materials spiraled so that areas of difficulty can be left temporarily and then returned to later?
- Is the presentation of instruction paced for various groups or individuals?
- Are the materials useful in their organizational schemata (e.g., units, page arrangements, illustrations)?

- Is the material teacher-directed or student-directed?

Skill 8.04 **Recognizing how cultural perspectives influence the relationship among families, schools, and communities, as related to effective instruction for students with disabilities**

The teacher should be familiar with the effects of cultural stereotypes and racism on the development of students with disabilities. The teacher should know that variations in beliefs, traditions, and values exist across and within cultures. Teachers should also be familiar with the characteristics and biases of their own cultures, as well as how these biases can impact their teaching, behavior, and communication.

The need to understand students' cultural backgrounds goes beyond fairness and acceptance; ignorance of a student's background can directly affect the success of instruction and assessment. The child's background experiences are crucial to reading comprehension. For example, some of the most important instructional strategies for comprehension involve "priming" or "activating" the child's prior experiences that are relevant to the material to be read. Children from different cultures come equipped with very different background experiences and the teacher may not know how to activate them because they are unfamiliar to the teacher.

Children in American culture will have experience with certain nursery rhymes, historical figures, even television shows and fictional characters. Students from other cultures might not share these experiences and might be confused by off-hand references to them by teachers and in literature. For example, one child from a background that did not include the Santa Claus figure was very confused by a holiday story that involved hanging stockings by the fire and finding them filled with candy the next morning. The only reason this child could imagine for hanging a stocking by the fire was to dry it out because it had gotten wet. The child, therefore, felt that the Santa figure was mean to put candy in a dirty, wet sock, where it would get mushy. Naturally enough, this child failed to identify the main idea of the story.

Educators need to ensure that they demonstrate positive regard for the cultures, religions, genders, and varying abilities of students and their families. This should include showing sensitivity to students with different cultural and ethnic backgrounds when designing the curriculum. Teachers should also convey to students how knowledge is developed from the vantage point of a particular culture. At the same time, teachers who use themes with a multicultural perspective should ensure that they are not teaching material that could be considered culturally insensitive or offensive. Culturally sensitive teaching creates a helpful, receptive, and enriched educational setting that permits all students to feel comfortable as they look at their attitudes and share their thoughts.

It is crucial that teachers develop an in-depth understanding of the influence of culture and language on students' academic performance. This will allow teachers to differentiate between genuine learning problems and cultural differences.

Multiculturalism is valuable for all students and all teachers; in unbiased classrooms, students hear the voices of a variety of different cultural groups. This enables students to understand the world from multiple ethnic and cultural perspectives, instead of just agreeing with the point of view of the mainstream culture.

Skill 8.05   Recognizing effective strategies for involving the individual and family in setting instructional goals and charting progress

Involving the special education student (when appropriate) and his or her family in setting instructional goals is necessary to develop a well-rounded IEP. When families help set goals for things that are important to the special education student, subsequent increased family cooperation and involvement are usually evident. Typically, the parent of the child knows the child best, so meshing the school goals and those of the family will provide a program that is most thorough in meeting the student's needs.

Progress on these mutually accepted goals, as well as those initiated by the school, can be charted or measured in a variety of ways. The methods used to track the goals should be those indicated in the goals and objectives section of the IEP.

- **Charting** is a formal tracking method of student behavior and progress. Often based on a functional behavioral assessment portion of the IEP, the chart will include behaviors (positive or negative), the time covered, and the frequency of the behavior, which is often shown with tally marks. A modified form of charting can be used by parents and teachers to link schoolwork with homework and maintain consistency in effort between home and school. Behavioral charts maintained by the student him or herself can also be very effective.
- **Anecdotal records** are a journaling of behaviors observed in the home or classroom. Such records could be notes kept by the classroom teacher or therapist, or notes from the parent (often in the form of paper notes, passbook entries, or emails) regarding student successes and challenges.
- **Observations** are a more focused form of anecdotal records when a specific activity, class, or time period is observed and the behaviors and skills of the individual student are recorded. Often, a comparison of student behavior in various settings gives information needed to write appropriate IEP goals.
- **Rating scales** are frequently used to assess a student's behavior or level of functioning in a particular environment (home, classroom, or

playground). These scales are often given to more than one person (parent, teacher, and/or therapist) to complete so that a more comprehensive picture of the student is obtained. Commonly used rating scales containing a component for professionals and parents include the Conners' Comprehensive Behavior Rating Scale (Connors 2008), the Vineland Adaptive Behavior Scale (Balla, Cicchetti, & Sparrow 2005), and the Child Development Inventory (Ireton & Ireton 1992).

Any of these methods can be used with some variety of home-school communication system such as a notebook that goes back and forth.

Skill 8.06   Demonstrating knowledge of assistive and instructional technologies for students with disabilities (e.g., alternative input and output devices)

ASSISTIVE TECHNOLOGIES

IDEA provides the following definition of an Assistive Technology device: "Any items, piece of equipment or product system, whether acquired commercially, off the shelf, modified, or customized that is used to increase, maintain or improve functional capabilities of children with disabilities." IDEA 2004 clarified that assistive technology "does not include a medical device that is surgically implanted, or the replacement of such device." Almost anything can be considered assistive technology if it can be used to increase, maintain, or improve the functioning of a person with a disability.

Visual Aids

For those with visual disorders, the Laser Cane and Sonic guide are two examples of electronic devices that have been in use for some time.

A newly developed machine, the Personal Companion, can respond to human voices and answer with a synthesized voice. The Personal Companion can "read" aloud sections from a morning newspaper delivered through telecommunications.

Advances in computer technology provide access to printed information for many people with visual impairments. Books are available on computer disks, allowing for a variety of outputs: voice, enlarged print, and Braille.

Personal computers with special printers can transform print to Braille, allowing teachers to produce copies of handouts, worksheets, tests, maps, charts, and other class materials in Braille.

Closed-Circuit Television (CCTV) can be used to enlarge the print found in printed texts and books.

Audio Aids

Talking books have been available through the Library of Congress since 1934, using specially designed cassette tapes, and, more recently, CDs. Modern CD readers (e.g., Daisy Reader) are not only for the blind. These CDs allow students with reading disabilities to use electronic menus to find specific text, reviews, or chapters and even to take notes or summaries. Regional resource and materials centers disseminate these machines. Newly devised systems that allow printed materials to be synthesized into speech are also available.

Similar programs translate the student's speech into print and can be very useful for students with writing disabilities.

Closed captions translate speech and sound on TV and videos for readers who cannot hear. Closed captioning has been required by law in the U.S. for a number of years and is available on virtually all TV stations, educational programs, CDs, and DVDs.

The Telecommunication Device for the Deaf (TDD) enables persons who have hearing impairments to make and receive telephone calls.

Hearing aids and other equipment that helps people make better use of their residual hearing are referred to as assistive listening devices (ALDs).

FM (frequency-modulated) transmission devices (auditory trainers) are used in some classrooms. To use them, the teacher speaks into a microphone and the sound is received directly by each student's receiver or hearing aid. This system reduces background noise, allows teachers to move freely around the room, and helps students benefit more from lectures.

Physical and Health Impairments

Technology has helped individuals with physical and health impairments to gain access to and control the environment around them, to communicate with others, and to take advantage of health care. Aids include high-tech devices, such as computers, but also low-tech devices, such as built-up spoons and crutches.

Mobility is assisted by use of lightweight or electric specialized wheelchairs. These include motorized chairs, computerized chairs, and chairs in which it is possible to rise. Electronic switches allow persons with only partial movement (e.g., head, neck, fingers, toes) to be more mobile.

Mobility is also enhanced by use of artificial limbs, personalized equipped vans, and electrical walking machines. Myoelectric (or bionic) limbs contain a sensor that picks up electric signals transmitted from the person's brain through the limb.

Speech/Communication

A communication board is a flat surface on which words, pictures, or both can be placed. The student is encouraged to point to the symbols of what he or she wants to communicate. Simple boards can be made from magazine or newspaper pictures. Others can be written on to display messages. More sophisticated boards incorporate an attachment that synthesizes a voice. Communication books perform the same function as communication boards.

Math

- **Calculators:** Students who have difficulty performing math calculations can benefit from the use of a calculator. Adapted calculators can be used for students with physical disabilities, and talking calculators are available for students with visual impairments.
- **On-screen electronic worksheets:** For some students with physical disabilities that affect writing, worksheets can be produced in an on-screen format, allowing the students to use a computer screen to answer the questions.
- **Manipulatives of all types:** Students who have difficulty acquiring or retaining math concepts often benefit from objects designed to provide a kinesthetic or visual illustration of the concept. These low-tech aids include such things as place value blocks, fraction strips, geared clocks, play money, etc.

Instructional Technologies

In addition to assistive technology to help an individual overcome a physical disability, there is a wide range of instructional technology available to help teachers accommodate varying student needs and learning styles.

The CD player is of particular benefit to students who learn best by auditory input. CDs frequently accompany commercial instructional programs (e.g., reading kits, programmed workbooks). They can accommodate earphones or headsets for single or group listening opportunities. Teacher-recorded CDs offer the opportunity for students to read along or follow story sequences with accompanying pictures, listen to stories for pleasure, practice spelling words, and learn to follow instructions. They can also be used to answer comprehension questions, discriminate auditory sounds, perform word study exercises, and, in general, maintain and motivate student interest.

Media such as DVDs and televisions provide opportunities for presenting instructional content to individuals or groups of students in a format that readers and nonreaders alike can understand. Depending on a school's policies, students may be allowed to go to a media center and view a video for pleasure. Teachers may also show part of a selected video and ask students to hypothesize what preceded or followed the action they saw.

The Overhead Projector (OVH) is an easy-to-use and easy-to-maintain visual communication device. A bright lamp source transmits light through the translucent material to a screen close to the machine. Transparencies can be purchased commercially or made from clear photocopies of materials.

Computers and Software

Computers can be valuable teaching tools. Software programs and adaptations enable learners with disabilities (physical, cognitive, and sensory) to profit from instruction in the classroom that they might not be able to receive otherwise. For example, tutorial programs simulate the teaching function of presentations, questions, and feedback. Games are effective as motivators and reinforcers.

Stages of learning

Some suggestions about selecting and using software were given by Male (1994). According to these findings, it is important to first make sure there is a curriculum correspondence between student learning goals and objectives and the use of computers. This should follow what Male calls "stages of learning." Software should be selected with these stages in mind:

1. **Acquisition:** Introduction of a new skill
2. **Proficiency:** Practice under supervision to achieve accuracy and speed
3. **Maintenance:** Continued practice without further instruction
4. **Generalization:** Application of the new skill in new settings and situations
5. **Adaptation:** Modifications of the task to meet new needs and the demands of varying situations

Computer-assisted instruction

Computers are used to provide a safe, stimulating learning environment for many students. The computer does not evaluate or offer subjective opinions about the student's work; it merely provides feedback about the correctness or incorrectness of each answer in a series. Smith & Luckasson (1992) state that the computer is like an effective teacher by the way in which it:

1. Provides immediate attention and feedback
2. Individualizes to the particular skill level
3. Allows students to work at their own pace

4. Makes corrections quickly
5. Produces a professional looking product
6. Keeps accurate records on correct answer and error rates
7. Ignores inappropriate behavior
8. Focuses on the particular response
9. Is nonjudgmental

Word processors and writing instruction

Many programs can assist students with writing disabilities by providing graphic organizers, word anticipation software, spell checkers, and even thesaurus options. The process approach to writing is encouraged, especially when using a word processor (Male, 1994). These stages include planning/prewriting, drafting, revising/editing, and sharing/publication.

Learn more about available Assistive Technologies here:
http://www.abilityhub.com

Skill 8.07   Demonstrating an understanding of effective collaboration among teachers and other professionals to facilitate students' use and independent management of assistive technologies in various settings

Determination of student need for assistive technology: Often, the special educator will identify the need for consultation or testing in an area in which a student is having difficulty. Testing or other professional evaluation might result in the trial or ongoing use of some form of assistive technology. If this technology proves effective, the team may later add the technology to the student's IEP.

Development of student skill using specific assistive technology: Students who have been identified as needing assistive technology require training in the use of the equipment. Sometimes a therapist or consultant will "push in" to the classroom, providing training for the student in the classroom setting. Other times, the student will practice using the assistive technology in a separate setting until a level of experience/expertise is reached. The assistive technology can then be used in the special education or inclusion classroom.

Communication of expected skill level in the classroom: As students begin to use assistive technology in the classroom, the desired use (including activity, location, and time) should be outlined for the special educator so that misunderstandings do not result in a student misusing or under-using the technology. The student will then have a level of accountability and be functioning to the best of his or her abilities.

Training of school personnel on use of assistive technology: Although special educators are often trained in using a variety of assistive devices, advances in technology make it necessary for professionals to participate in ongoing training for new or unfamiliar equipment. This training could be conducted by a knowledgeable therapist or consultant in the school district, or school personnel might need to attend a workshop off-campus. In an inclusion setting, both the special education teacher(s) and the general education teacher(s) will need to be trained.

Evaluation of student independent management of assistive technology in various settings: Ongoing evaluation of the student's use of the equipment is vital. This may be monitored through observation by the therapist or consultant, anecdotal records by the special educator, or some type of checklist. Often, an IEP goal will address how the use of the equipment as well as an evaluation of the student's performance with the equipment will be implemented.

Transitions and settings: While some technologies (e.g., a SmartBoard or calculator) can be moved from setting to setting by the student, others (e.g., computer, closed-circuit TV) are not so portable. Staff will need to coordinate when planning how portable technology will be moved from setting to setting as needed or how the student will move **to** the technology as needed in various lesson settings.

COMPETENCY 0009   UNDERSTAND STRATEGIES AND TECHNIQUES USED TO PROMOTE STUDENTS' LANGUAGE ARTS SKILLS IN A VARIETY OF SETTINGS

Skill 9.01   Identify types and characteristics of language arts difficulties associated with various disabilities

Language arts skills include both reading and writing skills. In order to understand the impact of various disabilities on reading and writing skills, it is necessary to be familiar with the typical development of these skills.

It should be noted that research shows that from the most basic foundation concepts required to learn the skills to the stages through which students move as they learn, reading and writing are two sides of the same coin. Both rely upon understanding the same metalinguistic principles: the alphabetic principle and sound-letter associations, the structure of language, and the conventions of writing. Regardless of the specific system or labels used to describe the stages of development, reading and writing skills will each follow complementary paths. For a given child, sometimes reading skills will outpace writing skills, or writing skills will outpace reading skills, but both will follow a similar path and each skill can be used to assist in learning the other. Specific learning disabilities (to be discussed later) can, however, impact one of these skills (either reading or writing) more heavily than the other.

TYPICAL SEQUENCE OF READING AND WRITING DEVELOPMENT

The U.S. Department of Education and the National Reading Panel (2000) have described a research-based sequence of typical reading development that begins at home and moves through preschool to about grade three, when a child begins to transition *from learning to read to reading to learn*. Although children progress through these stages at different rates and show strengths and weaknesses in differing areas, most will move through these stages in this order. For convenience, brief descriptions of the concurrent stages of writing development are included.

Age 3-4 through Pre-K: Developing Print Concepts

Children learn that print has meaning and that meaning does not change with successive readings. They learn print directionality. In English, this means that books are read from front (left) to back (right) and that print is read from left to right and top to bottom. They learn that pictures are related to print.

During this period, the child's language concepts are also developing. Chief among these is phonological awareness, the awareness of all the sound aspects of spoken language. Most critical for the later development of reading is phonemic awareness, the awareness that spoken words are made up of discrete sounds uttered in a specific order.

At this stage, when children scribble-write or use invented spelling, they reveal themselves as detectives of the written word, having watched parents and teachers make lists, write thank-you notes, or leave messages. Children show an understanding that print contains a message and they often draw-write to send a message. They might not be able to write many letters, but they will begin to draw shapes that resemble letters or use a few known letters (or approximations of letters) in their writing.

Kindergarten-First Grade: Beginning Alphabetic Concepts

During this phase, children learn to manipulate phonemes, or sounds, in words by deleting, adding, or substituting sounds in individual words and blending those sounds into new words orally. They also begin to understand the alphabetic principle that letters stand for sounds and that words have correct spellings. They can recognize and name most letters of the alphabet and they begin to identify the most common sounds of most letters. At this stage, they can also recognize high-frequency sight words and can begin to decode simple texts. They can make predictions about what is read to them and ask and answer questions about what they read.

Writing at this stage shows the child's emerging understanding of the alphabetic principle and phonics. Writers use very simple oral language structures and use at least some real letters. They may get only the first, last, or most noticeable letter/sound(s) when writing. They begin to show an understanding of the one-to-one correspondence between words in speech and words on the page (e.g., there are spaces between their words).

Second Grade: Expanded Phonics Knowledge and Decoding

The child's knowledge of phonics, the sound letter code, improves and he or she can decode both one- and two-syllable words and use context (both syntactic and semantic) cues to help decode unfamiliar words. The child can sequence events in a simple story, make brief oral summaries of material read, and begin to understand story elements and main ideas.

The child's writing shows the growing understanding of phonics, and invented spelling becomes more phonetic. Some frequently used words will be spelled correctly. When writing about topics that interest them and with which they have a rich background of information, students can use basic sentence structures with some variation in beginnings, and might begin to try to use "cool" words they encounter in reading or listening. Students begin to attempt to use punctuation and capitalization correctly.

Third Grade: Transition to Reading to Learn

Up to this point, children have been engaged in learning to read, in acquiring the many skills necessary to construct meaning from print, and to encode their own ideas in print through writing. Somewhere around third grade, children have acquired sufficient reading ability to use that ability to learn other information from content area texts. This transition process occurs gradually at rates individual to each student.

READING DISABILITIES

Reading is a complex process skill that involves the integration of many cognitive and perceptual skills. Most reading skills can be classified into two categories: decoding (the ability to identify and pronounce individual words) and comprehension (understanding the meaning of both individual words and connected text). Reading disabilities can affect one or both of these skill categories.

Torgeson and Wagner (1998) review research showing that (1) the most severe reading problems of children with learning disabilities lie at the word, rather than the text, level of processing (i.e., inability to accurately and fluently decode single words), and (2) the most common cognitive limitation of these children involves a dysfunction in the awareness of the phonological structure of words in oral language (p. 226).

Phonological Awareness

Flippo (2002) states that phonological awareness "refers to an awareness of *many* aspects of spoken language, including words within sentences, syllables within words, and phonemes within syllables and words…" **Phoneme awareness** is one part of phonological awareness, and is the understanding that spoken words are composed of tiny, individual sound units called phonemes. Children need a strong background in phonemic awareness in order for phonics instruction (sound-spelling relationships in print) to be effective.

The National Reading Panel (2000) specified six phoneme awareness skills crucial to learning to read:

- Phoneme isolation: Recognizing individual sounds (/g/ and /O/ in "go")
- Phoneme identification: Recognizing common sounds in different words (/b/ in boy, bike, and bell)
- Phoneme categorization: Recognizing sounds in sequence (bus, bun, rug)
- Phoneme blending: Hearing a series of individual phonemes, then blending them into a word (hearing /g/ /O/ and saying "go")
- Phoneme segmentation: Separating and counting out the sounds in a word (given "go" saying /g/ and /O/)

- Phoneme deletion: Recognizing what would be left if one phoneme is removed from a word (hear "flat" and remove the /f/ sound and state that "lat" would be left)

Most reading disabilities impact these phonological areas and will make it difficult for the student to decode individual words and read connected text without specific instructional interventions.

Reading Comprehension Deficits

Reading comprehension refers to a student's ability to understand what he or she is reading. Some students with reading comprehension difficulties are able to read a passage so fluently that you might assume they are highly proficient readers. However, when they are asked questions about what they have read, they have little or no understanding of the words. Students with this problem are sometimes referred to as word callers (Friend, 2005). It is always necessary to assess not only decoding but also the ability to understand what is being decoded.

The Impact of Reading/Writing Disabilities

Most language arts difficulties fall into one of four broad categories. Some students can, of course, exhibit more than one kind of difficulty. The specific instructional techniques and modifications each student needs will depend upon the specific problem. Since reading and writing are complementary skills, any reading disability will also impact writing skills.

1. **Reading/decoding problems** affect the child's ability to identify or remember words and are usually based in difficulties with the sound-letter code (see phonological awareness, above). These are problems with the mechanics of reading words and sentences. They impact all aspects of reading including comprehension if the child is required to decode on his or her own. Children with serious decoding issues expend so much effort decoding that they have nothing left for understanding what is being read. On the other hand, a child with decoding problems might have no difficulty comprehending material read to him or her.
2. **Reading comprehension problems** limit the child's ability to understand and recall what he or she has read. Such a child might be able to decode or read the words correctly, but does not understand them. This child does not understand material that is read to him or her, either. These problems are based in meaning and abstract inferences.

3. **Writing/encoding problems** limit the child's ability to correctly spell and write the words he or she wants to use. Often such children cannot spell phonetically and cannot read their own writing after they have finished it. They may, however, be quite good at composing ideas and organizing the concepts; they just can't write them down. Their problem is with the mechanics of writing.

4. **Writing/composing problems** involve limitations in the ability to construct sentences, frame or organize ideas, find the right words to use, or communicate ideas verbally or in writing. These children might be able to carry out the physical act of writing, have good handwriting, and be able to spell and capitalize well. Their problem is with the content of the message rather than the mechanics.

Dyslexia

Many students with reading and writing disabilities will have been diagnosed with some form of dyslexia. Dyslexia is a term used for a variety of language learning disorders that are often based on difficulties with phonological awareness and processing. Common symptoms include difficulty decoding words, poor fluency, poor writing and spelling, and sometimes comprehension difficulties as well. These difficulties are present in spite of normal intelligence and instructional methods. The National Association of Special Education Teachers (NASET) Learning Disabilities Report #3 (2008) describes over twenty types of dyslexia cited by the American Academy of Special Education Professionals' Educator's Diagnostic Manual of Disabilities and Disorders (2007). Teachers of students with reading and writing disabilities would do well to familiarize themselves with the more common forms of dyslexia.

Handwriting

There are many physical disabilities that can negatively impact handwriting skills. A purely physical inability to write legibly, however, is a very different class of disability and might not impact a student's composition or encoding skills at all. In other words, a student might be able to compose excellent expressive writing, and be able to spell and punctuate it properly, but not be able to physically manipulate a pencil for writing. Such students need assistive technology (see Skill 8.06) and/or accommodations to allow the student to demonstrate his or her writing skills.

Skill 9.02   Demonstrating familiarity with a range of approaches to language arts instruction that meet the needs of students with disabilities

There are many approaches and programs available for language arts instruction and an overview of such approaches is provided below. However, when choosing an approach or technique, teachers need to keep in mind that NCLB (see Skill 16.01) now holds K-3 teachers accountable for teaching reading using varied, *research-based approaches* with *measurable outcomes*. Therefore, whatever approach a teacher chooses should take into account current research on effective teaching methods.

RESEARCH ON CRITICAL COMPONENTS OF READING DEVELOPMENT

In 2000, the National Reading Panel released its now well-known report on teaching children to read. This report side-stepped the debate between phonics and whole language approaches and argued, essentially, that both letter-sound recognition and comprehension of the text are important for successful reading. The report identified five critical areas of reading instruction:

- **Phonemic Awareness**: The understanding that spoken words are made up of a sequence of individual sounds or phonemes. This is just one part of overall **phonological awareness**, the awareness of such aspects of spoken language as words as units, syllables within words, sentences, etc.
- **Phonics**: The process of linking sounds to letter symbols and combining them to make words
- **Fluency**: The ability to read with speed, accuracy, and proper expression without conscious attention, and to handle both word recognition and comprehension simultaneously
- **Vocabulary**: The part of comprehension based on the meaning of individual words in context
- **Comprehension**: The process of getting meaning or information from a text that occurs on multiple levels, from literal to abstract

Methods used to teach these skills are often featured in a "balanced literacy" curriculum that focuses on the use of skills in various instructional contexts. For example, a phonics component tailored to individual student needs is included; for independent reading, students choose books that interest them at their reading levels; with guided reading, teachers work with small groups of students to help them with their particular reading problems; with whole group reading, the entire class reads the same text and the teacher incorporates activities to help students learn phonics, comprehension, fluency and vocabulary. In addition to these components of balanced literacy, teachers incorporate writing so that students can learn the structures of communicating through text.

OVERVIEW OF APPROACHES TO READING INSTRUCTION
Beginning Reading Approaches

Methods of teaching beginning reading skills can be divided into two major categories: code emphasis and meaning emphasis. Both approaches have their supporters and their critics. Teachers may decide to blend aspects of both approaches to meet the individual needs of their students.

Bottom-up or code-emphasis approach

- Letter-sound regularity is stressed.
- Reading instruction begins with words that consist of letters or letter combinations that have the same sound in different words. Component letter-sound relationships are taught and mastered before new words are introduced.
- Examples: phonics, linguistics, modified alphabet, and programmed reading series such as the Merrill Linguistic Reading Program and DISTAR Reading.

Top-down or meaning-emphasis approach

- Reading for meaning is emphasized from the first stages of instruction.
- Programs begin with words that appear frequently, which are assumed to be familiar and easy to learn.
- Examples: whole language, language experience, and individualized reading programs

Developmental Reading Approaches

Developmental reading programs emphasize daily, sequential instruction. Instructional materials usually feature a series of books as the core of the program.

Basal reader program

Basal readers series form the core of many school reading programs from pre-primers to eighth grade. Teacher manuals provide a highly-structured and comprehensive scope and sequence, lesson plans, and objectives. Sometimes vocabulary is controlled from level to level, and reading skills cover word recognition, word attack, and comprehension.

Advantages of basal readers are the structured, sequential manner in which reading is taught and the comprehension-oriented lessons are already designed for the teacher.

A disadvantage of basal readers is the emphasis on teaching to a group rather than to the individual. Critics of basal readers claim that their structure could limit creativity and make it difficult to differentiate lessons for students with disabilities. A student with a severe reading disability might simply not be able to access the text of a basal reader. In addition, basal readers might not have adequate phonics development for students with disabilities in this area. Teachers might need to use alternate reading programs for students with disabilities.

Phonics approach

In this approach, word recognition is taught through grapheme-phoneme associations, with the goal of teaching the student to independently apply these skills to new words.

In a variation of a straight phonics program, an *onset-rime* or whole-word approach is used. This means that words are taught in word families (e.g., cat, hat, pat, and rat). The focus is on words that can be blended rather than on isolated sounds. Words are chosen on the basis of similar spelling patterns and irregularly spelled words are taught as sight words. The consistent visual patterns of the lessons guide students from familiar words to less familiar words and then to irregular words.

Critics of the phonics approach point out that the emphasis on pronunciation may lead to the student focusing more on decoding than comprehension. Some students could become confused by words that do not conform to the phonetic "rules." However, in many cases these apparent "exceptions" to a "rule" are actually the result of *other* rules or *orthographic tendencies* that can be learned. In addition, the extremely controlled vocabulary can result in awkward sentence structure and reading that does not follow normal oral prosody. However, advocates of phonics say that the programs are useful for remedial and developmental reading, and are often necessary for students with disabilities.

Whole language approach

In the whole language approach, reading is taught as a holistic, meaning-oriented activity and is not broken down into a collection of skills. This approach relies heavily on literature or trade books selected for a particular purpose. Reading is taught as part of a total language arts program, and the curriculum seeks to develop instruction in real problems and ideas. Phonics is not taught in a structured, systematic way. Students are assumed to develop their phonetic awareness through exposure to print. Writing is taught as a complement to reading.

While the integration of reading with writing is an advantage of the whole language approach, the approach has been criticized for the lack of direct instruction in specific skill strategies. Research has shown that the absence of systematic phonics instruction is a serious omission. When working with students with learning problems, more direct phonics instruction needs to be added to any whole language program.

Language experience approach

The language experience approach is similar to the whole language approach in that reading is considered a personal act, literature is emphasized, and students are encouraged to write about their own life experiences. Principles of this approach include:

- What students think about, they can talk about.
- What students say, they can write or dictate.
- What students write or dictate, they can read. (It should be noted, however, that this is often not true for students with disabilities such as dyslexia. Many students with disabilities can dictate an excellent composition, but when they write it down, they cannot read it back—see below.)

Although the emphasis on student experience and creativity stimulates interest and motivation and can be beneficial in the composition portion, this method shares the disadvantages of the whole language method, specifically the absence of a phonics component. Teachers would need to add this missing component into the program in some way. In addition, there is no set method of evaluating student progress in this approach.

Individualized reading approach

In this approach, students select their own reading materials according to interest and ability and progress at their own individual rates. Word recognition and comprehension are taught as the student needs them. The teacher's role is to diagnose errors and prescribe materials, although the final choice of materials is made by the students. Individual work may be supplemented by group activities with basal readers and workbooks for specific reading skills. The lack of systematic checks and developmental skills and emphasis on self-learning could be a disadvantage for students with learning problems. However, such an approach can be integrated into almost any global reading program and used to enhance student reading independence and enjoyment (see Skill 9.04).

Skill 9.03   Demonstrate knowledge of principles of and methods for assessing and developing students' reading and other language arts skills

READING

Based upon the National Reading Panel's research review (see Skill 9.02), whatever methods or programs a teacher chooses to use should focus on the five critical components listed in their report. The report not only reviewed research on these components, it also reviewed reading and intervention programs and techniques that research has shown to be most effective. Teachers would do well to become familiar with the research in the report.

Most reading intervention methods and programs separate the reading process into two major areas: decoding (phoneme awareness and phonics) and comprehension (understanding what is read), with fluency (the ability to read smoothly and automatically with comprehension) tying the two areas together.

Phoneme Awareness and Phonics

Because the ability to distinguish between individual sounds, or phonemes, within words is a prerequisite to the association of sounds with letters and manipulating sounds to blend words, the teaching of phonemic awareness is crucial to emergent literacy (early childhood K-2 reading instruction). Children need a strong background in phonemic awareness in order for phonics instruction (sound-spelling relationships in print) to be effective. Children with reading disabilities might need a great deal of instruction in phoneme awareness prior to and during phonics instruction.

Phonemic awareness

The key to phonemic awareness is that it can be taught with the students' eyes closed. In other words, it's all about sounds, not about ascribing written letters to sounds. Being phonemically aware means that the reader and listener can recognize and manipulate specific sounds in spoken words. Because phonemic awareness deals with *sounds* in words that are *spoken,* the majority of phonemic awareness tasks, activities, and exercises are oral.

Blevins (1997) describes the earlier work of theorist Marilyn Jager Adams in designing five types of phoneme awareness tasks that can be used in the classroom. These align well with the International Reading Associations' Reading Panel Report, *Teaching Children to Read* (2002) and its analysis of phoneme awareness skills.

1. **Task 1**: The ability to hear rhymes and alliteration. For example, the children listen to a poem, rhyming picture book, or song and identify the rhyming words they hear.
2. **Task 2**: The ability to do oddity tasks (recognize the member of a set that is different [odd] among the group). For example, the children look at pictures of a door, a dog, and a cat. The teacher asks which object starts with a different sound from the others.
3. **Task 3**: The ability to orally blend words and split syllables. For example, the children can say the first sound of a word (e.g., /b/) and then the rest of the word (/at/) and then put it together as a single word (bat), as in onsets and rimes.
4. **Task 4**: The ability to orally segment words; for example, the ability to count sounds. The children would be asked as a group to count the sounds in "sat" (/s/, /a/, /t/ = 3 sounds).
5. **Task 5**: The ability to do phonics manipulation tasks. For example, the children replace the "r" sound in rose with a "n" sound and say "nose."

Other instructional methods shown to be effective for teaching phonemic awareness include:

- Clapping the SOUNDS (not syllables) in words (e.g., "bat" has three sounds, /b/, /a/, /t/)
- Games where students must identify the beginning, middle, or end sound (not letter) of a word (e.g., "Find something that begins with the /t/ sound")
- Games with common nursery rhymes where the students change one sound in several words (e.g., "Jack and Jill went up the hill..." Now change Jack and Jill to begin like 'Mary')
- Using visual cues and movements to help children understand when the speaker goes from one sound to another (e.g., moving colored blocks around as the teacher changes the initial sound in "cat" to make it "bat")
- Singing familiar songs (e.g., Happy Birthday, Knick Knack Paddy Whack) and replacing key words with words that have a different ending or middle sound (oral segmentation)
- Dealing children a deck of picture cards and having them sound out the words for the pictures on their cards, or calling for a picture by asking for its first and second sound
- Onset and rhyme games in which children are given a beginning sound and told to blend it with a specific series of endings (e.g., "OK, start with /ch/ and add "eep," then "eet," etc.)
- Games like "I'm going on vacation and I'm taking a..." (something that begins or ends with a particular phoneme)

Phonics

Phonics refers to instruction in the letter/sound code of the language. Once the child can discriminate among the various phonemes of the language and manipulate them in verbally presented words, it is necessary to attach those sounds to certain letters and letter combinations.

Phonics instruction uses letters or groups of letter symbols and may be synthetic or analytic. In the synthetic method, letter sounds are learned before the student goes on to blend the sounds to form words. This usually means repeated drills on individual letters or letter combinations and sounds. Once the students can reliably produce a correct sound for a letter or combination of letters, the task of blending them into words begins.

The analytic method teaches letter sounds as integral parts of words. Regularly spelled sight words are memorized first, then the sounds in each are mapped out with the teacher's help. Both methods can be effective, but students with disabilities or limited phoneme awareness backgrounds may need at least some practice with a synthetic approach in order to master the code.

Programs that Teach Phoneme Awareness and Phonics

There are many programs available to teachers and choosing among them can be difficult. It is important to know the student population for which the intervention is intended and to select a program based upon individual needs rather than a universal standard. In *Building From the Best: Learning From What Works* (1999) The American Federation of Teachers describes five remedial reading programs that research had shown were effective for various populations and problems, and that include phonics instruction:

- **Direct Instruction (DI):** This is a very highly structured approach for at-risk students and involves mastery of early reading skills as well as comprehension and analysis. It has scripted lesson plans, research-based curriculum objectives, including extensive phoneme awareness activities, and involves achievement grouping of students, a rapid pace, and the use of outside coaches and facilitators.
- **Early Steps:** This is a tutorial-style program for reading and language arts intervention in the first grade. It presents a balanced approach including phoneme awareness and phonics as well as reading experiences based on the Reading Recovery model, word study, and a writing component.
- **Exemplary Center for Reading Instruction (ICRI):** This is a research based program for grades 1-12 based on early literacy instruction, word recognition, vocabulary, critical and inferential comprehension, writing, and study skills.
- **Lindamood-Bell:** This program for individual use with students in grades 1-12 involves a highly structured program for multisensory instruction in phoneme awareness and phonics; followed by word study, vocabulary, and spelling; and culminating in structured use of visualizing and verbalizing techniques to aid comprehension.
- **Reading Recovery:** This program involves pull-out tutorials for first grade students and is meant as a supplement to regular reading classwork and instruction. It includes literature-based activities that start with familiar material and move to new areas. It includes letter and word study and writing.

Other commonly used programs include:

- **The Wilson Reading Program** for decoding and encoding, an outgrowth of dyslexia research with the Orton-Gillingham phonics-based program. These are intensive, sequential phonics-based programs that teach word formation with a multisensory approach.
- **Phonografix**, a phonics and spelling program that teaches letter sound correspondence through use of "sound pictures" made of letter combinations
- **Open Court**, a reading program with a heavy emphasis on phonics

Whatever program or programs a teacher chooses, it is important to remember that students with reading disabilities might need many months of daily instruction in phoneme awareness and phonics in order to get master the code for reading and move on from "learning to read," to "reading to learn." Such instruction must also be closely integrated with instruction for comprehension (see below). Assessment of phoneme awareness and of phonics is usually built into these programs.

Comprehension

The National Reading Panel's Report (2000) described two major components of comprehension: understanding vocabulary and comprehension (being able to derive multiple levels of meaning from connected text).

Vocabulary

In its report, the National Reading Panel defined vocabulary as "the part of comprehension based on the meaning of individual words in context." Based on its review of research on methods of effectively teaching vocabulary skills, the panel made the following conclusions about vocabulary instruction as it relates to overall reading comprehension.

- There is a need for direct instruction of vocabulary items required for a specific text.
- Repetition and multiple exposures to vocabulary items are important. Students should be given items that will be likely to appear in many contexts.
- Learning in rich contexts is valuable for vocabulary learning. Vocabulary words should be those that the learner will find useful in many contexts. When vocabulary items are derived from content learning materials, the learner will be better equipped to deal with specific reading matter in content areas.
- Vocabulary tasks should be restructured as necessary. It is important to be certain that students fully understand what is asked of them in the context of reading rather than focusing only on the words to be learned.
- Vocabulary learning is effective when it entails active engagement in learning tasks.
- Computer technology can be used effectively to help teach vocabulary.
- Vocabulary can be acquired through incidental learning. Much of a student's vocabulary will have to be learned in the course of doing things other than explicit vocabulary learning. Repetition, richness of context, and motivation can also add to the efficacy of incidental learning of vocabulary.

- Dependence on a single vocabulary instruction method will not result in optimal learning. Research shows that a variety of methods can be used effectively with emphasis on the multimedia aspects of learning, the richness of context in which words are to be learned, and the number of exposures to words that learners receive.
- The panel found that a critical feature of effective classrooms is instruction of specific words that includes lessons and activities where students apply their vocabulary knowledge and strategies to reading and writing. Included in the activities were discussions where teachers and students talked about words, their features, and strategies for understanding unfamiliar words.

There are many methods for directly and explicitly teaching words. In fact, the panel found twenty-one methods that have been found effective in research projects. Many emphasize the underlying concept of a word and its connections to other words, such as semantic mapping and diagramming that use graphics. The keyword method uses words and illustrations that highlight salient features of meaning. Visualizing or drawing a picture, either by the student or by the teacher, was found to be effective. Many words cannot be learned in this way, of course, so it should be used as only one method among others. Effective classrooms provide multiple ways for students to learn and interact with words.

Vocabulary instruction for students with disabilities

Students with language and reading disabilities might have significant difficulties acquiring, remembering, or using vocabulary correctly. Word referents range from the literal ("dog" stands for a particular animal), to the very abstract ("analogous" stands for a concept concerning the relationship between abstract ideas). In order to properly comprehend and use words correctly, the word must be understood, stored, and retrieved when needed. It might also be necessary to hold a number of words and their referents in working memory while reading a complex passage or composing a sentence with them. A disability in any of these areas of attaching meaning to a word, storing it, or retrieving and working with it can seriously affect vocabulary development.

Children with such disabilities might not acquire vocabulary as efficiently as children without disabilities, even if they *are* in a language rich environment. Children with disabilities might need more explicit instruction, practice with strategies mentioned above, and accommodations to learn the vocabulary necessary to become good readers.

In particular, children with learning disabilities might not be able to use context without explicit training and practice. Some children will "read" or listen to a passage and be able to parrot back the words, but do not understand what these words mean in context. There are a number of strategies for explicitly teaching children how to use context to determine what a word means. One method for teaching students how to use context to determine the meaning of a word is to design a sort of "Mystery Word" game in which sentences with blanks or nonsense words are recorded on colorful cards and set up in a box for students. Students take a card or set of cards and try to figure out what word will fit in the blank. Context clues can be of two types:

1. **Syntax** clues are clues related to parts of speech and grammar; a word's job in the sentence (for example, in "The _____ ran up the wall," the word in the blank would have to be a noun of some sort).
2. **Semantic** clues are based on meaning in the sentence and the word (for example, in "My dad drove the _____ to work," the blank would have to be some sort of a vehicle, not a butterfly or feeling).

A set of sentences can be developed that provide increasing context clues to the meaning of the word. Children can guess each word and the teacher can guide the students to evaluate their guesses and clues and look at both syntactic and semantic context. The object in such lessons is not the actual vocabulary, but rather the *strategy* of using context to determine a word's meaning. Such an activity can be modified to include actual vocabulary words necessary for reading once the student has mastered the use of the strategy. Because some students with disabilities will have more problems with semantic clues, while others will have problems with syntactic clues, such lessons must be individualized for each problem type.

Another strategy for helping students with disabilities to acquire necessary vocabulary is to make the vocabulary as concrete as possible and present it in a multimedia manner. Whenever possible, illustrate the word with a picture or an accompanying action. If working memory is a problem, maintaining a visual bank of words or pictures from which to choose will help the student manipulate vocabulary correctly.

Methods for developing comprehension

Levels of comprehension

Comprehension involves understanding what is read, and can be delineated into categories of differentiated skills. Benjamin Bloom's taxonomy includes: knowledge, comprehension, application, analysis, synthesis, and evaluation. Thomas Barrett suggests that comprehension categories be classified as: literal meaning, reorganization, inference, evaluation, and appreciation. In both lists, difficulty increases as you move up the list (i.e., "knowledge" and "literal meaning" are the easiest to comprehend, and "evaluation" and "appreciation" are the most difficult).

Many students, especially those with disabilities, might need explicit instruction in the differences among these levels of comprehension and how to find clues in the text for each. Familiar fairy tales such as "Goldilocks and the Three Bears" or "The Three Little Pigs" can be adapted for this purpose. Children can be taught that some facts are *right there on the page* (literal comprehension). For example, the first pig used straw, the second used sticks, and the third used bricks. The teacher can demonstrate it is possible to point to a specific sentence that provides the information. Highlighters and sticky arrows can provide concrete evidence that the information is right in the text.

Children can be shown that other information will be right in the text but will be scattered, so it will be necessary to pull it together. For example, how did the wolf change his strategy as he tried to trick the pig? (each time he stated an earlier time to meet and HE turned up earlier, as well—this is all information that is IN the text, but in different places). Using color-coded highlighters or arrows can help children with this process. Use all red arrows for information relevant to one question, green for another, etc.

Children can be taught that other information can depend on what is already in THEIR heads, that is, what they know about similar situations (inferences). For example, they might speculate on how the town would now treat the third pig after the wolf was destroyed. They can be led through suggestive questions such as:

- What do you already know about wolves and pigs? (Wolves eat pigs, SO
- What can you guess about how the other pigs in town felt about the wolf? (They are afraid of him), AND
- How do people often react when someone saves them from something scary or dangerous? (They reward them and treat them like heroes), SO
- How might the town treat the third pig? (Like a hero; give him a parade, key to the town, elect him mayor, etc).

See Skill 9.05 for more detail on using nursery stories to analyze levels of comprehension.

For some tasks, particularly inferences, some modifications can be made for students with disabilities. For example, though inferential questions usually involve recall responses, they can be provided as multiple-choice recognition questions for students for whom recall is a problem.

General comprehension strategies

Use of comprehension skills before, during, and after reading

Before reading, it is helpful if students preview the text and ask themselves what it is about before they read it. Devices such as KWL charts and background webs can be useful before reading. Pre-reading strategies such as looking over the expository text subheads, illustrations, captions, and indices to get an idea about the book can also be helpful.

During reading, students can be continually asking whether the text confirms their predictions or answers their questions. Predictions and questions can be modified as reading progresses. Of course, after completing the text, students then review their predictions and verify whether they were correct.

After reading, each student can note: "I have found the answer to my question. This text is an excellent source of information for me about my question." (Or perhaps, "No, I have not found the answer to my question. This text is not a good source of information for me about my question. I will have to look for other resources.")

Storyboard panels, which are used by comic strip artists as well as television and film directors, are perfect for engaging children K-6 in a variety of comprehension strategies before, during, and after reading. They can storyboard the beginning of a story, read aloud, and then storyboard its predicted middle or end. Of course, after they experience or read the actual middle or end of the story, they can compare and contrast what they produced with its actual structure. They can play familiar literature identification games with a buddy or as part of a center by storyboarding one key scene or key characters from a book and challenging a partner or peer to identify the book and characters correctly.

Think alouds

Thinking aloud is one of the most effective strategies for teaching comprehension. As the teacher speaks aloud every thought that would normally be going on silently in her head, she demonstrates and explains the connections he or she is making while reading, and the students begin to understand how the teacher arrived at these connections. Students can practice their own think alouds by reviewing the questions they have chosen to set a purpose for reading.

Visualization

Visualization is the process of creating a mental picture corresponding to the words on the page. Generally, good readers have a mental image of what they are reading. When working with visualization, it can sometimes be helpful for students to take the additional step of drawing out the picture as they see it in their minds. Working with the teacher, the students can advance their comprehension even if key concepts are missing.

Self-monitoring

Students can be taught to stop at regular intervals (e.g., after each paragraph or page) and ask themselves whether they understand what they just read. If they find they did *not* understand, they can note questions or reread to try again.

Identifying main ideas

Identifying main ideas in an expository text is often difficult for students with reading disabilities, and it can be improved when the children have an explicit strategy for identifying important information. The child should be asked to be on the lookout for a **topic sentence** within the expository passage that **summarizes** the key information in the paragraph. This topic sentence can be highlighted in a particular color, and then the child can use another color to highlight all the sentences that "go with" that main sentence. Sometimes all the related sentences can be highlighted first, and *then* the topic sentence that summarizes the whole can be highlighted in a different color. These methods also allow students to refer back to the text when answering questions. Such scaffolding can be gradually reduced as students become more independent with this skill.

Graphic organizers

These can be very useful aids to comprehension. Students can record key points and use them for summaries. The amount of teacher support in this process can be gradually lessened as the students become more proficient.

Cloze activities

These activities can help students with memory disabilities retain and recall information. The teacher can reprint the reading passage with missing words and allow the student to fill in the blanks. This is a context-rich scaffold that can be gradually reduced as the child retains more and more of the information.

Fluency

In its report on teaching children to read (2000), the National Reading Panel defined fluency as the ability to read with speed, accuracy and proper expression without conscious attention and to handle both word recognition and comprehension simultaneously.

When students practice fluency, they practice reading connected pieces of text. In other words, instead of looking at a word as just a word, fluent readers read rapidly and smoothly, allowing their minds to focus on the comprehension of the text as a whole. Because reading fluency leads to reading comprehension, fluent readers typically enjoy reading more than students who apply all their energy to just sounding out the words.

Assessing fluency is usually done with *running records* and is a key part of assessment of all aspects of reading progress.

Running records

A running record is a formalized assessment for analyzing miscues when a student reads aloud. It can be combined with basic comprehension questions as well. It must be administered individually and one-on-one with a child, so it takes more time than a group assessment. However, it provides detailed information on the child's level of fluency, the readability of the text for the child, the cause of a student's errors, and the student's efforts to correct them.

There are many outlines and checklists available for conducting a running record. One method is presented below.

1. **Select a text:** If you want to see if the child is reading on instructional level, choose a book that the child has already read. If the purpose of the test is to see whether the child is ready to advance to the next level, choose a book from that level which the child has not yet seen.
2. **Introduce the text:** Briefly share the title and tell the child a bit about the plot and style of the book.
3. **Take the record:** Generally, with emergent readers in grades 1-2, there are only 100-150 words in a passage used to take a record. Note which words the child misreads or cannot read and carefully note the nature of the mistake (e.g., misread a visual cue by making the 'b' sound for the letter,'d'; used a word that looked similar but made no sense (e.g., horse for house); used a word that makes sense but is spelled differently (e.g., home for house, and so forth). Record words per minute and use a checklist for various characteristics of prosody and expression (e.g., voice lifts for questions, pauses for punctuation). There are a number of standard forms available for recording such behavior simply and easily and many of them have information on recording and analyzing errors, as well as formulae for evaluating responses and readability.
4. **Comprehension Check:** This can and should be done by inviting the child to retell the story. This retelling can then be used by you to ask further questions about characters, plot, setting and purpose, which allows you to observe and to record the child's level of comprehension

Calculating the reading level and the self-correction rate

Calculating the reading level lets you know if the book is at the level at which the child can read it independently or comfortably with guidance (instructional level), or if the book is at a level where reading it frustrates the child. When using a running record to assess the readability of a text for a particular child, look at the overall accuracy score:

- *Independent Level:* 95-100% suggests that the child can independently read the text and other texts on the same level.

- *Instructional Level*: 90-94% indicates that the text and other texts on the same level likely will present challenges to the child, but with guidance from you, a tutor, or a parent, the child will be able to master these texts and enjoy them. In fact, most reading instruction should occur at this level.
- Frustration Level: Below 90% means the material is too hard for the child to handle alone. Such material needs to be shared with the child in a shared reading situation or read to the child.

Silent reading refers to the inaudible reading of words or passages. Because the act of reading is done on a covert basis, the accuracy of the reading process can only be inferred through questions or activities required of the student following the reading. In addition, students can be given a purpose for silent reading (e.g., read to find out what the giant did with the treasure), and this can be assessed later. Silent reading is also simply a time to read for enjoyment, and what may be observed is the attention given to the printed material, the eye movements, an indication of relative pace, and body language signifying frustration or ease of reading.

WRITING

Teaching Writing to Students with Disabilities

As mentioned in Skill 9.01, writing/encoding disabilities will limit the student's ability to spell, use punctuation, even actually write out a thought, the mechanics of writing. Writing/composition disabilities will limit a child's ability to compose thoughts, recall words, and organize ideas. When teaching written communication to children with disabilities, therefore, it is often helpful to separate these two sets of skills and work on them separately until the child has mastered them. Doing this prevents a child's disability in one area from slowing down or restricting his or her progress in another area that is not impacted directly by the disability. In addition, the techniques used to help a child with composition and expression are different from those used to help with encoding and conventions, so separating the tasks makes it easier to provide training that is specific to the child's deficit.

For example, a child who is able to compose coherent, well-organized ideas but who cannot encode or spell the words needed to write them down might be allowed to dictate the composition to a teacher, peer, or computer. The student can then work on revising ideas for word choice, language, etc. In order to work on the encoding and conventions, the composition can be read back to the student, who can practice the encoding skills separately by writing down the composition. The teacher can provide whatever assistance is necessary to help the student learn the conventions and gradually reduce scaffolding over time. This allows the student to move ahead with expressive composition skills while working at a lower level on the more difficult (for him) conventions.

Alternatively, the student who can encode and use writing conventions well but who cannot express coherent ideas would need other kinds of help. If word finding is a problem for the student, the student and teacher might brainstorm a list of words relevant to the topic and record them in lists for the student to use in his composition. Graphic organizers of various sorts can help with organizational issues. Cloze procedures that allow the student to fill in key words (e.g., from the above-mentioned word bank) might help him or her to produce a coherent piece of writing. Less help would be needed for the student to actually write the composition down once the ideas are clear.

Teaching the writing process

Whatever the child's disability, approaching writing as a process rather than merely a product is an effective way to improve writing in all areas. Each phase of the writing process has strategies that help the student develop metacognitive skills and proficiency.

Prewriting: During this planning stage, the student must choose (or be given) a purpose, find a topic, establish an audience, decide how the paper will be organized, and experiment with ideas. Strategies for generating ideas might include listing, brainstorming, interest inventories, or free writing.

Organizing Content: This phase includes graphic organizers that represent the relationships among ideas visually. Depending upon the student's writing ability, the teacher might provide an appropriate graphic organizer or the student might be taught to choose from among an assortment. Types of organizers might include concept or semantic maps, cluster maps, cause and effect maps, chronological event maps, opinion and argument maps, and main idea and detail maps.

Drafting: In this phase, ideas are developed and the writer makes connections among the ideas. Mechanics should not be considered, and the student should not spend too much time on this phase. Learner activities include focusing on the ideas, not the content, consulting the teacher or peer about the content, and reading the piece or a portion of the piece to defocus and generate new ideas.

Revising: After the drafts have been written, the student can reorganize ideas, add details, and edit the paper for mistakes in grammar and spelling. Improving word choice can be done at this stage as well. Sections of the paper can be removed or reorganized. Strategies include putting the paper aside for a day or two; asking the teacher or a peer for feedback; using scissors and tape to reorganize sections of the paper (a VERY useful tactic for some students with disabilities); and using the computer to aid in revision (also useful for students with disabilities).

Final Draft: In this stage, the writer gives the paper a final edit, reads the paper to see that everything makes sense, and makes mechanical corrections in spelling, punctuation, etc. Some of the things that a student can do to prepare the final draft include using a checklist to check the final copy for errors (critical for some students with disabilities); reading the story into a tape recorder and playing it back with a written copy to listen for grammatical errors and pauses where punctuation marks should be; and reading the paper one sentence at a time to identify sentence fragments.

Skill 9.04   Recognize strategies for promoting students' enjoyment and independent involvement in reading and writing

READING FOR ENJOYMENT

There are two key principles to remember when promoting students' enjoyment of reading:

1. Students will both read more and enjoy reading more when they may *read what they want to read.* It is absolutely critical that the teacher know each child's interests and sees to it that the student has access to reading material on those topics. It is not necessary for the material to be strictly "educational" for it to improve reading ability, either. Any time the child spends reading for enjoyment is also time spent practicing and improving reading skills.
2. Students will both read more and enjoy reading more if the material that interests them *is available at their independent reading level* (see Skill 9.03). No matter how interesting the child thinks the material is, if it is at their frustration level they will not spend as much time reading it and will not enjoy it as much. This means it is also critical for the teacher to be sure that students have access to high-interest material that is written at a level accessible to students with reading disabilities.

When students are able to independently use reading skills for enjoyment, a key goal of literacy development has been attained. Initially, special education teachers might choose books that have already been read in class, have a high correlation between text and pictures, and are interesting to students. These can be kept in a classroom reading area for students to reread independently. Note that the emergent reader might, at first, be paraphrasing the story or reciting the words from memory instead of actually reading the words. Special education teachers can also select a set of books from which to choose during library time. Books that are hi/lo (high interest/low reading level) are often good choices for the student with significant reading delays. As students progress in reading skills, the special educator should change the materials that are available for the students to read.

After a certain level of reading is reached, special education students might enjoy participating in reading reward programs such as Accelerated Reader, Reading Counts, Book It, or others through which the child can acquire prizes, food coupons, or tickets to theme parks and sporting events. It is the role of the special educator to evaluate if the amount of required reading is realistic for the student with disabilities or if it should be modified per individual needs.

Students with disabilities who also come from diverse cultural or linguistic backgrounds will need materials that are even more specific to their needs. Many publishers now print books with the bilingual child in mind.

In addition to traditional print books, students might be motivated to read classroom magazines or graphic novels independently, because these typically have engaging illustrations and topics. Students often enjoy reading text or directions for games and activities on the computer; the typical shortened text for computer materials, graphics, audio components, and interactive features of computer materials can be very appealing to many students with disabilities. Another consideration is box or board games that incorporate reading skills, such as Scrabble Jr. and Boggle Jr.

WRITING FOR ENJOYMENT

As with reading, the two key principles to remember when promoting independent writing for enjoyment are:

1. Children will write more if they are allowed *to write what they want to write.* Children need *authentic* reasons to write, reasons that are important to *them.* There will be many occasions on which they will write something assigned by the teacher. The teacher must be alert for opportunities for the child to write about something important to him or her (e.g., perhaps a cousin has entered the military and is stationed far away—the student could write a letter or draw a picture with a caption; perhaps a holiday is near; perhaps the student objects to something on the school menu—he or she could write a letter of complaint to the cafeteria; if the child suddenly thinks of a cool story about a monster—he or she should write it down). A daily journal, "free writing" time, or time when students are allowed to pass notes can be very helpful.
2. Children will write more and enjoy it more if they feel successful at it and are not overwhelmed by the task. Not every piece of writing or journal entry needs to be developed through all the writing steps and finalized. Quick ideas and expressions can be useful and important in themselves.

In order for students to feel successful, it is often necessary for the teacher to provide scaffolding and prompting, because some students are so scared of writing that they simply will not attempt anything. This can be particularly true of students with disabilities, whose writing, like their reading, may have previously been judged inadequate. The teacher might need to plan ahead and design a scaffolding procedure that systematically and sequentially reduces teacher involvement in written production by students. If the teacher keeps the above two principles in mind throughout the procedure, it can be very helpful.

The precise degree of teacher assistance will vary depending upon student need. The student might select a topic and generate ideas for the beginning of a graphic organizer but get lost in the middle or at the end. At each step the teacher can provide a motivational prompt ("Keep thinking, you'll get it"), a content prompt ("What do you think the dog will do?") or even a literal prompt ("Let's write that the dog jumped the fence and see where it goes from there"), depending upon what the child needs.

USING READING TO ENHANCE WRITING

Often overlooked in the classroom is the importance of using high-interest reading materials to teach writing skills. The teacher should make a practice of calling attention to "cool" writing whenever reading anything for any purpose whatsoever. If the story being read uses squiggly text letters when talking about a ghost, call attention to it, ask why the author did it, and suggest that students may use that technique in their own writing. If an author uses words that students think are "really cool," let them write down the words for use in their own writing. If they read a funny account of a school event in a comic book, remind them that they can use that technique in their own writing. If a writer used dark, somber words in a mystery, call attention to the fact. If a student likes a particular author or book series, help the student analyze why they like it and suggest that the student try some of the same techniques in his or her own writing. There are many ways to use reading to help students improve and enjoy writing.

Please refer to Skill 6.01 to read about how to employ other motivational strategies.

Skill 9.05   Apply strategies for promoting students' use of critical-thinking and problem-solving skills in language arts

Please also refer to Skill 9.03 for another look at the use of folktales to illustrate levels of comprehension.

Most educators recognize that comprehension covers a wide continuum of lower-to-higher level thinking skills. The following steps make up one way of displaying the continuum, beginning on the low side of the spectrum:

1. **Literal** indicates an understanding of the primary, concrete and discrete facts and meaning of words, sentences, or passages.
2. **Inferential** involves an understanding of the deeper meanings that are not literally stated in a phrase, sentence, or passage.

3. **Evaluation** signifies a judgment made by comparing ideas or information presented in the written passage with other experiences, knowledge, or values.
4. **Appreciation** involves an emotional response to the written selection.

The teacher can also determine the student's level of comprehension using Barrett's (1968) Taxonomy of Cognitive and Affective Dimensions of Reading Comprehension. These steps can stimulate thinking across a continuum of comprehension levels. In the following example, the teacher is asking questions about the story of "Goldilocks and the Three Bears."

Literal Comprehension focuses on ideas and information that are explicitly stated in the selection.

1. Literal Recognition requires the student to locate or identify ideas and information explicitly stated in the reading selection. For recognition questions, the text should be available for the child or alternative answers must be given from which the child selects one.

   - *Recognition of details.* Where did the three bears live?
   - *Recognition of main ideas.* Why did the three bears go out for a walk? Note that a 'why' question is only a literal question IF the answer is clearly stated in the text. If readers must pull clues together from different parts of the text or use their own background knowledge or judgment it would be an inference question.
   - *Recognition of sequence.* Whose porridge did Goldilocks taste first, Mama's, Papa's, or Baby Bear's?
   - *Recognition of comparisons.* Whose porridge was too hot? Too cold? Just right?
   - *Recognition of cause-and-effect relationships.* Why didn't Papa Bear and Mama Bear's chairs break into pieces like Baby Bear's chair? Again, such a question would be literal ONLY IF the cause and effect relationship is clearly stated in the text, and would be inferential if the student needs to combine clues or use information from outside the text.
   - *Recognition of character traits.* Which words can you find in the story that describe Goldilocks?

   In any of the above cases, the teacher can provide the answers or the teacher can have the child show in the pictures or read in the text the part of the story pertaining to the question. The objective is to access the child's literal comprehension—not his or her memory.

2. <u>Literal Recall</u> requires the student to produce from memory ideas and information explicitly stated in the reading selection. In this case, the child does not have the story to review, but must pull information from memory.

    - *Recall of details.* What were the names of the three bears?
    - *Recall of main ideas.* Why did Goldilocks go into the bears' house? (See above note about 'why' questions.)
    - *Recall of a sequence.* In order, name the things belonging to the three bears that Goldilocks tried.
    - *Recall of comparisons.* Whose bed was too hard? Too soft? Just right?
    - *Recall of cause-and-effect relationships.* Why did Goldilocks go to sleep in Baby Bear's bed?
    - *Recall of character traits.* What words in the story describe each of the three bears?

    In the above cases, the teacher does not give the answer unless the student cannot provide it him or herself. The purpose is to test the child's recall of stated facts.

3. <u>Reorganization</u> requires the student to analyze, synthesize, and/or organize ideas or information explicitly stated in the selection. This is sometimes considered a simple form of inference. The information is explicitly stated in the text, but it is not all in the same place; it must be pulled together, and sometimes background knowledge or experience must be used as well.

    - *Classifying:* List the things Goldilocks discovered to be "just right" in the story.
    - *Outlining:* Outline each thing Goldilocks tried, whether it was just right or did not suit her.
    - *Summarizing:* Tell me in just a few sentences what happened in the story.
    - *Synthesizing:* Predict what other things Goldilocks might have tried if the bears had had a daughter.

4. <u>Inferential comprehension</u> is demonstrated by the student when he or she "uses the ideas and information explicitly stated in the selection, his [or her] intuition, and his [or her] personal experiences as a basis for conjectures and hypotheses," according to Barrett (cited in Ekwall & Shanker, 1983, p. 67).

    - *Inferring supporting details.* Why do you think Goldilocks found Baby Bear's things to be just right?

- *Inferring main ideas.* What did the bear family learn about leaving their house unlocked?
- *Inferring sequence.* At what point did the bears discover that someone was in their house?
- *Inferring comparisons.* Compare the furniture mentioned in the story. Which was adult size and which was a child's size?
- *Inferring cause-and-effect relationships.* What made the bears suspect that someone was in their house?
- *Inferring character traits.* Which of the bears was the most irritated by Goldilocks' intrusion?
- *Predicting outcomes.* Do you think Goldilocks ever went back to visit the bears' house again?
- *Interpreting figurative language.* What did the author mean when he wrote, "The trees in the deep forest howled a sad song in the wind?"

5. <u>Evaluation</u> requires the student to make a judgment by comparing ideas presented in the selection with external criteria provided by the teacher, through some other external source, or with internal criteria provided by the student.

- *Judgment of reality or fantasy.* Do you suppose that the story of "Goldilocks and the Three Bears" really happened? Why or why not?
- *Judgment of fact or opinion.* Judge whether Baby Bear's furniture really was just right for Goldilocks. Why or why not?
- *Judgment of adequacy and validity.* Give your opinion as to whether it was a good idea for the bears to take a walk while their porridge cooled.
- *Judgment of appropriateness.* Do you think it was safe for Goldilocks to enter an empty house? Why or why not?
- *Judgment of worth, desirability, and acceptability.* Was Goldilocks a guest or an intruder in the bears' home?

6. <u>Appreciation</u> deals with the psychological and aesthetic impact of the selection on the reader.

- *Emotional response to the content.* How did you feel when the three bears found Goldilocks asleep in Baby Bear's bed?
- *Identification with characters or incidents.* How do you suppose Goldilocks felt when she awakened and saw the three bears?
- *Reaction to the author's use of language.* Why do you think the author called the bears Papa, Mama, and Baby instead of Mr. Bear, Mrs. Bear, and Jimmy Bear?
- *Imagery.* What is meant by the phrase, "His bed is as hard as a rock"?

As teachers design lesson plans in all reading and content areas, it is important to plan for questioning at many levels of comprehension and structure activities based on these levels. For students with disabilities, the more abstract levels of comprehension involving inferences might be particularly difficult. Students with memory deficits will find pulling information together from different places in the text in order to draw a conclusion particularly difficult.

As mentioned in Skill 9.03, it can help to make the steps in comprehension as concrete as possible. Use of graphic organizers, highlighters and sticky arrows to mark information in the text can help students with memory deficits as well as those for whom inference is a challenge. For some students it might be necessary to list a set of clues and then provide a list of three inferences or conclusions and ask which follows from the clues. Cooperative groups can be VERY helpful here. Assign each group a different question and have them discuss among themselves how each clue they have applies, then report to the whole class group and discuss again. Students with disabilities might need a great deal of practice like this and many will continue to need accommodations (e.g., highlighters, multiple choice lists) for some time.

Skill 9.06   Demonstrating knowledge of strategies for integrating language arts skills across the content areas

Language arts skills (e.g., reading, writing, listening, speaking) will be used across all curriculum areas throughout the student's educational career. In spite of this fact, reading and writing are often treated as distinct subjects and inadequate time is spent helping students learn how to apply these skills in other areas. In addition, much of the reading instruction found in lower elementary schools emphasizes fiction over nonfiction

Although reading and appreciating literature, poetry, drama, etc. are important, research has shown that students' ability to comprehend nonfiction or expository text is critical to their success on standardized tests, in their future education, and in adult life. Duke, Bennett-Armistead, and Roberts (2002) describe studies showing that nonfiction periodicals represent the single most common form of adult reading. They further explain that understanding informational text is key to future educational success. It is, therefore, essential that reading (and writing) instruction include strategies for understanding and using information found in nonfiction text in content areas.

READING NONFICTION: USING COMMON TEXT FEATURES

Regardless of the specific subject matter, there are certain common text features children will encounter when reading nonfiction, and understanding the significance of these features significantly enhances comprehension of the text. This is particularly important because nonfiction texts often are very *dense* in terms of amount of information conveyed.

Understanding the arrangement of nonfiction text with section and chapter titles, heads and subheads set in bold type, and other unique organizational devices can provide students with powerful tools to be successful. Students who use such headings as the main points can than fill in additional learning by reading the information below that heading. They can turn the heading into a question and use it to generate practice answers from the text. Also, when looking for a specific piece of information students can utilize the Table of Contents and Index, which are generally a part of expository texts. By understanding such common text features, students save valuable time and decrease the amount of rereading required to understand the content of the text.

Additionally, charts, graphs, maps, diagrams, captions, and photos in the text can work in the same way as looking up unknown words in the glossary. They can provide more insight and clarify the concepts and ideas the author is conveying. However, like other forms of comprehension, students need instruction in how to interpret these features and apply the information in them to questions that arise. All too often a student will insist that the information "isn't in there," only to find that it IS there—in a diagram or the caption to an illustration.

READING: USING NONFICTION TEXT STRUCTURES

In spite of research demonstrating the importance of learning to read and write nonfiction (see above), surveys have shown that the vast majority of reading in primary grades is fiction. Far less attention is paid to nonfiction. This is a critical omission, because nonfiction text structures are more varied and difficult than those of fiction. Most fiction follows a fairly standard structure that is chronological in nature and can be outlined in terms of story grammar markers that list setting, characters, problem or initiating event, a sequence of events, and a resolution. Nonfiction text structures follow many different forms and it is important to teach strategies for comprehending them.

The following are six of the most common types of expository texts to which the children should be introduced through modeled reading and a teacher-facilitated walk through.

Description Process (Main Idea and Supporting Details)

This type of text usually describes a particular topic or provides the identifying characteristics of a topic, or presents factual information that illustrates a main idea or more global fact. It is very common in science and social studies texts as well as in persuasive writing. Within this type of text, the child reader has to use all of his or her basic reading strategies because these types of expository texts do not have explicit clue words. The student must figure out what the main idea of the selection is and, if possible, locate a topic sentence that expresses that main idea. To make matters more difficult, not all selections have topic sentences; sometimes the main idea is implied. Differentially highlighting main ideas and details can help, as can the use of graphic organizers that let the student state the topic or main idea and then briefly list descriptive details. Writing exercises that use this text structure might include describing something important or interesting to the child.

Causation or Cause-Effect Text

This text appears in content area textbooks, newspapers, magazines, advertisements, and on some content area and general information Web sites. Students should be taught to take note of certain clue words such as: *therefore, the reasons for, as a result of, because, in consequence of,* and *since.* These clues point to statements of cause and effect relationships. Again, students can differentially highlight cause and effect in the text and use graphic organizers to help with comprehension.

Comparison Text

This is an expository text that is centered on the contrasts and similarities between two or more objects or ideas. Many social studies, art, and science textbooks, as well as other nonfiction books, include this structure. Sometimes newspaper columnists use it as well in their editorial commentary.

Again, strategies for helping children comprehend the comparison and contrast intended by the author include the use of key clue words and phrases. Among these are: *like, unlike, resemble, different, different from, similar to, in contrast with, in comparison to,* and *in a different vein.* It is important that when children examine texts that are talking about illustrated or photographed entities they can also review graphic representations for clues to support or contradict the text. Graphic organizers such as Venn diagrams can be very useful for recording and summarizing details. Cloze frameworks or sentence templates can form a bridge to writing compare and contrast paragraphs that use this structure.

Collection Text ("How to")

This is an expository text that presents ideas in a group. The writer's goal is to present a set of related points or ideas. Another name for this structure of expository writing is a listing or a sequence. The author frequently uses clue words such *as first, second, third, finally, and next* to alert the reader to the sequence. Based on how well the writer structures the sequence of points or ideas, the reader should be able to make connections.

Recipe-making is a simple collection text that can be literally modeled for young children. Walking through a simple recipe (e.g., instructions on the back of a box for making hot cereal or a brownie mix) with children and actually producing the food can help children construct meaning from the instructions and pay close attention to collection texts in the future. A variety of writing exercises can also be constructed for this type of text structure.

Response Structure

This is an expository text that presents a question or problem followed by an answer or a solution. Of course, entire mathematics textbooks, and some science and social studies textbooks, are organized around this type of structure. Again, it is important to walk the child reader through the excerpt and to sensitize the child to the clue words that signal this type of structure. These words include, but are not limited to: *the problem is, the questions is, you need to solve for, one probable solution would be, an intervention could be, the concern is,* and *another way to solve this would be.* It can be helpful for the child to highlight the question or questions in some way.

A number of news magazines (e.g., *Time For Kids, Sports Illustrated for Kids*) bring current events into the classroom written at various grade levels. Children see their parents and other adults reading newspapers and magazines all the time. Many of the text structures and features they will need to learn are found in and taught through such high-interest publications. Writing assignments can be tailored to model this form of writing as well (e.g., children put out their own newspapers or create their own timelines).

It is also essential to be sure that high-interest nonfiction material is available in a range of reading levels for students with reading disabilities. Many publishers (e.g., Rigby, National Geographic Windows on Literacy) provide nonfiction readers at multiple reading levels. See Skill 5.03 for techniques of modifying text to simplify the reading level when such published materials are not available.

In particular, the reading strategies of summarizing, answering questions, generating questions, using graphic organizers, using text structure and marking, monitoring comprehension, and discussing are useful in science, mathematics, and social studies.

Please refer to Skill 10.03 for special implications of reading and writing skills in mathematics.

COMPETENCY 0010 UNDERSTAND STRATEGIES AND TECHNIQUES USED TO PROMOTE STUDENTS' MATHEMATICS SKILLS IN A VARIETY OF SETTINGS

Skill 10.01 Identify types and characteristics of reasoning and calculation difficulties typically observed in students with disabilities

DEVELOPMENTAL STAGES RELEVANT TO MATH

In order to understand the impact of various disabilities on learning math skills, it is first necessary to understand something about the developmental processes that influence the child's acquisition of mathematic concepts. Hatfield, et al. (2005) describe the child's developing sense of number and math concepts in terms of Piaget's observations on child development.

Preoperational Stage

Although movement through developmental stages is highly individual in terms of exact age, most preschool and first grade children are still in what Piaget calls the *Preoperational Stage.* They are aware that objects have a reality outside that of the child him or herself, and that objects have properties, which they can describe in a limited way. However, they do not yet understand many of the concepts that are critical to basic, underlying math concepts, and they need a great deal of interaction with objects and manipulatives, as well as guiding questions and time, to develop these concepts.

Concrete Operational Stage (Grade 2—Middle or High School)

By second grade, many children are beginning to enter the *Concrete Operational Stage*, during which a number of concepts critical to the development of math sense can be learned. Children at this stage can act on operations, that is, they can understand an *operation* on an object. They can begin to understand relationships between objects (e.g., size and order) and can carry out operations on objects and *reverse* operations on objects.

At this stage, children can learn to sort and classify objects according to a variety of criteria. They can understand that an entire group can be a *part* or *subset* of another group. They can successively compare objects and *put them in order*. Most important of all for developing math concepts, they can begin to *conserve number* or to understand that the number of objects remains the same even when their arrangement or appearance changes. These concepts are critical to the ability to understand the nature of addition and subtraction, as well as other operations in math.

Formal Operational Stage

By the time children enter middle or high school, many of them will be at the *Formal Operational Stage* and they will be capable of learning to conduct operations on other operations independent of any objects or concrete stimuli.

A delay or deficit in any of these developmental levels can result in a learning disability that affects math skills. Of particular significance is any delay in developing conservation of number (or volume, etc.) as described above. This concept is so central to any development of math skills and concepts that children with any delay in developing it will experience a significant and global math disability. Although they might be able to memorize various math facts, they will be unable to understand underlying concepts and principles, such as place value, and will not be able to master problem solving skills until this underlying concept is mastered. For this reason, much remedial work will focus on this developmental milestone until it is mastered (see later skills in this section).

DEVELOPMENT OF SPECIFIC MATH CONCEPTS AND PROCESSES

Reid (1988) describes four processes that are directly related to an understanding of numbers. Children typically begin learning these processes in early childhood through the opportunities provided by their caretakers.

- Describing: Characterizing objects, sets, or events in terms of their attributes, such as calling all cats "kitties" whether they are tigers or house cats
- Classifying: Sorting objects, sets, or events in terms of one or more criteria, such as color, size, or shape (e.g., black cats versus white cats versus tabby cats)
- Comparing: Determining whether two objects, sets, or events are similar or different on the basis of a specified attribute, such as differentiating quadrilaterals from triangles on the basis of the number of sides
- Ordering: Comparing two or more objects, sets, or events, such as ordering children in a family on the basis of age or on the basis of height

Children who do not master these processes, either due to a disability or a lack of opportunities to explore them at home, will have difficulties when they enter school. These processes all require the abstract mental ability to separate an object from its attributes and see the abstract attribute (e.g., color, size, and living/nonliving) as independent of the object. Number and size are attributes and math skills will falter if the child does not understand this.

It should be noted that this disability will also impact progress in the language arts and content areas, where the child might be unable to compare and contrast, distinguish main ideas from details, or evaluate clues in reading. Treatment of this type of disability will need to occur across content areas.

Children usually begin learning the following concepts during early childhood:

- Equalizing: Making two or more objects or sets alike on an attribute, such as putting more milk into a glass so that it matches the amount of milk in another glass
- Joining: Putting together two or more sets with a common attribute to make one set, such as buying packets of trading cards to create a complete series
- Separating: Dividing an object or set into two or more sets, such as passing out cookies from a bag to a group of children so that each child gets three cookies
- Measuring: Attaching a number to an attribute, such as three cups of flour or ten gallons of gas
- Patterns: Recognizing, developing, and repeating patterns, such as secret code messages or designs in a carpet or tile floor

Like other math concepts, these build upon and assume mastery of those that occur earlier. Pattern recognition, particularly, depends upon the earlier mastery of separating an attribute from an object. When students are asked to recognize a pattern, they are being asked to identify the repetitive nature of something. This requires at least two prerequisite skills:

- Identifying similarities
- Detecting differences

Prior to beginning any lessons on pattern recognition, the teacher needs to ensure that students have these two prerequisite skills and provide remedial help for those that do not have them. Disabilities that affect pattern recognition will impact both math computational and reasoning skills. Computation skills will be affected because many of them build upon patterns (e.g., adding one to a number moves it up ordinally and subtracting one moves it down). Math reasoning requires recognizing patterns not only in math but also in the strategies used to solve math problems.

Most children are not developmentally ready to understand the following concepts until after they enter school:

- Understanding and working with numbers larger than ten: They may be able to recite larger numbers but are not able to compare or add them.
- Part-whole concept: The idea of one number as part of another number
- Numerical notation: Place value, additive system, and the zero symbol

These all build upon mastery of earlier skills and will be affected by any disability that affects the earlier skills.

SPECIFIC LEARNING DISABILITIES THAT AFFECT MATH SKILLS

Bley and Thornton (2001) provide a comprehensive table of specific disabilities and the effect of each on math skills (p. 6-7) as well as more detailed analyses of each. A brief overview of these includes:

- **Executive functioning disabilities** affect pattern recognition, applying operations to word problems, and solving multi-step problems.
- **Visual and auditory figure-ground disabilities** affect pattern recognition, multiple step operations, counting on from a previous sequence, keeping place value straight and visualizing groups.
- **Perceptual closure disabilities** impact simple reading of multi-digit numbers, pattern recognition and all aspects of algebraic reasoning.
- **Perceptual discrimination disabilities and reversals** impact differentiating coins, clocks, multi-digit numbers, operational signs, and place value.
- **Spatial-temporal disabilities** make writing and aligning numbers, especially fractions, difficult and impact the ability to understand before/after concepts and size differences.
- **Short-term and working memory disabilities** affect retention of newly learned material, copying numbers, counting on from a midpoint, multi-step computations and solving multi-step, multi-operational word problems.
- **Long-term memory disabilities** affect retention of basic facts and steps in longer operations.
- **Sequential memory disabilities** affect simply reading numbers correctly, all complex operations and multi-step problems, time telling, and equations.
- **Receptive and expressive language disabilities** affect understanding word problems and explaining answers, math vocabulary and symbols, and counting on from a midpoint.

Skill 10.02 Demonstrating knowledge of principles and methods for improving students' computation and reasoning skills

AN OVERVIEW OF PRINCIPLES OF MATH INSTRUCTION AT ALL LEVELS

Based on the child's development as outlined above, Baratta-Lorton (1978) described three levels of instruction necessary to help a child move through any mathematics curriculum. Modern research has consistently confirmed this approach to teaching math.

- **Concept Level:** At this level, the child needs *repeated and varied* interaction with manipulatives. The child needs to interact intensively with a variety of objects, to see patterns, combinations and relationships among the objects before the child can internalize concepts. When introducing any new concept, this is the level at which the child will spend the most time. It is important to remember that the objects are not being used by the teacher to demonstrate concepts, but by the child to *discover* concepts and relationships. The teacher's role is to ask questions that trigger higher-order thinking and learning from the child.
- **Connecting Level:** At this level, the child learns to assign symbols or representations to the objects and the operations carried out on the objects. However, the objects or manipulatives are still very present and part of the process. Labeling the objects and operations with symbols in the presence of the objects or manipulatives serves as a connection from the concrete level to the next level. The child can move on from this level more quickly and whenever he or she is ready to do so.
- **Symbolic Level:** At this level, the child can use symbols without manipulatives. The child understands the abstract concepts behind the symbols and can operate on and with symbols alone.

The National Council of Teachers of Mathematics (NCTM)'s 2000 outline of principles upon which mathematics instruction should be based provides a similar process by which math concepts should be taught. This document states that instruction and exploration should go through three stages of *representation* (the procedure for modeling and interpreting organization of objects and mathematical operations).

- **Concrete Representations:** The extensive exploration and use of objects and manipulatives to discover and then demonstrate operations and relationships
- **Pictorial Representations (semi-abstract):** The use of concrete pictures of objects and actions often in the presence of the objects as discoveries and demonstrations are made
- **Symbolic Representations (abstract):** The use of symbols exclusively to conduct operations, explorations and discoveries about math concepts

The NCTM report goes on to describe a mathematics program based on NCTM standards and current research as having the following general characteristics.

- Children will be actively engaged in exploring math concepts and *doing* math. There will be hands-on, concrete exploration, as well talking about, reading about, and writing about math.
- Students will be encouraged to "stretch" their math sense and "think like mathematicians." High standards will be expected, but the learning setting will be safe enough for children to take risks and make mistakes in order to learn and enjoy learning.

- Teachers will be asking questions that stimulate children to make new discoveries and connections and to reveal concepts they already know.
- Cooperative learning will take place. Children will learn from talking to one another about math and from working together.
- Math will be part of the "real world" and connections to that real world will be made for all activities and concepts.
- Content taught will cover a wide range of topics and applications, not only computation, but the concepts behind computation and use, and the math language to discuss these connections.

A review of research by David Allsopp (in Allsopp, Kyger, & Lovin, 2007) suggests additional general practices:

- Teaching problem-solving strategies is more effective than exclusively using rote practice.
- Concrete instruction, persistently applied throughout the levels of mathematics curriculum, is effective in helping students develop computation and problem-solving skills and preparing for abstract mathematics work.
- Ongoing assessment of students' performance, as well as sharing and discussing their progress and successes with them, improves learning outcomes.
- Engaging students as active participants in their learning by encouraging and teaching metacognitive behaviors like goal setting, self-monitoring, and self-talk boosts math proficiency. The same outcome is true for showing them how to apply these skills not only to their mathematics work but also to general problem solving.
- Well-planned cooperative learning activities, such as peer tutoring and work groups, can offer students opportunities for meaningful practice and skill enhancement.

USING THESE PRINCIPLES TO IMPROVE COMPUTATIONAL AND REASONING SKILLS

Teaching Conceptual Reasoning from Simple to Complex

Early math readiness skills involve primitive practice in quantification and, as mentioned above, should be taught with extensive interaction with manipulatives of all sorts to ensure a firm grounding in basic mathematical reasoning. Although these skills overlap somewhat, it is beneficial to teach them in this order:

1. **One-to-one Matching**: Children can be asked to match the items in two groups one by one and to describe what they find (e.g., which group has more?)
2. **Rote Counting**: Naming the numbers in correct sequence, without really understanding what the numbers mean

3. **Selection of Correct Number of Objects**: For counting to become meaningful, children must learn the conservation of number described earlier. Prior to this they will assume that a difference in the alignment or shape of a group will affect the number of objects in the group. Such students will need many chances to interact with equal groups of varied things, moving them around, counting and recounting, discussing observations that the longer line could have the same number as the shorter line because the objects in it are further apart, etc. This can only be done with manipulatives. Teaching the child a rote rule (e.g., "The total number does not change when the shape changes") will not have the same effect upon the child's *conceptual* reasoning about numbers.

4. **Ordinality and Cardinality:** *Ordinality* refers to the relative position or order of an object within a set in relation to the other objects, like first, second, etc. *Cardinality* answers the question of "How many?" When counting, children use numbers cardinally as they say "one" for the first object, "two" for the second, and so on.

5. **Sequencing Numbers to Ten:** Prior work in comparing and ordering quantities is gradually extended. Children learn that five, which is more than three, comes after three in counting sequence.

6. **Zero:** Developmental work with zero occurs after learning the 1 to 10 sequence. The meaning of zero as "none at all" is easier for children to understand when they can use it in relation to a change in known quantities. For example, "There were two cookies on the plate. My dad and I each had one. Now they are all gone."

7. **Symbols:** At the beginning of the pictorial representation stage of instruction, students learn to name number symbols as they see them, including the greater and less than symbols, and to use the number symbols, choosing a model in the presence of the objects. Later, they will learn to name and use symbols even when the objects are no longer present.

8. **Sight Groups:** Children need to practice recognizing—without counting—the number of objects in groups having four or fewer items. Throw a group of three objects on one board and a group of four on another and challenge children to say which is bigger and to name the number in each group (quickly). Eventually, children will learn to sight sub-groups with larger numbers of objects.

9. **Writing Numerals:** After children have learned to recognize a numeral and associate it with the correct number of objects, writing is begun. However, even when the focus is on writing, continued reference to quantities named should be made.

10. **Sequencing Tasks:** Earlier work, in which children used one-to-one matching to tell whether a group has more, less, or as many objects as another, is extended. Children come to recognize that when a number means more, it comes after another in the process of counting. Conversely, when a number means less, it comes before another in counting.

The stages just described serve as precursors in the development of number concepts. The conceptual understanding of number concepts further extends into mathematical operations, place value, regroupings, and decimals later.

Teaching Computation and Basic Facts

When teaching basic computation, lessons should follow the progression from concrete to pictorial to symbolic described above. For example, before introducing addition facts provide extensive practice with manipulatives letting students identify the number in two groups and physically put them together ("adding") to demonstrate the concept of addition. The process would follow this progression:

- **Concrete:** Give students two cups, one with three buttons in it and the other with four in it, and tell them to put them together and count them, demonstrating 3 + 4 = 7.
- **Semi-concrete:** Use pictures of three buttons and four buttons to illustrate 3 + 4 = 7, or have students draw the three buttons in one cup and the four in the other, and so forth.
- **Abstract**: The student solves 3 + 4 = 7 without using manipulatives or pictures.

This step-by-step process would be repeated *every time a new operation is taught.* In each case, the student practices the operation concretely, then adds symbols, then uses symbols alone. This also applies to higher levels of math, such as learning place value. In fact, place value concepts are so critical for understanding our math system that it is recommended that extensive practice using manipulatives to combine and label quantities in a variety of base number systems take place *before* addressing our base ten place value system (see Hatfield et al, p. 200-203).

Because memorization of basic facts is an important skill for efficient computation, care should be taken to teach these facts in a systematic, efficient fashion. For example:

- Teach addition facts in this order: +0, +1, doubles, near doubles (i.e., doubles +1 and –1), group to 10, and teach the commutative property of addition (you can switch around the numbers: 5+4 is the same as 4+5) from the start.
- Teach subtraction facts in this order: -0, -the whole, -1, then fact families with addition.
- Teach multiplication facts in this order: x1, x0, skip count by 2, 5, 10, 3; then x doubles and x9.
- Teach division as part of fact families with multiplication and locating missing factors.

Teaching basic facts in this manner reduces the cognitive load of memorization and helps teach principles behind the facts.

Please refer to Skill 10.05 for details on modifying lessons for students with disabilities.

Skill 10.03   Applying strategies for promoting students' use of critical-thinking and problem-solving skills in mathematics

PROBLEM SOLVING

The skills of analysis and interpretation are necessary for problem solving. Students with some learning disabilities find problem solving difficult, with the result that they avoid activities associated with it. Skills necessary for problem solving include:

- **Identification of the main idea:** What is the problem about?
- **Main question of the problem:** What is the problem asking for?
- **Identifying important facts(and ignoring irrelevant ones):** What information is necessary to solve the problem?
- **Choosing a strategy and an operation:** How will the student solve the problem and with what operation?
- **Solve the problem:** Perform the computation.
- **Check accuracy of computation and compare the answer to the main question:** Does the answer seem reasonable?
- **If solution is incorrect:** Repeat the steps, or perhaps try a different method.
- Explaining how the answer was obtained and justifying the answer are increasingly demanded as part of modern standards-based curricula.

Identify Effective Teaching Methods for Developing the Use of Math SPkills in Problem Solving

Developing critical thinking and problem-solving skills in mathematics goes beyond simply solving "word problems" in a math textbook. Problem solving is the process of applying previously acquired knowledge to new and novel situations, and it involves more than simply reading word problems, deciding on correct conceptual procedures, and performing the computations. It involves posing questions; analyzing situations; hypothesizing, translating, and illustrating results; drawing diagrams; using trial and error; and *explaining* results.

Children will need to learn a variety of problem-solving strategies to keep in their personal "toolkit" for solving mathematical problems in school and in everyday life. Some of these strategies include:

- Acting out the problem or using manipulatives

- Drawing pictures, graphs, or tables
- Identifying simpler problems with similar solutions
- Guessing and checking possible solutions
- Using a flow chart to outline the problem or the steps in it
- Constructing 3D models
- Looking for patterns
- Working backward
- Developing their own idiosyncratic strategy

Simply learning such strategies is not enough. They can be used to solve most textbook word problems, which tend to be "goal oriented" and involve practice using a recently learned computational skill or problem solving strategy to find an answer. While this is important practice, students must also learn the *process* of problem solving, and this requires a different type of instruction. Some techniques to help children become active, confident problem solvers, regardless of the level or type of problem, include:

- Address problem solving outside of math and help students learn how to transfer what they learn to math. For example, find time in the day to present small problems to the class and spend time soliciting ideas on how to solve these problems. Teachers can use things like fables and folktales as starting point; just don't include the solution (e.g., tell about the crow and the water pitcher but don't tell what the crow did to get the water; let the students figure out a solution). Shannon (1994) presents a variety of folktales that can be used as problem-solving starters.
- Let students attempt their own ways of solving rather than prescribing a particular way as correct. While many math problems have only one correct answer, many have more than one correct answer (e.g., "Which of these toys could Tom buy with his $10?" might have more than one answer, and many higher math problems require a range of answers). In addition, there might be a number of ways to arrive at a correct answer.
- Discuss each child's method and highlight the multiple ways to solve a problem (e.g., "Ok, you added, Tom drew a picture, let's see what Sue did").
- Help students to identify similarities and differences among various problems. Present two or three at a time and, rather than asking for a solution, ask students to identify how the problems are similar and how they are different. This can lead to recognizing patterns and types of problems and choosing appropriate strategies.
- Use cooperative learning groups; assign a problem and let children work together. A variation of a common procedure used in reading can be very useful here. Assign each student a "job" (e.g., one looks for vocabulary terms critical to the solution, one looks for numbers and amounts, one looks for operations, one for relevant versus irrelevant information, one does computation, etc).

- When assessing students, look not only at whether the students' answers are correct but also for whether they used an appropriate strategy, accurately identified relevant information, and so forth. Let students see that this aspect of problem solving is important to you (and to their scores).
- Routinely ask students to explain how they solved a problem, what they tried that failed, why they chose the strategy or strategies that they did, and ask for this in a variety of forms (e.g., orally, in pictures, in written expression).

In addition to the above specifics, teachers should include the following in their planning for math instruction:

1. Allot time for the development of successful problem-solving skills. It is a complex process.
2. Be sure prerequisite skills have been adequately developed. Problem-solving instruction can begin at the earliest elementary level, but, for math problems, be sure that either the requisite math skills for a particular problem have been mastered or that a template or calculator is available.
3. Use error analysis to diagnose areas of difficulty. One error in procedure or choice of mathematical operation, once corrected, will eliminate subsequent mistakes following the initial error. Look for patterns of similar mistakes to prevent a series of identical errors. Instruct children on the usage of error analysis to perform self-appraisal of their own work.
4. Teach students appropriate terminology and "good math language" (see Skill 10.05 for more on this). Many words have a different meaning when used in a mathematical context rather than in everyday life.
5. Have students estimate answers. Teach them how to check their computed answer to determine how reasonable it is.

Skill 10.04 Demonstrating familiarity with techniques for encouraging students' application of mathematics skills in a variety of contexts, including practical daily living situations

Application of math skills to a variety of real-world contexts requires that students generalize or transfer those skills from the setting in which they are learned to a different setting in which they will be used (e.g., daily home life and work). This generalization will be far more likely to occur if the instructional setting mirrors the home or job setting. Although specific settings and techniques will vary depending upon the individual student's needs, math skills learned and practiced in a setting as close to the real-world setting as possible will be more likely to transfer to that real-world setting.

Applying principles of generalization specifically to math, the following practices can help students learn to use their math skills in real world contexts.

Use many and varied real-world-style problems in teaching to deepen application of learned skills. Once a computational or problem-solving skill has been studied, design real-world problems that need to be solved using it. For example, use grocery store flyers for a variety of exercises in both computation and problem solving.

Use consistency in initial teaching situations and later introduce variety in format, procedure, and use of examples.

Have the same information presented by different teachers, in different settings, and under varying conditions. This requires good collaboration among various teachers and professionals (See Competency 6), but it will be helpful if all the teachers working with the student are aware of what is currently being taught in math. If the students are currently learning addition with regrouping in math class, the personal finance instructor could use those skills to help students balance mock checkbooks; if multiplication is the current topic, ask the shop teacher to involve students in determining how many nails are needed for a certain number of boards, and so forth.

Include a continuous reinforcement schedule at first, later changing to delayed and intermittent schedules as instruction progresses.

Teach students to actively look for ways a particular skill might be used and record instances of this generalization. Cooperative learning can be used here: For example, assign a small group to brainstorm ways to use the four basic math operations in the grocery store or the baseball field.

Associate naturally occurring stimuli when possible (e.g., the above use of grocery flyers). Arranging for practice in the real life setting can greatly enhance generalization (e.g., a field trip to the grocery store).

Real-world applications of mathematics abound and offer highly-motivating opportunities for computational practice. The development of number sense and mathematical reasoning can give students confidence in their mathematical abilities. Finding the mathematical connections in outdoor games, planning for the purchase of lunch, comparing heights among classmates, calculating the time until recess, and figuring out which sports team is headed for the playoffs are just a few examples of real-world applications.

The Special Connections Project at the University of Kansas suggests a number of strategies in its paper entitled "Creating Authentic Mathematics Learning Contexts" (*http://www.specialconnections.ku.edu/cgi-bin/cgiwrap/specconn/main.php?cat=instruction&section=main&subsection=math/learningcontexts*):

- **Begin where the students are:** Students' ages, interests, and experiences are excellent clues to the kinds of contexts that will offer the most compelling learning opportunities, whether school-, family-, or community-related.
- **Document interests:** Comparing and contrasting them can help identify patterns and differences and assist with lesson and activity planning. Documenting and reviewing this information (e.g., student names, hobbies, interests, family activities, etc.) could be an activity to share with students.
- **Model the desired concept, skill, or strategy explicitly and within the real-world context:** Observing a problem-solving approach and its outcome helps to ground students in the math and begins to strengthen associations between mathematical concepts and real-life situations.
- **Reinforce the associations** by demonstrating the relevance of the concept, skill, or strategy being taught to the "authentic context."
- **Offer opportunities for guided, supported practice** of the concept, skill, or strategy; this includes feedback, redirection, remodeling, and acknowledgement of progress and successes.

Skill 10.05   Evaluating, selecting, and adapting instructional strategies, materials, and resources to individualize instruction and facilitate student achievement in mathematics

As discussed in Skill 10.01, physical, perceptual and learning disabilities can negatively impact acquiring math skills in many ways. In math instruction, teachers must focus on each student's observed strengths and weaknesses and relevant information from the student's IEP, then task-analyze the concepts, skills, and strategies to be taught in terms of prerequisite skills and individual student readiness.

Research reviewed in the NCTM journal article, "Planning Strategies for Students with Special Needs" (*Teaching Children Mathematics*, 2004), suggests that the next step in deciding on strategies, materials, and resources is to identify the "barriers" to success that the students' disabilities might present as they work toward the objectives of the curriculum and their IEPs. This information can help direct teachers' thinking about proactive solutions, including the selection and/or adaptation of the best strategies, materials, and resources. (Please refer to the following skills for general information: Skill 5.03 for accommodations, Skill 8.03 for selection and modification of materials, and Skill 7.02 for principles of differentiated instruction).

REMEMBERING THE LEVELS OF ABSTRACTION IN MATH STUDY

Critical to math instruction for students with learning disabilities is the understanding that many students with disabilities will need to spend more time at the concrete concept level of study (see Skill 10.02) before moving on to the more abstract pictorial or symbolic levels. Similarly, once arriving at the pictorial representation level, students with disabilities might need to spend more time at that level before moving on to the symbolic level. In fact, one of the first and most effective instructional strategies a teacher can use when a student encounters difficulty in any area of math is simply readdressing the skill with concrete manipulatives at the concept level and giving the student more time to work at that level. More time at the pictorial level *in the presence of the manipulatives* can also be effective.

SPECIFIC STRATEGIES FOR TEACHING STUDENTS WITH DISABILITIES

The specific strategies used in a given lesson will, of course, depend upon the individual student's needs and the requirements of the lesson objectives. However, some types of strategies will commonly be helpful for many students with disabilities.

- Spending more time at the concrete level (see Skill 9.03)
  - More time for the student to interact with and to explore manipulatives
  - Use of concrete objects and manipulatives to illustrate operations and concepts, often while talking about them
  - More use of visuals and pictures as you work
- Cueing systems: Using boxes and circles to set off and contain relevant information
- Organizing aids, diagrams and charts
- Formatting workbook pages with less information displayed centrally with lots of empty space around it (particularly useful for students with visual and attention issues)
- Providing templates from which to work
- Minimizing copying from the book or doing the copying for the student
- Color coding material or using color cues for concepts and operations
- Using concept charts for choosing operations
- Using sticky arrows for highlighting the problem or relevant information
- Presenting sequence and flow charts to show steps in solutions
- Listing of possible strategies and criteria for choosing
- Using language of math aids: For many students with disabilities, it is the language of math that is most difficult.
  - Model and talk aloud as you work problems and encourage the students to do so under your supervision; this helps the students learn the reasoning process, the correct math words to use, and problem solving strategies.

o **Do** the operation manually or have the student do it and **talk** about it as you do it.
o Explicitly teach math vocabulary using visuals and objects.
o Rephrase a student's words to include usage of math terminology and reward use of correct math terms.

Other useful strategies can include:

- Varying learning modalities (visual, kinesthetic, tactile, aural)
- Integrating technology (calculators, computers, game consoles)
- Developing a range of engaging activities (games, music, storytelling)
- Using real-world problem solving (fundraising, school-wide projects, shopping, cooking, budgeting)
- Adopting a cross-curricular approach (studying historical events strongly influenced by math, music theory)
- Adaptations (extended wait time, recorded lessons, concept videos, ergonomic work areas, mixed-ability learning groups)

Making It Real

In a paper published by the ERIC Clearinghouse on Disabilities and Gifted Education, author Cynthia Warger (2002, p. 2-3) writes, "…for students with disabilities to do better in math, math must be meaningful for them. Both knowing and doing mathematics must be emphasized to enhance the quality of mathematics instruction and learning for students with disabilities." Many of the techniques discussed in Skill 10.04 for helping students generalize math skills to the real world can also be used to make math more meaningful and concrete for students.

Differentiated Instruction in Math

Please refer to Skill 7.02 for a description of differentiated instruction.
It will often be necessary to differentiate the math lessons to accommodate varying student needs. For example, typical objectives in late elementary grades involve organizing and displaying data using pictures, tallies, tables, charts, and a variety of types of graphs. An IEP objective in this area modified for different students' abilities might look like this:

- **Basic level:** Student will count and tally a selection of objects supplied by the teacher and construct a bar graph with a one-to-one scale using manipulatives such as stickers or blocks on a form provided by the teacher.
- **Moderate level:** Student will tally a selection of objects supplied by the teacher, then use a template for a bar or pictograph and record the data on the graph using teacher assistance to select an appropriate scale or key amount.

- **Mastery level:** Student will tally numerical data on a topic provided by the teacher, then select an appropriate type of graph for display and construct the graph including all necessary scales, keys, and labels.

Differentiation with Basic Facts, Memorization and Sequential Tasks

As mentioned in Skill 10.01, deficits in short-term memory, working memory, or long-term memory can have a significant impact on developing math skills. Some students with disabilities simply may not be able to memorize basic math facts or will take so long learning them that it will seriously delay their ability to learn more abstract, higher-level operations. Although students with these disabilities might not be able to memorize math facts, they **might** be perfectly capable of understanding the underlying math *concepts* and solving math problems if given accommodations such as number lines and calculators.

Alternatively, there might be students with other math or language disabilities who can easily memorize math facts but do not understand the concepts underlying the processes. These students might be able to follow a rote algorithm or computational method, but will struggle to choose the correct operation or know what to do with the answer once they have it. These students will need additional instruction in understanding the concepts behind the math and/or templates, flow charts, and strategies for determining what the answer to a problem means.

The key is to provide a combination of differentiated instruction and accommodations so that a student's disability in one area of math does not prevent the student from progressing in other areas of math where there is greater strength.

COMPETENCY 0011   UNDERSTAND STRATEGIES AND TECHNIQUES USED TO PROMOTE STUDENTS' ACQUISITION OF FUNCTIONAL LIVING SKILLS

Skill 11.01   Demonstrating knowledge of methods for teaching students with disabilities to use problem solving, decision-making, and other cognitive strategies to meet their own needs

See Skill 10.03 for details on developing problem solving skills.

In order for students to apply critical thinking and problem solving skills learned in school to decisions relevant to functional life needs, students must be able to *generalize* or *transfer* these skills from the school setting to the functional living setting of home life, jobs, and leisure. Generalization training is a procedure in which a behavior is reinforced in each of a series of situations until the student begins to more automatically apply the learned behavior to new situations. The more similar two situations are, the easier it is for the student to transfer learned behavior to the new situation.

This is particularly true of functional skills involved in independent living and the workplace. Skills learned in the school setting are far more likely to generalize to home life or the workplace if the school setting resembles the home or work setting.

Even when the settings are deliberately made as similar as possible, however, many students with disabilities will need instruction specifically designed to help them think about how to apply what they have learned in school to real life problems. These are higher-order or critical thinking skills because they require students to think about thinking. For example, these skills can be found in:

- Balancing a checkbook and analyzing bills for overcharges
- Comparing shopping ads or catalogue deals
- Following news stories
- Reading a TV guide and planning to record shows
- Gathering information/data from diverse sources to plan a project
- Following a sequence of directions in a recipe or on the job
- Looking for cause and effect relationships (e.g., why is the dog barking or why is the baby crying?)
- Appropriate responses and use of community resources (e.g., call the electrical company if the power is out, call the doctor and my work supervisor if I am sick)
- Evaluating information relevant to making a given decision (e.g., deciding which movie to go to might involve cost, time, duration, personal interest, available transportation)

Both the math problem-solving strategies and the techniques for helping students to apply them to real life discussed in Skill 10.03 can be adapted for use with many functional life skills. General techniques for improving the transfer of problem solving skills listed in Skill 10.03 might be modified as follows:

- Use of the cooperative learning groups or whole -discussions of how to solve problems might involve common home life and job related problems rather than folktales or math. Role playing can be particularly effective in cooperative groups for this purpose.
- Allowing students or groups of students to try their own solutions and then discussing various approaches that might work can help them learn that there may be more than one solution to or method for solving a problem. For example, if the proposed problem is how to get to work on time, solutions might include walking (depending on the distance), biking, a bus route, subway, driving or carpooling, or even a taxi.
- Collaboration among teachers (see Skill 11.02)
- Helping students identify similarities in functional problems might involve helping them see that getting to work on time and getting to a movie on time involve many of the same skills, for example.

A modification of the analysis of math word problems can be used as a general problem solving strategy for functional life problems. For example, students can ask themselves:

- What is the problem or decision, or what do I want to do? (Main idea)
- What do I need in order to do it? (Information needed to solve)
- What do I need to find out that I don't already know? (relevant information)
- How can I find out what I need to know? (Strategy or plan)
- Solve the problem or make a decision
- Check to see if decision or solution actually gets me what I wanted.

Attention to learner needs during planning is essential. It includes identifying the things students already know or need to know; matching learner needs with instructional elements such as content, materials, activities, and goals; and determining whether or not students have performed at an acceptable level following instruction.

The ability to create a personal chart of students' functional learning and emotional growth found within the performance-based assessment of individualized portfolios can be useful for both students and teachers. Teachers can use semester portfolios to gauge student progress and the personal growth of students who are constantly trying to apply their learning to new situations. When a student studies to master a functional skill and makes a visual of his or her learning, it can help connect the learning to a higher level of thinking that can be generalized to new situations that were not specifically studied in class.

Skill 11.02   Demonstrate an understanding of effective collaboration among teachers and other professionals to facilitate students' maintenance and generalization of skills across learning environments.

Please refer to Skills 10.03 and 11.01 for details on methods for improving generalization and transfer of skills from classroom to daily life.

ARRANGING OBJECTIVES TO ENHANCE TRANSFER OF LEARNING

Transfer of learning occurs when experience with one task influences performance on another task. Positive transfer occurs when the required responses and the stimuli are similar, such as moving from baseball to handball or from field hockey to soccer. Negative transfer occurs when the stimuli remain similar but the required responses change, such as shifting from soccer to football, tennis to racquetball, or boxing to sports karate. As mentioned in previous skills, instructional procedures should stress the similar features between the activities and the dimensions that are transferable. Specific information should emphasize when stimuli in the old and new situations are the same and when responses used in the old situation apply to the new.

To facilitate learning, instructional objectives should be arranged according to their patterns of similarity. Objectives involving similar responses should be closely sequenced so the possibility for positive transfer is stressed. Likewise, learning objectives that involve different responses should be programmed to emphasize and explicitly teach the difference to minimize negative transfer.

For example, students should have little difficulty transferring handwriting instruction to writing information on an employment form; however, there might be some negative transfer when moving from manuscript to cursive writing. By using transitional methods and focusing on the similarities between manuscript and cursive writing, negative transfer can be reduced.

When addressing basic skills in the classroom, it is important to keep the ultimate uses of those skills in mind in order to improve positive transfer and minimize negative transfer. For example, the arrangement of many traditional practice worksheets for addition and subtraction could actually produce some negative transfer when applied to a critical life skill: balancing a checkbook. Although column addition is often taught in school, most subtraction problems involve only two numbers at a time. Checkbooks require successive, sequential subtraction; in each case the number obtained as a difference becomes the "starting" number from which the next number is subtracted. Also, the operation switches from subtraction to addition when a deposit is made. Both these processes might be difficult for some students with disabilities. In order to minimize negative transfer, classroom worksheets might need to be modified to include such skills.

Collaboration to Enhance Generalization of Skills

Please refer to Skills 6.02, 6.03, and 6.06 for general guidelines on collaboration among teachers and other professionals.

When the goal is to promote students' acquisition of functional life skills, collaboration among various teachers and specialists to provide reinforcement of these generalization skills might involve several teachers working on related skills in different subjects. The strategy of designing math worksheets to reflect functional skills, mentioned above, is one example of collaboration. Others might include the following:

- One functional life skill is getting to work on time. In this instance, the reading teacher might have a lesson on how to read diagrams such as bus and subway lines, while the social studies teacher covers street maps, and the math teacher works on elapsed time using bus and job schedules.
- In a decision-making problem about choosing among possible residences in which to live with your pet dog, the reading teacher might cover reading ads and lease arrangements, the science teacher might include a unit on the physical needs of the pet, social studies might address how to find out about local ordinances, and math could involve costs to support the pet, or even the amount of fencing material (and its cost) for building a fence for the dog.

Skill 11.03 Demonstrate familiarity with strategies for linking life skills instruction to employment and independent, community, and personal living

Please refer to Skills 10.04 and 11.01 for methods of instruction designed to help students generalize skills learned in school to daily life and employment.

Adaptive life skills are the skills that people need to function independently at home, school, and in the community. These include communication and social skills (e.g., intermingling and communicating with other people); independent living skills (e.g., shopping, budgeting, and cleaning); personal care skills (e.g., eating, dressing, and grooming); employment/work skills (e.g., following directions, completing assignments, and being punctual for work); and functional academics (e.g., reading, solving math problems, and telling time).

Although most students acquire adaptive behavior skills through practical experiences, students with disabilities might need direct instruction in order to acquire them and to transfer them to various life situations. The specific curriculum content needs to follow objectives in the student's IEP and be appropriate for the student's long-term functional goals.

LINKING INSTRUCTION TO EMPLOYMENT AND COMMUNITY LIFE

Community-referenced instruction and community-based instruction are two forms of functional instruction designed to help students with disabilities acquire proficiency in the skills they will need to live and function in the wider community. Instruction focuses on adaptive behavior and daily living skills, as well as work skills in a community setting.

Community-Referenced Instruction (CRI)

Community-referenced instruction was discussed in detail in Skill 7.05. It involves classroom instruction that specifically targets skills needed in daily life and is designed to reflect the functional setting as closely as possible. It is usually coordinated with *Community-Based Instruction*, below.

Community-Based Instruction (CBI)

Community-based instruction refers to regular and systematic instruction in specific, functional skills that takes place in the natural community setting in which the specific skill(s) will actually be used. This instruction can also include use of accommodations needed for the skill to be used in the community setting. For example, for a student who needs to learn how to use public transportation, CBI would involve mapping the route the student needs to use and providing systematic instruction and practice finding a bus stop, standing in line at the stop, recognizing the correct bus, getting on, and notifying the driver when he or she needs to get off the bus. All of this would take place on the real bus and along the relevant route.

To be effective, CBI involves three major components:

1. **Analyzing Student Need:** All goals and objectives must be tied to the student's needs as stated in the IEP. Goals should be consistent with state learning standards for the student's grade and level of development. Elementary students will, obviously, need different types of CBI from high school students who may be preparing for the world of work. For students 14 years of age or older, there should be explicit transition goals in the IEP (Skill 11.07 addresses transition in detail). This part of the analysis will also focus on what skills relevant to the goal or objective the student already has.
2. **Ecological Inventory:** An ecological inventory is a detailed analysis of the specific community setting in which the skill is to be used. In the public transportation example used above, it might include the locations where the student gets on and off the bus, including landmarks en route; the types of buses used on the route and access to the bus; the maps and labels used; the type of device (cord, button, etc.) for requesting a stop; and other relevant factors in the environment. This inventory would also

include an analysis of the fundamental skills necessary to achieve the objective relative to skills the student might already have that will be helpful.

3. **Task Breakdown and Analysis:** Once the inventory is done, it is necessary to make a step-by-step analysis of the objective behavior or skill and provide a breakdown of the hierarchy of skills necessary for the student to learn in order to achieve the objective. This would involve integrating the skills the student already has with those he does not have so lesson plans and activities can be designed to help him acquire the missing skills. It then involves repeated practice of each level of the skill in the setting in which it is to be used.

In many cases, CRI and CBI are used together to maximize learning. Some beginning skills can initially be taught in the school setting with practice moving to the community setting when a certain level of proficiency is acquired. Often, CRI and CBI are interwoven throughout the student's educational experience. In elementary school, for example, the emphasis is on CRI, with the student practicing skills in a school setting (e.g., making choices and paying for cafeteria lunch, raising a hand to ask for guidance from a teacher). Carefully designed role-playing activities are often a part of CRI. In middle school and high school, more and more instruction will shift into the community in CBI (e.g., choosing and buying lunch at a fast food chain, asking a clerk for help finding something).

It should be noted that a *field trip*, an activity common in many educational settings, is **not** a form of CRI or CBI. Field trips can help students become acquainted with a particular community setting. However, CRI and CBI involve far more systematic and detailed analyses of skills and lessons, as well as repeated practice in the relevant setting. Watching someone else doing something might be a useful first step, but is does not constitute training or practice.

Skill 11.04   Demonstrating knowledge of methods, including collaboration among professionals in a variety of settings, for promoting students' development of independence to the fullest extent possible (e.g., self-advocacy skills, self-management strategies, independent use of assistive devices, person-centered planning)

Please also refer to Skills 6.03 and 6.06 for strategies for collaboration and Skill 6.05 for details on self-advocacy. Refer to Skill 5.02 for information on use of assistive technology.

As mentioned in Skill 6.05, self-advocacy training must be present in all aspects of the child's education. Students need to be aware of their own strengths and disabilities, their needs for accommodation, their legal rights (this is of critical importance not only at school but as they enter adult life), and they need to have a strategy or template for applying this knowledge in various settings. There are many ways to accomplish this. One method suggested by Mastropieri and Scruggs (2000) is the *IPLAN* approach:

- *I*nventory: Student participates in a self-inventory of strengths, skills, disabilities, learning styles, and needed accommodations, and studies this inventory.
- *P*: Student *P*rovides teachers with a copy of the inventory or a summary of its results.
- *L*: Student *L*istens to each teacher's comments
- *A*: Students *A*sks any questions that might be helpful.
- *N:* Student *N*ames his or her goals for each teacher.

This approach, of course, requires collaboration and communication among the various teachers and professionals in the student's life as they coordinate their responses and plans based on the student's *IPLAN*. This approach is easily adaptable for use in adult life. The student can prepare a letter or resume outlining these points when entering post-secondary training or even a new job.

Independence is an integral part of self-advocacy and most students with disabilities also require explicit instruction and practice to become more independent. As mentioned in the earlier skill sections, teachers must design instruction to allow the student to experience success when exercising independence. One thing teachers can do to help students achieve greater independence is to provide training in self-monitoring, self-instruction, and self-recording.

Many students with disabilities benefit from learning to record their own behaviors, grades, scores, and even feelings. Depending upon the particular objective, the student is given a recording sheet and keeps a record of some important behavior. It might be a checklist of work attempted, finished, and unfinished a day's end, or there might be regular auditory signals or times when the student would record on- or off-task behavior, paying attention, etc. Other such checklists might record student feelings. Students can be taught to provide rewards for themselves if they meet a prearranged criterion on such checklists. The key is to improve the student's self-knowledge and self-direction.

Self-instruction often accompanies self-recording. Students can learn to "talk" to themselves and provide their own instruction depending upon the results they record. For example, the student who records off-task behavior might be taught to use a phrase like "Hey! Get back to work!" or, when recording on-task behavior, might say to himself, "I've been working for 15 minutes; I deserve a break," and so forth. Not only do such techniques teach independence, but they are also metacognitive skills that can be used throughout the student's adult life.

Effective use of such self-recording and instruction procedures, like self-advocacy instruction, require a lot of collaboration among the various adults in a child's life. All teachers and specialists at school must be consistent in their use of these methods. It can even be useful to enlist help from parents and outside tutors in these efforts.

Fostering independence also affects the choice of accommodations and procedures in every class. When an evaluation of a child's needs determines that an accommodation or modification of some sort is necessary for the child to be successful, care must be taken to *choose the accommodation that allows for the greatest independence*. For example, if a child needs to dictate written compositions, some programs suggest the child dictate to a teacher or even a classmate. However, neither of these accommodations promotes independence as much as dictating to a recording device or a computer. Dictating to *another person* forces the child to ask for help and means she cannot do it on her own. Dictating to a computer with voice recognition software that will print her composition as she speaks allows her to complete the entire activity independently, provided she has been taught to use the computer.

All such efforts are based in a *person-centered planning* approach. IDEA 2004 requires that as students begin to prepare to enter the adult world, their IEPs reflect their individual goals, aspirations, needs and strengths. Recent changes in the regulations governing Transition Planning (see Skill 11.07) require person-first language and even reflect the child's own words wherever possible. In planning for improved independence and self-advocacy, the emphasis must be on the individual child.

Skill 11.05 Recognizing that cultural, linguistic, and gender differences need to be taken into account when developing instructional content, materials, resources, and strategies for promoting students' functional living skills

Please refer to Skills 1.05 and 4.07 for discussion of many multicultural issues, and to Skills 3.08 and 7.08 for language issues.

Writing functional living skills curriculum for a student requires understanding that a disability does not define the whole person. Students are more than the sum of the effects of their disabilities. Cultural, linguistic and gender characteristics also help define the student, and these characteristics must be taken into account in person-centered instructional planning (see Skill 11.04). Such issues can directly impact the student's and the student's family's conceptions of what constitute important functional skills.

The American Association of Intellectual and Developmental Disabilities (formerly, the American Association of Mental Retardation) reminds us of the impact culture has on everyone's development by adding two prerequisites to the diagnosis of mental retardation:

- Limitations in present functioning must be considered within the context of community environments typical of the individual's age peers and culture.
- Valid assessment considers cultural and linguistic diversity, as well as differences in communication, sensory, motor, and behavioral factors.

Teachers must recognize these facts in relation to everyday life for their students. Interviewing parents is a way of including them in the development of a functional skills program; it also allows the teacher to learn what is considered a cultural norm in the student's home life. Neither the teacher nor the IEP team who designs the child's goals can assume that parents from diverse cultures will automatically agree with American assumptions about desirable functional skills or the methods used to teach them.

For example, many mainstream American families would list future independence as a goal for a child with a disability. They hope that even a child with a severe disability will be able to live and work as independently as possible. However, from some cultural perspectives this goal would be unthinkable. The emphasis on extended family and the manner in which each cares for the other throughout all stages of life might lead some parents to look with horror on the prospect of a child with a disability ever living alone or functioning independently. Their assumption might be that the best and most appropriate goal is for the child to find a way to fit in and contribute to the family while being sheltered *at home* with siblings and relatives.

Gender can also create sensitive issues with regard to functional skills curricula and instruction. Some cultures and sub-cultural groups have very specific and distinct ideas about appropriate male and female roles in society, and these ideas might impact what is considered an appropriate functional skill. Some cultural groups, for example, consider family food preparation and cooking to be appropriate skills for women, but not for men. Regardless of whether the teacher agrees with the viewpoint or not, it is the teacher's responsibility to take it into consideration when designing instruction.

If, for example, the functional life skill being addressed is preparing food, the teacher sensitive to such a (male) child's background might enlist parental help in finding out what a culturally acceptable method of meeting the need for meals would be for a male who does not have a woman in the house, then use that to design instruction. In all cases, the planned method of instruction, as well as any materials used, must be culturally sensitive as well as practically effective.

The following is a set of instructional methods commonly used for teaching functional skills with brief comments or modification about how to use them to avoid cultural conflict:

- Use the think aloud process. Teachers should state simple questions and answer them as part of the thought process while demonstrating a specific skill. Allowing students, particularly those from diverse backgrounds, to think aloud reinforces the concept that there can be many different ways to think about and solve a problem.

- Create opportunities for students to ask open-ended questions regarding the skill to be completed. Encourage students from diverse backgrounds to ask why this skill is important. Are there differences in this country that make a skill important here even though it might not be as useful in another environment?

- Provide multiple examples of how to attain a skill. Encourage students from all cultures to describe how they would solve the problem or use the skill (or whether they would use the skill at all). Materials comparing how something is accomplished in various cultures can be helpful: for example, pictures showing how someone gets to work in a variety of settings.

- Include the use of culturally diverse and even student-designed art to show how a skill can be completed and how it might be used.

- Use scaffolding, which allows for a skill to be taught through small steps. Reach a small objective and build upon each one to reach a selected skill. Be aware of each student's learning style, particularly as it relates to cultural background. Some students from cultures with strong oral traditions might prefer to have an oral description and be talked through each step. Others might want written steps, and many will want concurrent demonstrations as they move through the steps. The teacher must be able to integrate effective instructional strategies with cultural and learning preferences.

Skill 11.06 Demonstrate understanding of the development and use of a task analysis

See Skill 3.01 for the definition of task analysis and an example of a task analysis of a common household functional skill. See Skills 7.05 and 11.03 for the use of a task analysis in designing instruction for community and job skills.

The breakdown of functional and job skills into small sequential steps (task analysis) is an important component of both instructional design and assessment for functional life skills. Previous skills provided examples of task analysis for instructional practice, but task analysis can also be used to plan assessment and as a learning strategy for students themselves.

A teacher can use a set of behavioral specifications that are the result of the task analysis to prepare rubrics and assessments that will measure the student's progress toward functional life objectives. Such assessments are criterion measurements, and if the task analysis identified which skills will be needed to perform a task successfully, then the criterion measurements can identify whether the student possesses the necessary skills or knowledge for that task.

The level of performance that is acceptable is the "criterion level."

Criterion measurements must be developed along certain guidelines if they are to accurately measure a task and its sub-skills. Johnson and Morasky (1977) give the following guidelines for establishing criterion measurement:

1. Criterion measurement must directly evaluate a student's ability to perform a task.
2. Criterion measurements should cover the range of possible situations in order to be considered an adequate measure.
3. Criterion measurements should measure whether or not a student can perform the task without additional or outside assistance. They should not give any information that the student is expected to possess.
4. All responses in the criterion measurement should be relevant to the task being measured.

Behavioral objectives offer descriptive statements defining the task that the student will perform. They state the conditions under which the task will occur and show the criterion measurement required for mastery. For the instruction to be meaningful, there must be a precise correspondence between the capabilities determined in a criterion measurement and the behavioral demands of the objective.

Teaching Students to Use Task Analyses

Learning to apply a task analysis to personal goals can be a very useful functional life skill in itself. Students can be taught to break down their own classroom tasks into small, manageable steps and self-monitor (see Skill 11.04) to keep track of their progress toward the objective. This can be done with both classroom assignments and homework assignments.

Students can initially be given a checklist of steps to follow to complete a task or a rubric of criteria to evaluate, and can record their progress on their own. Next they might be given a Cloze-style blank template for recording steps or criteria on their own (e.g. "My first step will be ___, then, I will ___") and they can gradually learn to break down tasks on their own and evaluate their own progress. This skill can be used throughout adulthood and will contribute to increased independence and self-advocacy (see Skills 6.05 and 11.04)

Skill 11.07 **Demonstrating knowledge of instructional techniques and strategies that promote successful transitions (e.g., from home to school; preschool to grade school; classroom to classroom; school to school; school to adult life roles, employment, or post-secondary education or training)**

Please refer to Skill 5.06 for National Early Childhood Transition Center (NECTC) guidelines for transitions prior to secondary school. See Skill 6.01 for discussion of techniques to manage classroom and class-to-class transitions.

SCHOOL TO ADULT LIFE ROLES

IDEA 2004 requires those receiving special education services to have transition plans. Planning for transition into the world after school requires the input of the student, parents, teacher, and others involved in delivering services. Planning should be based on the student's individual strengths, preferences, and interests. Indeed, recent changes to the requirements for IEP transition planning require student voice in all transition plans. Goals and objectives must reflect the student's priorities and interests.

Ideally, such post-school student objectives should be realistic. This is more likely to be the case if the student's educational experiences have included many of the techniques for fostering student independence and self-advocacy, such as student self-recording and self-instruction described in earlier skills (e.g., Skills 6.05, 7.05, 11.03, and 11.04). The acquisition of these skills produces a student who can be a productive member of the transition planning team. If the student's goals are too unrealistic, however, some guidance toward "alternatives" for the future should be provided.

Transition planning must look into providing instruction and training in vocational programming whenever possible and where related services outside the school environment can be tied into making a student's transition successful. It is also possible for transition planning to provide job opportunities that could lead beyond the school years, and possibly to the ability to achieve what could be considered "normal" independence.

New York state school districts often refer students finishing their school careers to the state's established departments for Vocational and Educational Services for Individuals with Disabilities (VESID), which will coordinate the delivery of additionally needed services beyond the secondary level of education. This department offers continued support in college environments and training schools; they also assist those with disabilities in finding jobs. (See Skill 15.07 for more on VESID.)

Other community resources that can assist with the transition to the "real world" environment to provide continuity as the emerging adult leaves the protective school environment should be pointed out to both the student and his or her parent(s).

SPECIFIC TRANSITION SERVICES

Transition services will be different for each student and should be explicitly outlined in the IEP. Transition services must take into account the student's interests and preferences. Evaluation of career interests, aptitudes, skills, and training should be considered. Specific transition activities that must be addressed, unless the CSE team finds it unnecessary, include: (a) instruction, (b) community experiences, and (c) the development of objectives related to employment and other post-school areas.

Instruction

The instruction part of the transition plan deals with school instruction. Students should have a portfolio completed upon graduation. They should research and plan for further education and/or training after high school. Goals and objectives created for this transition domain depend on the nature and severity of the student's disability, the student's interests in further education, plans made for accommodations needed in future education and training, and identification of post-secondary institutions that offer the requested training or education.

Community Experiences

This part of the transition plan investigates how the student utilizes community resources. These resources include places for recreation, transportation services, agencies, and advocacy services. It is essential for students to deal with the following areas:

- Recreation and leisure (e.g., movies, YMCA, religious activities)
- Personal and social skills (e.g., calling friends, religious groups, going out to eat)
- Mobility and transportation (e.g., passing a driver's license test or utilizing Dial-A-Ride)
- Agency access (e.g., utilizing a phone book and making calls)
- System advocacy (e.g., having a list of advocacy groups to contact)
- Citizenship and legal issues (e.g., registering to vote)

Development of Employment

This segment of the transition plan investigates becoming employed. Students should complete a career interest inventory. They should have chances to investigate different careers. Many work skill activities can take place within the classroom, home, and community. Refer to Skills 7.05 and 11.03 for information about community-referenced and community-based instruction.

Daily Living Skills

This segment of the transition plan is also important. Living away from home can be an enormous undertaking for people with disabilities. Numerous skills are needed to live and function as an adult. In order to live as independently as possible, a person should have an income, know how to cook, clean, shop, pay bills, get to a job, and have a social life. Some living situations might entail independent living, shared living with a roommate, or supported living in a group home. Areas that might need to be considered include: personal and social skills; living options; income and finances; medical needs; and community resources and transportation.

Please refer to Skills 15.06 and 15.07 for more information.

COMPETENCY 0012   UNDERSTAND STRATEGIES AND TECHNIQUES USED TO IMPROVE THE SOCIAL COMPETENCE OF STUDENTS WITH DISABILITIES

Skill 12.01   Identify social skills needed for various educational and functional living environments, as well as for personal and social behavior in various settings

Early in the debate about inclusion, Salend and Lutz (1984) summarized the social skills that general and special education teachers considered essential for successful inclusion. Many of these skills showed up on a more recent review (Mastropieri and Scruggs, 2000) of research on social skills needed both in school inclusion settings and in the movement to community and job settings after school. The skills on these lists can be sorted into several broad categories.

Interacting Positively with Others

Skills in this category include:

Conversational Skills such as starting a conversation, joining a conversation without interrupting, give and take in conversation, ending conversation politely, listening skills, use of appropriate tone and loudness of voice, eye contact and appropriate distance, telling the truth, and appropriate language

"Play" and Interaction Skills such as sharing, taking turns, inviting and including others, encouraging and praising others, and respecting others' viewpoints

Problem Solving and Coping Skills Include:

Assertiveness Skills such as asking for clarifications; making, negotiating, and denying requests; exhibiting politeness; attempting a task before asking for help or giving up; and asking for help when necessary

Self-regulating Skills such as staying calm, listing possible solutions, handling name calling and teasing, accepting correction and taking responsibility for one's actions, giving positive feedback to oneself, and expressing feelings in words

Work- and Class-Related Skills Include:

Task-Related Skills such as on-task behavior, attention to task, completion of task, following directions, doing your best, obeying rules, and starting on time

Job-Related Skills such as being prepared (dress, paperwork), listening skills, and thinking before answering interview questions

Skill 12.02   Demonstrate knowledge of effective social skills instruction and reinforcement by educators and other professionals across a variety of educational settings

Social skills and adaptive behaviors can be learned in several ways. Most children learn through **Incidental Learning or Teaching**. That is, they learn through everyday experiences, observing those around them, and seeing the consequences of their own and others' behavior. Children with disabilities, such as Autism Spectrum Disorders, ADHD, etc., might not learn appropriate social skills in this manner. Some children can learn through **Peer tutoring** or **Peer Interaction,** where the student is paired on a daily basis with a socially competent peer who serves as a model. The student is instructed to watch and imitate the model.

However, many students with disabilities will need **Direct Skills Instruction** in order to learn appropriate social skills and adaptive behaviors. Direct skills instruction involves a systematic curriculum with objectives, exercises, and assessments that must be implemented by a teacher or counselor.

SELECTING SOCIAL SKILLS CURRICULA AND TECHNIQUES

There are many direct skills instruction curricula available. The choice of curriculum will, of course, depend on the age, setting, and specific skills needed, and the specific disabilities in the student population. Whatever curriculum is chosen, however, it should be a **Validated Social Skills Curriculum**, that is, one that has been research-tested for effectiveness. Such curricula will have certain key features. Typically, such a curriculum will include the following general topics or areas of behavior:

- Interpersonal or peer relationships
- Conflict management
- Self awareness of feelings and words to describe feelings
- Coping strategies for strong feelings
- Classroom behavior expectations
- Conversational rules of give and take
- Problem solving strategies for when things go wrong
- Interpretation of body language and nonverbal cues
- Community or group dynamics and behavior
- Older students may also need job related social skills

Methods used should include these research-based techniques:

- Modeling of appropriate behaviors by both teachers and age-appropriate models
- Explicit instruction in Why, With Whom, Where, When, and How the behavior being taught should be used

- Role playing and lifelike practice
- Extensive and repeated practice
- Explicit feedback and reinforcement
- Practice in multiple and realistic settings to encourage generalization and transfer
- Cooperative group activities

PRAGMATICS AND NONVERBAL COMMUNICATION

As discussed in Skill 1.04, pragmatics refers to the contextual and nonverbal aspects of communication skills. Children with disabilities might perceive facial expressions and gestures differently from their non-disabled peers. There are several kinds of activities to use in developing a child's pragmatic understanding of and sensitivity to other people. Examples of these activities include:

- Offer an assortment of facial pictures to the child and ask the child to identify or classify the faces according to the emotion that appears in the picture. Allow the child to compare his or her reactions to those of the other students. This works well as a cooperative task. The happy face "emoticons" available online and in word processing programs are excellent resources for this sort of activity.
- Compare common gestures through a mixture of acting and discussion. For example, demonstrate a gesture and ask for its meaning, or play a game in which each student performs a gesture while others explain what it means.
- Shows and movies are available in which famous people and cartoon characters utilize gestures. Children can be asked what a particular gesture means.
- Tape recording with playback can be used to present social sounds. Again, play a game wherein the activity focuses the student's attention on one narrow issue—in this case, the sound and its precise social meaning.
- Pairs of students can be formed for exercises in reading each other's gestures and nonverbal communications.

SOCIAL SITUATIONS

Inherent differences in appearances and motions among children with disabilities cause some of them to develop behavior problems in social situations. It is necessary to remediate this situation in order to provide as normal a life and adulthood as possible.

Below are some activities that strengthen a child's skills in social situations.

- Anticipate the consequences of social actions. Have the students act out roles, tell stories, and discuss the consequences that flow from their actions.

- Gain appropriate independence. Students can be given exercises in going places alone. For the very young, and for those with development issues, this might consist of finding a location within the room. Go on a field trip into the city. Allow older students to make purchases on their own. Using play money in the classroom for younger children could also be beneficial.
- Make ethical and/or moral judgments. Read an unfinished story and ask the student to finish it at the point where a judgment is to be made. This requires an independent critique of the choices made by the characters in the story.
- Plan and execute: Children with disabilities can be allowed to plan an outing, a game, a party, or an exercise.

Social Skills "Autopsies"

One strategy for helping students understand the consequences of their own social actions and plan strategies for future social actions is the *Social Skills Autopsy* (Lavoie, 2005). This is an analysis carried out by student and teacher (or even a cooperative group) following either a failed social interaction or problem OR a particularly successful social interaction. It is meant to be an upbeat, positive action, and can even be infused with some humor based on the autopsy metaphor (e.g., "Well, that game's over and dead—let's cut it up and find out what happened").

It is important to note that the autopsy is *not* intended as punishment or criticism. Children with learning disabilities usually learn best *in the natural setting,* and this technique is designed to address the issue *right when it happens* in the context in which the child will learn best. In a social autopsy, the goal is to talk together in order to:

- Determine the cause or causes of the social success or failure (someone might make a written list or dictate a list into a recorder like TV coroners, etc.)
- Analyze the effects (e.g., the extent of the damage or the positive influence)
- Plan for the future (e.g., a list of things NOT to do or to be sure to do next time)

Skill 12.03 Demonstrate familiarity with instructional techniques that promote the student's self-awareness, self-control, self-reliance, self-esteem, and personal empowerment

Instructional techniques for these skills have been covered in earlier skill sections. For details on fostering self-advocacy and independence, refer to Skills 6.05 and 11.04. Skill 11.04 also addresses techniques for learning to self-monitor and develop self-awareness and control.

SELF-CONCEPT AND SELF-ESTEEM

Self-concept can be defined as the collective attitudes or feelings that one holds about oneself. Positive self-esteem comes from positive attitudes and a feeling of empowerment and competency. Children with disabilities perceive, early in life, that they are deficient in skills that seem easier for their peers without disabilities. They also receive expressions of surprise or even disgust from both adults and children in response to their differing appearance and actions, again resulting in damage to the self-concept. For these reasons, the special education teacher will want to direct special and continuing effort to bettering each child's own perception of him or herself.

- The poor self-concept of a child with disabilities can cause that student, at times, to act out over inappropriate things. The teacher can ignore this behavior, thereby reducing the amount of negative conditioning in the child's life, unless the behavior is dangerous to others or too distracting to the total group. Furthermore, the teacher can praise this child, quickly and frequently, for the correct responses he or she makes, remembering that these responses might require special effort on the student's part. Further correction, when needed, can be done tactfully and in private.

- The teacher should pull the child whose poor self-concept manifests itself in withdrawn behavior gently into as many social situations as possible. This child must be encouraged to share experiences with the class, to serve as teacher helper for projects, and to be part of small groups for tasks. Again, praise for performing these group and public acts is most effective if done immediately.

- The teacher can plan in advance to structure the classroom experiences so that aversive situations will be avoided. Thus, settings that stimulate the aggressive child to act out can be redesigned, and situations that stimulate group participation can be set up in advance for the child who acts in a withdrawn manner.

- Positive self-esteem comes from the experiences of overcoming obstacles and of successfully meeting goals. Therefore, realistic goal setting and structuring the environment to make success more likely are good ways to help bolster self-esteem.

- Frequent, positive, and immediate are the best terms to describe the teacher feedback required by children with disabilities. Praise for very small correct acts should be given immediately and repeated when each correct act is repeated. However, praise should be honest and very specific, clearly stating what the child has done that is worthy of praise. Criticism or outright scolding should be done, whenever possible, in private. When it must be done, the teacher should first revisit the total day's interactions with that student to ensure that the number and qualitative content of verbal stimuli is heavily on the positive side.

- The teacher must have a strategy for use with the child who persists in negative behavior outbursts. One system is to intervene immediately and break the situation down into three components. First, the teacher requires the child to identify the worst possible outcome from the situation—the thing that he or she fears the most. To do this task, the child must be required to state the situation in the most factual way he or she can. Second, the student should state what would really happen if this worst possible outcome happened and evaluate the likelihood of it happening. Third, the student must state an action or attitude that can be adopted after examining the consequences in a new light. This process has been termed *rational emotive therapy*.

Skill 12.04 Recognizing effective strategies across a range of educational settings for preparing students to live harmoniously and productively in a diverse society

Effective teaching and learning for students begins with teachers who can demonstrate sensitivity for diversity in teaching and relationships within school communities. Teachers must be responsive to including culturally appropriate and diverse resources in their curriculum and instructional practices. It should be remembered that cultural diversity, though critically important, is only one form of diversity. Religion (or lack of it), gender, family structure, socioeconomic status, lifestyle, learning styles, and the presence of disabilities themselves are also aspects of diversity that must be incorporated into instruction.

Exposing students to sensitive room decorations and posters that show positive and inclusive messages is one way to demonstrate appreciation for diversity. Teachers should also continuously make cultural connections that are relevant and empowering for all students, including academic and behavioral expectations. Cultural sensitivity must be communicated beyond the classroom with parents and community members to establish and maintain relationships.

Other artifacts that could reflect teacher/student sensitivity to diversity might consist of the following:

- Student portfolios reflecting diverse perspectives
- Journals and reflections from field trips or guest speakers from diverse cultural backgrounds
- Printed materials and wall displays from multicultural perspectives
- Parent/guardian letters in a variety of languages reflecting cultural diversity
- Projects that include cultural history and diverse inclusions
- Disaggregated student data reflecting cultural groups
- Classroom climate of professionalism that fosters diversity and cultural inclusion

By changing the thinking patterns of students to become more culturally inclusive in the 21st century, teachers are addressing the globalization of our world.

Skill 12.05 Demonstrating knowledge of strategies for integrating social skills across curricula

Earlier skill sections addressed the topic of collaboration in detail. Skills 6.02, 6.03, 6.06, 6.08 will be particularly helpful in addressing this issue.

Whatever approach to social skills instruction is chosen for a particular student, it is essential that all the teachers, professionals and other staff involved with the child be "on board" with the approach so methods can be consistently applied across all settings. If a Direct Skills Instruction approach is being used, all those who work with the student should be made aware of the current lesson and any decisions about application. If the Social Autopsy approach is used as recommended, it will be necessary for everyone involved with the student to know how to use it appropriately and be committed to doing so. Even parents can be enlisted to be sure home methods are consistent with school methods.

In addition, efforts at improving the student's self-esteem should be consistent across all settings, and this will require that professionals meet and consult (see the above-mentioned skills) to ensure this consistency. Depending upon the particular student's needs, there are several methods that might improve this collaboration:

- A Communication Notebook or Checklist can be passed from teacher to teacher, class to class, from class to specialist, home to parents, or to anyone involved with the student. It can contain brief guidelines or reminders of current goals and procedures (e.g., "watch for and reward on-task behavior or sharing," a list of that week's direct instruction social skills, "Use social autopsy"). This can help maintain consistency in instruction and reinforcement and improve generalization of skills. Teachers can add notes of significant events or suggestions so everyone stays informed.
- Periodic observations can be made using checklists modeled on those discussed in Skills 3.01 and 3.02. Depending upon the needs of the specific student, this might include frequency, duration or interval measures, or even a multiple baseline design. Such periodic observation would also allow evaluation of whether methods are being applied successfully across all settings and allow modification or even retraining (of student OR teachers) if necessary.

COMPETENCY 0013 UNDERSTAND THE DEVELOPMENT AND IMPLEMENTATION OF BEHAVIOR INTERVENTIONS

Skill 13.01 Demonstrating familiarity with a variety of effective behavior management techniques appropriate to the needs of students with disabilities, based on the individual's IEP

See Skill 6.01 for techniques appropriate for students with disabilities and Skill 13.07 for Functional Behavioral Assessments and formal Behavior Intervention Plans.

The specific behavior management techniques used will be as varied as the students and their IEPs. Teachers should be familiar with a number of approaches and the situations in which they are appropriate in order to use them selectively when particular student behaviors and situations occur. In many cases, a student's IEP will actually specify a particular approach.

LIFE-SPACE INTERVIEW (REDI & WINEMAN, 1952)

The life-space interview is a here-and-now intervention built around the child's life experiences. Its purpose is to help the child develop a conscious awareness of distorted perceptions, particularly perceptions affecting how the child reacts to the behaviors and pressures of other persons. It is sometimes referred to as "emotional first aide."

Example

Jack, a 10-year-old fifth grader enrolled in Mr. Bird's resource room, is creating difficulties for himself, his classmates, and his teachers. His unacceptable social behaviors have caused him to be ignored, rejected, or used as a scapegoat by other students.

Essentially, Jack believes he is unacceptable to his peers and feels that others are making fun of him or rejecting him, even when they are being friendly. His reaction to this feeling is to try to isolate himself by placing his backpack over his head, walking down the hallways sideways with his face to the wall, and so on.

Mr. Bird and other staff decide to use a life-space interview, and each time Jack engaged in the behavior, he was immediately removed by a supportive adult, who discussed the incident with Jack. These actions allowed Jack to plan a more acceptable response. Jack returned to the setting in which the behavior occurred and continued his daily schedule.

Over time, and after many life-space interviews, Jack increased his capacity to differentiate between social acceptance and rejection.

Life Interview Guidelines:

- Be polite to the student and do not begin the interview until the student has control of his or her emotions.
- Sit, kneel, or stand to establish eye contact. Talk with, never at, the student.
- When unsure about the history of the incident, investigate. Do not conduct an interview on the basis of second- or third-hand information or rumors.
- Ask questions to obtain a grasp of the incident but do not probe areas of unconscious motivation; limit the use of "why?"
- Listen to the individual and try to comprehend his or her perception of the incident.
- Encourage the student to ask questions and respond politely.
- Try to reduce any shame or guilt the student might be feeling.
- Facilitate the student's efforts to communicate what he or she wishes to say.
- Work carefully and patiently with the individual to develop a mutually acceptable plan of action for the future.

REALITY THERAPY

In reality therapy, the therapist or teacher confronts students about whether their present behavior is helping them or hurting them. Confrontational questions assist the individual in taking responsibility for his or her behavior. Responsibility is seen as the ability to fulfill one's personal needs in a manner that does not deprive other individuals of their ability to fulfill their needs.

The teacher acts as a facilitator to help the student develop a plan to resolve troublesome behavior. The student generally feels more responsible for enacting the plan if it is written and signed.

Example

Kyle, a tenth-grade student, had superior academic potential but was flunking several subjects. Mr. Scott, Kyle's favorite teacher, decided to use the reality therapy approach with Kyle because he and Kyle were friends; he cared about Kyle, and he knew Kyle knew that.

In their first session, Mr. Scott confronted Kyle with questions like, "What are you doing?"; "Is it helping you?"; "If not, what else could you do to help yourself?" Mr. Scott found that Kyle would not work in any class if he did not like the teacher. If he felt the teacher was too demanding, unfriendly, etc., he just gave up and refused to study.

Once Kyle recognized that his behavior was harmful to himself, he and Mr. Scott developed a plan. During the next few months, they met regularly to monitor

Kyle's progress and to write and revise the plan as needed. Kyle learned to accept responsibility for his behavior. His grades improved dramatically.

Reality Interview Guidelines:

- Be personal. Demonstrate that a teacher can be a friend who cares about the student. It is helpful if this relationship already exists.
- Focus the therapeutic process on present behavior, not past behavior. Accept expressed feelings, but, again, do not probe into unconscious motivators. *Confront* by asking what, how, and who (not why) questions.
- Do not preach, moralize, or make judgments about the behavior.
- Help the student make a practical plan to increase responsible behavior.
- Encourage the student to make a commitment to the plan.
- Do not accept excuses for irresponsible behavior. When a plan fails or cannot be implemented, develop another.
- Do not punish the student for irresponsible behavior. Try to allow the student to realize the logical consequences of the behavior unless the consequences are unreasonably harmful.

TRANSACTIONAL ANALYSIS

Transactional analysis is considered a rational approach to understanding human behavior. It is based on the assumption that individuals can learn to have trust in themselves, think for themselves, make their own decisions, and express personal feelings. As such, this approach can be useful in improving self-advocacy and independence. This approach assumes that each person has a number of facets or components to their personality and that day-to-day experience serve as stimuli that evoke memories of past situations and elicit behavior based on emotional reactions to those past events.

Although there are many types of transactions, there are three major ones:

1. Complementary transactions are predictable reactions received from a person in response to an act. For example, a common response of a student to being given an assignment might be that the child grumbles a little but does it.
2. Cross transactions occur when someone gets an unpredictable response from another individual. For example, an unexpected response from a student who usually does his work might be, "No way, I won't do it. It's boring."
3. Ulterior transactions have a hidden message, so what is stated is not the real message being sent. For example, a student says, "This is boring! My stomach hurts. I need a drink. When is school over?" Instead of saying, "I don't get this and I need help." the student complains about all sorts of other things.

Teachers can use transactional analysis to help "decode" the student's comments and behavior and help the student figure out what he or she really feels and needs.

ROLE-PLAYING AND PSYCHODRAMA

Psychodrama and role-paying, originally developed for therapeutic purposes, can help a student clarify feelings and understand reality in three ways.

1. It can focus on real occurrences. An incident can be reenacted and the participants told to attend to the feelings that are aroused, or an incident can be reenacted with the participants changing roles and attending to the feelings of the aroused by these new roles. A student might be directed to deliver a soliloquy (monologue) to recreate an emotionally loaded event. Emphasis here is on expressing feelings that were hidden or held back when the event first occurred.
2. It can focus on significant others. The student can portray a significant person in his or her life about whom a great amount of conflict is felt.
3. It can focus on processes and feelings occurring in new situations. Directions for this type of role-playing may be very specific, with the students provided with special characters and actions, or directions can be vague, allowing students to form their own characters.

Role-playing and psychodrama techniques have been incorporated into several effective education programs concerned specifically with clarification of values and standards.

Example

George, a 13-year-old eighth grader, was shorter than the other children in his grade and his classmates were constantly making fun of his size, calling him "runt," "shorty," "midget," and "dwarf." Because he was a sensitive person, he began to withdraw. His teacher was very concerned about George's mental wellbeing and his classmates' lack of consideration. She believed that role-playing might be a method of helping the whole class, including George, gain insight into their behavior.

As the students began to empathize with the feelings of the characters they were role-playing, George became more accepted and less of a target of their hurtful behavior. George began playing with the others more readily during free time.

CONTINGENCY MANAGEMENT (BEHAVIOR MODIFICATION) IN THE CLASSROOM

The term contingency management refers to the planned, systematic relationship established between a behavior and a consequence. This is an approach that teachers use to modify behaviors by managing the consequences of those behaviors. Contingency management incorporates the systematic use of reinforcement and punishment to develop, maintain, or change behavior. The following guidelines can be used in developing a contingency management plan:

1. Decide what to measure: A desired target behavior is specified and defined.
2. Select a measurement strategy: The behavior must be observable and measurable, as in frequency and duration (see Skill 3.01).
3. Establish a baseline: The level of the behavior prior to implementing a treatment plan or an intervention must be established.
4. Design a contingency plan: Reinforcers or punishers are selected that correspond with behavioral consequences.
5. Implement the contingency plan: Teachers collect data, provide reinforcement or punishment for the behavioral occurrences in accordance with the schedule selected for use, and record behavioral measurements on a graph.
6. Evaluate the program: Teachers modify the contingency management plan as needed. Modifications can be achieved by: (1) a reversal to baseline to determine the effects of treatment on behavior, (2) changing the reinforcer or punisher if needed, or (3) implementing a new treatment.

Contingency management depends upon the skillful use of reinforcement and an understanding of motivation. Motivation and reinforcement can be intrinsic or extrinsic. *Intrinsic* reinforcement comes from within the individual, internal satisfaction of curiosity, a desire to succeed, feeling of pride or accomplishment, etc. *Extrinsic* reinforcement comes from outside and is basically a reward given to the individual by someone else.

When teachers use reinforcement to help shape a student's behavior, they are generally using some type of extrinsic reinforcer (i.e., the teacher supplies the reward). There are several types of extrinsic reinforcers that the teacher might use, including:

- Primary or edible reinforcers such as snacks
- Physical reinforcers, that is, forms of appropriate positive contact such as a "high five" slap or pat on the shoulder
- Tangible reinforcers such as those used in a token economy: stars, stickers, class "money" that can be traded for small prizes or privileges

- Social reinforcers such as smiles, claps, situation-specific praise and friendly comments

Reinforcement Schedules

Whatever form of reinforcement is used, it can be helpful to understand the effects of various reinforcement schedules, because each affects learned behavior differently.

- **Continuous Reinforcement** is reinforcement given every single time the desired behavior occurs. It is most useful for building and establishing new behavior patterns. For example, if you are trying to teach a student to wait his turn patiently without barging in, during the initial stage of this process you would reward him every time he waits patiently.
- **Partial Reinforcement** is reinforcement given only some of the time, not every time the behavior occurs. It is usually used *after* the behavior is occurring fairly regularly in order to wean the student off continuous reinforcement and make the behavior less resistant to extinction. There are several types of partial reinforcement schedules and the teacher should choose the one that suits the student, the student's stage of learning, and the particular behavior and type of reinforcer.

A contingency management plan can be very useful in the classroom setting. In most classrooms, teachers specify what behaviors are expected and the contingencies for performing those behaviors. Contingencies are stated in the form of "If…then…" statements. Contingency management can take the form of various treatment techniques, including token economies, contingency contracting, and precision teaching.

Students can be involved in the process of designing, implementing, and evaluating a contingency management plan. They can decide on behaviors that are in need of modification, select their reinforcers, assist in data collection, record the data on graphs, and evaluate the effectiveness of the contingency or treatment plan. The ultimate goal of allowing students to participate in contingency management is to encourage them to use the procedures they have been taught to manage their own behaviors. As with self-recording, the transition from teacher-managed to student-managed programs must be gradual, and students should be explicitly taught how to use self-reinforcement or self-punishment.

BACKWARD CHAINING AND APPLICABLE SITUATIONS

Behavioral chaining is a procedure in which individual responses are reinforced for occurring in sequence to form a complex behavior. Each link is subsequently paired with its preceding one; thus, each link serves as a conditioned reinforcer for the link immediately preceding it. Behavior chains can be acquired by having each step in the chain verbally prompted or demonstrated. The prompts can then be faded and the links combined, with reinforcement occurring after the last link has been performed.

In backward chaining, the components of the chain are determined by a form of task analysis that reverses the order of the steps like sub-skills necessary to successfully complete the target task. The teacher models the task in correct order, and then each sub-skill is modeled in reverse order from beginning to end. The student practices the modeled sub-skills, usually last step first, and upon mastery of it, goes back to the correct order until the task is completed. In this way, the final link or target behavior is consistently reinforced and preceding links are built upon one at a time.

An example of backward chaining would be teaching a child to undress himself. The child is given the instruction, "Jimmy, take your jacket off," and his jacket is unzipped and lifted off the shoulders and down the arms until only the cuffs remain on Jimmy's wrists. If he does not pull the jacket the rest of the way off, he is physically guided to do so. He is given a reinforcer following removal of the garment. During the next session, the procedure is repeated, but the sleeve is left on his arms. In subsequent sessions, both arms are left in the sleeves, and then the jacket is left zipped. The instruction, "Jimmy, take your jacket off," is always presented, and a reinforcer is given only when the task is completed. The removal of each garment is taught in this manner and the component steps are combined until the instruction has acquired stimulus.

Backward chaining can be used to teach other self-help skills such as toileting, grooming, and eating. Many academic and pre-academic readiness skills can be effectively taught using this procedure as well. Steps leading up to the final one are provided, with prompting occurring on the last step, and reinforcements delivered following the behavior. Each step in the program is prompted until the student can perform the entire sequence by him or herself. The backward chaining procedure may be of greatest assistance when a student experiences limited receptive abilities or imitative behavior.

Skill 13.02   Demonstrating an understanding of effective collaboration among teachers and other professionals to identify appropriate modifications to the learning environment (i.e., schedule and physical arrangement) to manage inappropriate behaviors

Please refer to Skills 6.02, 6.03, and 6.06 for detailed discussion of methods of collaboration.

Teachers of exceptional students are expected to manage many roles and responsibilities, not only concerning their students, but also with respect to students' caregivers and other educational, medical, therapeutic, and administrative professionals. Because the needs of exceptional students are by definition multidisciplinary, a teacher of exceptional children often serves as the hub of a many-spoked wheel while communicating, consulting, and collaborating with the various stakeholders in a child's educational life. Managing these relationships effectively can be a challenge, but it is central to successful work in exceptional education.

Each professional should share information from his or her area of expertise with the team. For example, the child's previous teacher might be able to offer some suggestions about modifications that were previously successful, or the speech pathologist might have noticed an issue with background noise that would be relevant. The team should communicate often to verify the success or failure of the modifications and to adjust or add modifications as needed.

SCHEDULING

As noted in Skill 6.02, efficient scheduling is a critical prerequisite for successful delivery of services to students with disabilities. Administrators must work closely with all those involved in delivery of services to maximize time on task, instructional time, and practicality. Scheduling issues can be very complex because most providers are working with multiple students and all their individual schedules must be coordinated. Not only is it important to ensure the child is receiving the necessary classes and extra assistance, but the time of the day each subject is being taught is extremely important as well. For example, if the student is more alert and focused in the afternoon, he or she might need to take the weakest academic courses in the afternoon. Also, the nurse might know that the child takes medication after lunch that makes him or her drowsy or not as alert; therefore, that child might need to take the weakest academic courses in the morning.

PHYSICAL ARRANGEMENTS

Physical arrangement is another important area to discuss with other professionals. The current special education teacher and any previous teacher can offer suggestions based on their prior knowledge of the child. For example, the child might function better in the front of the class or away from the windows. A physical therapist might suggest that the child be seated near the door. Therefore, it is essential that the team collaborate to discuss potential modifications of the child's learning environment. Many such accommodations will be recorded in the child's IEP, but it is necessary to monitor and ensure consistent application in all settings.

One aspect of the physical arrangement is the juxtaposition of service locations. When setting up the child's schedule, it is important to take into consideration any movement from area to area that the child must make on a regular basis. For example, a child in an inclusion third grade room might still need to move to another location for speech or OT services and the route to those services, as well as the timing (will the fifth graders be crowding the hall on their way to lunch at that time? etc.), will need coordination.

Skill 13.03 Understanding the importance of ongoing communication about behavior interventions among the student, the student's teachers, and the student's parents/guardians

Please refer to Skill 13.07 for information on Behavior Intervention Plans (BIP).

Whether interventions are part of a formal BIP (Skill 13.07), prereferral efforts (Skill 4.01), or implementation of IEP requirements, it is important that the plan be put into place with input from all the people who work with the student, including the student, parents, teachers, support teachers, and other service providers. In this way, all parties involved can agree on expectations as well as rewards or consequences.

It is essential that application of the provisions of the intervention plan be consistent across all settings. For example, if a reward or punishment is established in the general education classroom, then it must be reinforced in other classrooms as well as the home setting. This allows the student to see consistency, which will make the contingencies more effective.

It is important that all parties ensure ongoing communication on a weekly, if not daily, basis to ensure that proper feedback and follow-up is taking place. The behavior intervention plan should define behaviors and consequences and it should be adaptable to different places, such as the classroom, playground, after-school program, daycare, etc. In order to maintain consistency, proper communication must occur on an ongoing basis. The communication notebook or checklist described in Skill 12.05 can be a useful tool for this purpose.

Skill 13.04 Recognizing that teacher attitudes and behaviors positively or negatively influence the behavior of students with disabilities

The attitude of the teacher can have either a positive or a negative impact on student performance. A teacher's expectations of the student's potential performance have been shown to have a powerful effect on a child's ultimate success. In addition, attitudes will shape the teacher's behavior toward the student, and this will, in turn, affect student behavior. For example, some of the behavior management techniques (discussed in Skill 13.01) depend heavily upon the teacher's past attitude toward the student and the establishment of a positive relationship between student and teacher.

Negative teacher attitudes toward students with disabilities are particularly detrimental to the handicapped students mainstreamed in general education classrooms. This is related to the phenomenon known as the self-fulfilling prophecy. The term "self-fulfilling prophecy" in the educational context refers to the documented phenomenon in which a teacher's expectations about a student strongly influence both the teacher's perceptions of the student and the student's self-image and behavior.

Teachers are more likely to notice behaviors that reinforce their expectations, so when evaluating a student's behavior they are more likely to report and record those behaviors that fit their expectations. Therefore, if the teacher expects the student to fail, the student is more likely to be *judged* to have failed, regardless of the student's objective behaviors, while that same student might be *judged* to have succeeded if the teacher expected him to succeed, because the teacher in each case is more likely to see and record behaviors that fit expectations.

In addition, the teacher's expectations can have a powerful effect on the student's self-image and confidence about success or failure. A student who feels the teacher's high expectations both for behavioral standards and for the student's ability to meet them will typically make more of an effort and be less likely to give up than a student who feels that the teacher already considers him a failure. This effort and confidence (or lack of) contributes to a self-fulfilling prophecy effect in the classroom.

Researchers in psychology and education have investigated this occurrence and discovered that many people are sensitive to verbal and nonverbal cues from others regarding how they expect to be treated. As a result, they may consciously and unconsciously change their behavior and attitudes to conform to another person's expectations. Depending on the expectation, this can be either advantageous or detrimental.

The teacher's attitude toward a student can be shaped by a number of variables, including race, ethnicity, disability, behavior, appearance, social class, and past experience with other students from similar groups. All of these variables can impact the teacher's attitude toward the student and how well the student will achieve academically. The teacher has a responsibility to not allow personal negative attitudes toward a student to impact interactions with the student. If the teacher is able to communicate to all students that they have great potential, and is optimistic regarding this, then each student should excel in some aspect of his or her educational endeavor.

It can be difficult for teachers to maintain a positive attitude at all times with all students, but it is important to be encouraging. Every student has the potential to be successful in school. Communication with other professionals and service providers can often help a teacher maintain a positive attitude toward a particular child. It can be very helpful to hear other teachers describe positive attributes noticed in other settings. For example, a classroom teacher who is constantly annoyed by an active, talkative child's behavior during silent desk work might benefit from hearing the physical education teacher describe how this child helps other students in the gym, constantly praising and encouraging them, and telling them how well they are doing. Seeing the positive aspects of all that talkative behavior can help the teacher maintain a better attitude toward the student in question.

Teachers should utilize their verbal communication skills to ensure that the things they communicate to students are said in the most positive manner possible. For example, instead of saying, "You talk too much," it would be more positive to state, "You have excellent verbal communication skills and are very sociable. Please use those skills for good purpose."

For teachers to rise above their prejudices and preset attitudes, it is important that teachers be given training and support services to enable them to deal with students who come from backgrounds the teacher has difficulty accepting or understanding. It is also essential that teachers *understand their own attitudes and prejudices*. See Skill 13.08 for methods to help teachers do this.

Skill 13.05   Identifying effective strategies for crisis prevention and intervention

According to the Center for Effective Collaboration and Practice (USDE 1998), most schools are safe; however, violence from surrounding communities has begun to make its way into schools. Fortunately, there are ways to intervene and prevent crisis in our schools.

EARLY WARNING SIGNS

First, administrators, teachers, families, students, support staff, and community leaders must be trained and/or informed on early warning signs that a student might be approaching a crisis breakdown. It should also be emphasized not to use these warning signs to inappropriately label or stigmatize individual students because they might display some of the following early warning signs.

- Social withdrawal
- Excessive feelings of isolation
- Excessive feelings of rejection
- Being a victim of violence
- Feelings of being picked on and persecuted
- Low school interest and poor academic performance
- Expression of violence in writings and drawings
- Uncontrolled anger
- Patterns of impulsive and chronic hitting, intimidating, and bullying
- History of discipline problems
- Past history of violent and aggressive behavior
- Intolerance for differences and prejudicial attitudes
- Drug use and alcohol use

- Affiliation with gangs
- Inappropriate access to, possession of, and use of firearms
- Serious threats of violence

These early signs mean that teachers should begin to intervene and try to assist the student to identify the problem and find a positive solution. Many of the methods discussed in Skill 13.01 can be used effectively in these situations.

IMMINENT WARNING SIGNS

Early warning signs and imminent warning signs differ in that imminent warning signs require an immediate response. Imminent warning signs indicate that a student is very close to behaving in a way that is potentially dangerous to self and/or others. Imminent warning signs can include:

- Serious physical fighting with peers or family members
- Severe destruction of property
- Severe rage for seemingly minor reasons
- Detailed threats of lethal violence
- Possession and/or use of firearms and other weapons
- Other self-injurious behaviors or threats of suicide

When imminent signs are seen, school staff must follow the school board policies in place. These typically include reporting the warning signs to a designated person or persons. It is the teacher's responsibility to be familiar with the school crisis intervention plans.

INTERVENTION AND PREVENTION PLANS

Every school system's plan might be different, but the plan should be derived from some of the following suggestions.

Share responsibility by establishing a partnership with the child, school, home, and community. Schools should collaborate with community agencies to coordinate the plan. They should also render services to students who might need assistance. The community involvement should include child and family service agencies, law enforcement and juvenile justice systems, mental health agencies, businesses, faith and ethnic leaders, and other community agencies.

An important aspect of this at the school level is the establishment of a culture of trust and support among students and staff. If students feel they can trust teachers and staff and feel comfortable discussing sensitive issues with them, they are more likely to provide information about themselves or others that will help staff recognize the early warning signs.

Inform parents and listen to them when early warning signs are observed. Effective and safe schools make persistent efforts to involve parents by informing them routinely about school discipline policies, procedures, and rules; informing them about their children's behavior (both good and bad); involving them in making decisions concerning school-wide disciplinary policies and procedures; and encouraging them to participate in prevention.

Maintain confidentiality and parents' rights to privacy. Parental involvement and consent is required before personally identifiable information is shared with other agencies except in the case of emergencies or suspicion of abuse.

Develop the capacity of staff, students, and families to intervene. Schools should provide the entire school community—teachers, students, parents, and support staff—with training and support in responding to imminent warning signs, preventing violence, and intervening safely and effectively. Interventions must be monitored by professionals who are trained in this area.

Support students in being responsible for their actions. Schools and members of the community should encourage students to see themselves as responsible for their actions and actively engage them in planning, implementing, and evaluating violence prevention initiatives.

Simplify staff requests for urgent assistance. Many school systems and community agencies have complex legalistic referral systems with timelines and waiting lists. This should be a simple process that does not prevent someone from requesting assistance.

Drill and Practice. Most schools are required to have drills and to provide practice to ensure that everyone is informed of proper procedures to follow if emergencies occur. In addition to violence caused by a student, the emergency can also be an intruder in the building, a bomb threat, a natural disaster, or a fire.

Skill 13.06   Demonstrating an understanding of ethical considerations, laws, rules and regulations, and procedural safeguards regarding behavior interventions, including the concept of least restrictive intervention consistent with the needs of the individuals with disabilities

In general, school personnel can discipline students with disabilities for the same amount of time and with the same disciplinary methods as students without disabilities so long as a change of placement does not occur and the behavior being disciplined is not a manifestation of their disability. According to IDEA, a student may be removed for up to ten school days for each separate act of misconduct without a change of placement occurring.

The IEP team and additional qualified staff must assess whether the behavior in question is part of the student's disability before a disabled student's placement can be modified as a result of disciplinary action (See Manifest Determination, below). However, the IEP team may decide that a modification of placement is required in order to provide a free, appropriate public education (FAPE) in the least restrictive environment.

IDEA 97 broadened the schools' rights to take a disciplinary action against children with disabilities when those students bring a weapon to school, knowingly possess or use illegal drugs, or sell or solicit the sale of a controlled substance while at school or school functions. Under such circumstances, school staff can place a student in an interim alternative educational setting without the consent of the parent for the same timeframe that a student without a disability could be placed, but not more than forty-five calendar days.

The district has to give all IEP services to a student with a disability who has been taken from his current placement for more than ten school days in the school year as a result of disciplinary action.

The Code of Federal Regulations also requires that a functional behavioral assessment (FBA, see Skill 13.07) must be done before a student can be removed from a placement. After the FBA is performed, the IEP team must convene to create a positive Behavior Intervention Plan (BIP, see Skill 13.07) that addresses the behavior in question and make sure that the plan is put into place. Information from the FBA is utilized to create meaningful interventions and plan for instruction in replacement behaviors. The IEP team must review the positive BIP and how it is implemented to decide if changes are needed to make the plan more effective.

MANIFEST DETERMINATION REVIEW

Under IDEA 97, suspensions and disciplinary consequences can result in an alternative educational placement. This possibility is to be weighed by a Manifest Determination Review, which is held by an IEP team within 10 days of the disciplinary action. Its purpose is to decide whether the misbehavior that resulted in disciplinary action was a *manifestation* of the disability itself. This review team has the sole responsibility of determining the answers to the following questions:

1. Does the child's disability impair his or her understanding of the impact and consequences of the behavior under disciplinary action?

2. Did the child's disability impair the ability of the child to control the behavior subject to discipline?

If the behavior is determined to be related to the student's disability, then the current placement remains in effect; the student's placement cannot be changed as a form of discipline. When no relationship between the inappropriate behavior and the student's disability is established, IDEA 97 uses FAPE to allow the relevant disciplinary procedures described above. Those measures applicable to children without disabilities may be applied to the child with a disability in the same manner in which they would be normally applied. Of course, as mentioned above, the IEP team may decide that intervention measures are not effective and that the child needs a different placement in order to succeed in what is, for that child, the least restrictive environment.

Skill 13.07 Demonstrating an understanding of how to develop, implement, and evaluate a Functional Behavior Assessment (FBA)

A functional behavior assessment (FBA) is a method of gathering information to assess why problem behaviors occur and what to do about them. An FBA can be useful any time a student's behavior interferes with the educational success of the student or others in the student's environment. The data from a functional behavioral assessment (FBA) can be used to create a positive behavioral intervention plan (BIP).

As mentioned in Skill 13.06, IDEA specifically calls for an FBA when a child with a disability has his or her present placement modified for disciplinary reasons. IDEA 2004 states that in such a case, the FBA must be written by a team and parental permission is required. However, if no change in placement is being considered and no new testing is required, the FBA does not require formal parental permission. IDEA does not elaborate on how an FBA should be specifically written, because the procedures can vary depending on the specific child. Even so, there are several specific elements that should be a part of any FBA. An FBA often leads to a behavioral intervention plan (BIP).

The first step is to identify the particular behavior that must be modified. If the child has numerous problem behaviors, it is necessary to prioritize and select one or two behaviors most in need of modification. The most typical order of procedures is as follows:

1. Identify and define the behaviors that need to be modified. Behavior should be precisely defined in concrete, objective terms that pinpoint a measurable act (e.g., "Tells teacher and students to 'shut up'" rather than "is rude"). Such definitions usually include onset, duration and intensity.

2. Identify antecedents and possible triggers for the behavior (i.e., find out when, where, with whom and during what activity the behaviors are most likely to occur). The team will ask these types of questions: What is unique about the surroundings where behaviors are and are not an issue? Could they be linked to how the child and teacher get along? Does the number of other students or the work a child is requested to do trigger the difficulty? Could the time of day or a child's frame of mind affect the behaviors? Was there a bus problem or an argument in the hallway? Are the behaviors likely to happen in a precise set of conditions or a specific location? What events seem to encourage the difficult behaviors?

3. Assemble data on the child's performance from as many resources as feasible. Collect baseline data. Develop a hypothesis about why difficult behaviors transpire; that is, *what does the child get out of the behaviors* (the function of the behaviors). Determine what happens *after* the behaviors. This is a critical step. Each behavior occurs for a reason; it accomplishes something for the child. Modifying it is much easier if one can identify its function for a particular child.

4. Single out other behaviors that can be taught that will fulfill the same purpose for the child. A child's IEP or BIP should concentrate on teaching skills. Sometimes, school discipline policies are not successful in rectifying problem behaviors because the child does not learn what the school staff intended through the use of punishments such as suspension. The child may learn instead that problem behaviors are useful in meeting a need, such as being noticed by peers. When this is true, it is difficult to defend punishment, by itself, as effective in changing problem behaviors. (See BIP below)

5. Modify any environmental factors that might contribute to the behaviors (e.g., if it appears the behavior is the result of hunger just before lunch, provide a regular snack time). This is the intervention phase.

6. Test the hypothesis. Observe and record information on the child's behavior under the new procedures and use the information to evaluate the success of the interventions. Modify or fine-tune as required.

If children have behaviors that place them or others at risk they might require a crisis intervention plan. See Skill 13.05 for details.

ESSENTIAL ELEMENTS OF A BEHAVIOR INTERVENTION PLAN

A behavior intervention plan (BIP) is a specific intervention, usually based on information obtained in the FBA and designed to reinforce or teach positive behavior skills and/or alter the environment to assist in the acquisition of those skills. It is based on the procedures numbered 4 through 6 above. The essential elements of a behavior intervention plan are as follows:

- Skills training in more appropriate behaviors that serve the same function as the inappropriate behavior

- Support mechanisms (across all settings) to help the child use the new behavior
- Modifications to be made in classrooms or other environments to decrease or remove problem behavior
- Individualized procedures. It is necessary to remember that a procedure that works with one child demonstrating a particular behavior (say, hitting) might not work with another simply because the function of that behavior differs from child to child.
- Before and after measures that help determine the effectiveness of the plan (this should be part of the original FBA that led to the BIP).

Please refer to Skill 13.01 for details on behavior management techniques that might be part of the BIP

The Behavior Intervention Plan (BIP) should be evaluated to make sure that it is being followed and to make sure that it is working effectively. A BIP that is written into a child's IEP should be reviewed at least annually, but a BIP can be reviewed whenever any member of the team feels that a review is necessary.

The parent/guardian and the behavioral intervention case manager or qualified designee may make minor modifications in accordance with law without a CSE meeting. The IEP team may also include in the plan contingency schedules for altering specified procedures, as well as their frequency or their duration, without reconvening the IEP team.

Skill 13.08   Recognizing the importance of teacher self-assessment/reflection in the development and implementation of behavior interventions

As discussed in Skill 13.04, research shows that teacher attitudes, learning and teaching styles, and expectations have a profound impact on all aspects of a child's educational experience and can positively or negatively affect his or her success in achieving learning objectives. This is particularly true when behavior interventions are necessary, because in these situations something has already gone wrong, stress levels might be up, and the stakes are high.

Sometimes a teacher's attitude, nonverbal communication, or teaching approach might even be one component of the problem. The FBA may show that a student's misbehavior occurs following a particular type of correction or reprimand or during a particular type of task the teacher did not realize was the cause of a problem. At other times, the teacher's attitude or approach might not be related to the *cause* of a problem, but it might affect the teacher's ability or willingness to implement a particular part of a BIP.

It is critical, then, that teachers be *self-aware*, particularly of all their own attitudes or tendencies toward particular attitudes, as well as of their own preferred learning and teaching styles and modes of communication. This awareness will help them be objective and base their responses on the child's needs rather than their own.

One way to do this is simple self-reflection. Teachers might, for example, use the "social autopsy" procedure discussed in Skill 12.03 *on themselves* to discover anything in their own approach that affects a difficult situation. It might also be useful for teachers to use various assessments scales and checklists (see Skills 3.02 and 3.04) to analyze their own learning and teaching styles and personality characteristics. Then, when teachers conduct such assessments on students, they can compare student profiles with their own to anticipate potential conflicts or problems.

SUBAREA III.   WORKING IN A COLLABORATIVE PROFESSIONAL
                ENVIRONMENT

COMPETENCY 0014   UNDERSTAND HOW TO ESTABLISH PARTNERSHIPS
                   WITH STUDENTS WITH DISABILITIES AND THEIR
                   FAMILIES TO ENHANCE STUDENTS' ABILITY TO
                   ACHIEVE DESIRED LEARNING OUTCOMES

Skill 14.01   Identifying effective strategies for collaborating with students
               with disabilities to promote their development of self-advocacy
               skills

Earlier skill sections have addressed most components of this skill. Skills 6.05
and 8.05 discussed instructional techniques for improving self-advocacy and
independence. Skill 8.05 particularly discussed involving the student in setting up
goals and objectives. The problem-solving and decision-making skills covered in
Skill 11.01 are a form of self-advocacy that can be applied in many real-life
situations. These skills directly involve the student in the learning process. The
IPLAN, self-monitoring, self-recording, and self-instructional behaviors described
in Skill 11.04 are directly relevant to involving the student in developing self-
advocacy.

The key when using any or all of the previously described techniques is that
planning must be *person-centered* and the person around whom the plan is
centered is the child. Note that the child, not the disability, is at the center of all
the aforementioned techniques. At every step the child is involved, to the extent
feasible, in determining needs, developing plans of action, and evaluating results.
When this approach begins very early in the child's educational life and gradually
moves more and more responsibility onto the child as the child grows,
improvements in self-advocacy and independence will be seen.

Skill 14.02   Applying strategies for assisting parents/guardians in
               becoming active participants in the educational team

The best resource a teacher has in reaching a student contact with the student's
parents and/or guardians. Good teaching recognizes this fact and seeks to
strengthen this bond through communication.

The first contact a teacher has with parents should be before the school year
starts and should go beyond generic letters stating the required supplies.
Parents are used to hearing that their child has done something bad or wrong
when they receive a phone call from a teacher. However, parents should be
contacted whenever possible to give positive feedback. For example, when a
teacher calls John's mother to say, "John got an 'A' on the test today," the
teacher has just encouraged her to maintain open communication lines. Try to
give three positive calls for every negative call you must give.

Parent-teacher conferences are scheduled at regular intervals throughout the school year and provide excellent opportunities to discuss children's progress, what they are learning, and how it might relate to future plans for their academic growth. It is not unusual for the parent or teacher to ask for a conference outside of the scheduled parent-teacher conference days. These meetings should be looked at as opportunities to support that student's success.

Using the following strategies will help you before, during, and after these meetings.

Before the Conference:

1. Be prepared. The parents/guardians might be interested in seeing their child's records, so you should be ready to share the student's portfolios, assessments, and other pertinent information. Make sure preparation for these meetings allows you to share the grades of the individual child without giving the information of another.
2. Check to see if there are any possible mistakes in your record keeping.
3. Write down at least three positive comments you would like to share with the parent, in addition to any concerns you might have.
4. Schedule a set amount of time for each conference. Don't overbook yourself. Remember that some conferences should be allotted more time than others.
5. Anticipating parents' questions will also provide you with the opportunity to appear professional when these questions come up.
6. Remember, the goal of the conference goes beyond simple communication; it is the opportunity to forge an alliance to work together for the betterment of the child.
7. Ask your mentor for suggestions in preparing for the conference.

During the Conference:

1. Maintain a professional decorum. Remember, the student's needs come first.
2. Remember this is your opportunity to learn about the student from his or her parents. You must show that you value their information.
3. Don't monopolize the time. While you might have things you consider important to share, parents need opportunities to voice their own concerns as well.
4. Be an active listener. If you must take notes, let the parents know why you have chosen to do this.
5. Remember to ask for suggestions. Get the "inside information" on the strategies that work for the parents. This enables you to show a united front.
6. Provide closure. Orally summarize the conference at the end. If another conference is needed, schedule one at this time.

Please refer to Skill 14.06 for information on interpreting test scores for parents.

After the conference:

1. Review your notes. This will help you prepare a course of action.
2. Follow through. If you and the parent agreed upon a strategy or something that needed to be done on your part, make sure you follow through.
3. Share any pertinent information with others who work with the student.
4. Commit yourself to maintaining the strength of the parent-school connection.
5. Document the time, place, and participants for future reference.

Modern technology has opened two more venues for communicating with parents. School/classroom Web sites are written with the intent of sharing regularly with parents and guardians. Many teachers now post their plans for the marking period and provide extra-credit and homework on these websites.

Email is now a major mode of communication. Most parents have email accounts and are more than willing to give you their email addresses to keep in contact. However, many school systems forbid the use of email for sharing any personal confidential information about a student. Email is simply not secure enough to meet the standards of confidentiality required in special education. Stick to generic and public information (e.g., date of open house or winter concert) in emails.

Skill 14.03 Demonstrating familiarity with typical concerns of parents/guardians of students with disabilities and with strategies for planning an individualized program that addresses these concerns

Most parents share some basic goals for their children. They want their children to grow up to be healthy, happy members of society who lead independent lives with productive employment. Parents of students with disabilities are no different, although the path that their children take might have additional turns and obstacles along the way.

HEALTH

Many children with disabilities have associated health problems or are at risk for health problems. Many also take medication(s) routinely for health or behavioral conditions. Parents of students with disabilities are concerned with their children's long-range health, the cost of health care (as children and later as adults), and the effects of medication on their child's behavior, health, and schoolwork, as well as confidentiality regarding medication.

HAPPINESS

The quality of life for more severely disabled children is different from that of the general population. Even students with less severe physical conditions (for example, a learning disability) might have lower self-esteem because they feel "stupid" or "different." Students with disabilities often have difficulty making friends, which can also impact happiness. Parents of students with disabilities feel the emotional impact of the disability on their children and are anxious to help their children feel good about themselves and fit in with the general population of their peers.

INDEPENDENCE

Initially, parents of students with disabilities might be somewhat overprotective of their child. Eventually, however, most parents begin to focus on ways to help their child function independently.

Young children with disabilities might be working on self-care types of independence, such as dressing, feeding, and toilet use. Elementary students might be working on asking for assistance, completing work, and being prepared for class with materials (books, papers, etc.). High school students might be working on driving, future job skills, or preparation for post-secondary education. Any or all of these types of goals can be written into the IEP.

JOB TRAINING

IDEA 2004 addresses the need for students with disabilities to be prepared for jobs or post-secondary education in order to be independent, productive members of society.

Job training goals and objectives for the student with a disability might be vocational, such as food service, mechanical, or carpentry. Job training goals for other students might include appropriate high school coursework to prepare for a college program.

PRODUCTIVITY

Ultimately, the goal of the parents and the school is for the student to become a productive member of society who can support him or herself financially and live independently. This type of productivity is achieved when the student becomes an adult with a measure of good health, positive self-esteem, the ability to interact positively with others, independent personal and work skills, and job training.

PARTICULAR STAGES OF CONCERN

Parents of students with special needs deal with increased concerns when the child is going into a new stage of development. Some of these times include: when the child is first identified as having a disability, entrance into an early childhood special education program, kindergarten (when it is evident that the disability remains despite services received thus far), third grade (when the student is expected to use more skills independently), junior high school, and entrance into high school.

Additional IEP goals and objectives might be warranted at these times, because the student is expected to use a new set of skills or might be entering a new educational setting.

It should be noted that parents are often more concerned when a younger, non-disabled sibling surpasses the child with the disability in some skill (such as feeding or reading). Previously, the parents may not have fully been aware of what most children can do at a particular age.

Parental Concerns about Homework

Although parents express positive feelings about homework, many have concerns about their children's homework, including their personal limitations in subject-matter knowledge and effective helping strategies. More research is needed on how school personnel can effectively support parental homework help.

Interactive homework assignments

The development of interactive homework assignments (homework that requires parent-child interaction as part of the activity) has shown promise as a way of supporting parent involvement and student achievement. Homework activities that are explicitly designed to be interactive have shown positive results for increasing achievement in several subject areas, including science and the language arts. Well-designed interactive assignments can have a number of positive outcomes: they can help students to practice study skills, to prepare for class, to participate in learning activities, and to develop personal responsibility for homework. These assignments can also promote parent-child relations, develop parent-teacher communication, and fulfill policy directives from administrators.

Skill 14.04   **Recognizing the effects of cultural and environmental influences (e.g., cultural and linguistic diversity, socioeconomic level, abuse, neglect, substance abuse) on students and their families**

Previous skill sections have addressed several aspects of cultural variables that affect the learning environment. Skill 1.05 addresses cultural attitudes toward disabilities; Skills 3.04 and 3.07 address testing bias and laws about bias; Skill 8.04 addresses cultural factors impacting relationships among families and schools; and Skill 11.05 addresses cultural implications for functional living skills.

CULTURAL BACKGROUND

Research is beginning to document the ways in which cultural minority parents interact with their children to support learning. The research mostly focuses on how these interactions differ from more mainstream or middle-class approaches. Some studies, for example, explore the non-traditional ways in which Hispanic parents are involved in their children's education; ways that are not necessarily recognized by educators as parent involvement.

Espinosa (1995), for example, discusses three major factors common to many Hispanic cultures that impact student performance in school:

- The typically more authoritarian, directed conversation between adults and children means that some Hispanic children may be unaccustomed to the give and take in discussion found in many mainstream American classrooms.
- The typical Hispanic approach views a sharp division between school and home responsibilities, expecting the school to take care of education and the parents to take care of the home. In some cases parents might even feel it would be intrusive and insulting to interfere in school matters.
- Hispanic culture typically believes in strong family ties and is more person-centered than task-centered. Individuals might pay as much attention to nonverbal communication signals as to actual words. The person-centered approach might conflict with typical-task oriented approach in mainstream American classrooms.

Espinosa reviews several techniques that improve relationships with students and families from Hispanic backgrounds with the above characteristics:

- Use the personal approach and face-to-face communication rather than generic informational letters or flyers
- Ensure your communication approach is non-judgmental. Teachers should be alert for unconscious attitudes (see Skills 13.04 and 13.08) that might negatively affect nonverbal cues.

- Persevere and maintain the personal contact over a long period of time; do not assume that because you made one pleasant contact a bond has formed.
- Be flexible in policies and approach and conscious of the particular child's background. Although the above characteristics are typical of many, there is also great diversity within any cultural group.

Guidelines such as these can be helpful, particularly since Hispanic children represent the fastest-growing minority in the country and approximately three-fourths of the children designated as Limited English Proficiency (LEP) in our schools. However, there are many cultural groups represented in the American classroom and teachers need to learn as much as they can about each child's specific background in order to teach most effectively.

EDUCATIONAL BACKGROUND

In addition to factors outlined above, and regardless of the culture or language involved, a child's previous access to education can affect the validity of many of the tests used to diagnose special education needs. Kirk, et al (2003) discuss research showing that children with school experience simply *think differently* from those with little or no school experience. They report that at least some school experience is needed before most students learn to categorize objects, reason logically, or make inferences. Children without any school experience tend to rely on individual experience instead of using and manipulating information independently. Because these skills are typically tested on IQ tests that are at the heart of many special needs screening batteries, children from backgrounds that involve little or no formal schooling might be inappropriately diagnosed with disabilities and overrepresented in the special education population.

OTHER FACTORS

Other factors that can influence students with disabilities and their families include abuse, neglect, and substance abuse.

Abuse

Whether abuse occurs to the child or to a parent, the effect transcends the immediate situation to interaction with others in the home, school, and community. If the child with a disability is the one who is abused, he or she might be distrustful of others. The child might also continue the cycle of behavior by acting out in abusive ways towards others. In addition, the strain a disability can put on a family increases the probability of abuse of a child with a disability.

If a parent of the child with a disability is being abused, the child might feel responsible and might even try to protect the abused parent. A parent who is being abused will be less likely to be able to attend to the needs of the child with a disability. The parent might be secretive about the fact that the abuse even occurs.

Neglect

If a child with a disability is neglected physically or emotionally, he or she may exhibit a number of behaviors, among them an exacerbation of the effects of the disability itself. The child will most likely be distrustful of adults, might horde classroom materials or snacks, or be unfocused on school work.

In instances (or suspected instances) of abuse and neglect, the special educator is a mandated reporter to the appropriate agency, such as the New York Office of Children and Family Services.

Substance Abuse

If a child with a disability or a parent is involved in substance abuse, that abuse will have a negative effect in the areas of finances, health, productivity, and safety. It is important for the special education teacher to be aware of signs of substance abuse. The teacher should be proactive in teaching drug awareness. He or she should also know the appropriate school channels for getting help for the student, as well as community agencies that can help parents involved in substance abuse.

Skill 14.05 Demonstrating knowledge of factors that promote effective collaboration in a culturally-responsive program that fosters respectful and beneficial relationships among students, families, and educators

Techniques discussed in the previous section (Skill 14.04) are relevant to promoting collaboration in a culturally-responsive program. Other skills relevant to this area include: Skill 1.05 (cultural attitudes toward disabilities); Skills 3.04 and 3.07 (testing bias and laws about bias); Skill 8.04 (cultural factors impacting relationships among families and school); and Skill 11.05 (cultural implications for functional living skills).

STUDENTS

Useful standards have been developed by the Council for Exceptional Children (2010) that outline best practices in communicating and relating to children and their families. For example, CEC guidelines suggest that effective teachers:

- Offer students a safe and supportive learning environment, including clearly-expressed and reasonable expectations for behavior
- Create learning environments that encourage self-advocacy and

developmentally appropriate independence
- Offer learning environments that promote active participation in independent and group activities

Such an environment is an excellent foundation for building rapport and trust with students and for communicating a teacher's respect for students and the expectation that each student takes a measure of responsibility for his or her educational development. Ideally, mutual trust and respect will afford teachers opportunities to learn about and engage students' ideas, preferences, and abilities.

PARENTS AND FAMILIES

Families know their children and they are a valuable resource for teachers of exceptional students. Often an insight or observation from a family member, or the family member's reinforcement of school standards or activities, can mean the difference between success and frustration in a teacher's work with the student. Suggestions for relationship building and collaboration with parents and families include:

- Using laypersons' terms when communicating with families and making the communication available in the language of the home
- Searching out and engaging family members' knowledge and skills in providing services, both educational and therapeutic, to the student
- Exploring and discussing the concerns of families and helping them find tactics for addressing those concerns
- Planning collaborative meetings with children and their families and assisting them in becoming active contributors to their educational team
- Ensuring that communication with and about families is confidential and conducted with respect for their privacy
- Offering parents accurate and professionally presented information about the pedagogical and therapeutic work being done with their child
- Keeping parents abreast of their rights, of the kinds of practices that might violate these rights, and of available recourse if needed
- Acknowledging and respecting cultural differences

Please refer to Skill 14.06 for more on communicating with families, and to Skill 15.03 for more information on collaborating with educators.

Skill 14.06   Demonstrating an understanding of how to communicate effectively and to adapt communication techniques and strategies in response to the characteristics and needs of students and their families

Effective communication strategies are particularly important when dealing with families of students with disabilities. Many of the topics about which special educators must communicate with students and families are emotionally laden and there is often a history of stress and misunderstanding to overcome. As mentioned in Skill 14.04, face-to-face communication is often the best way to communicate effectively. In addition to principles of communication discussed in previous sections, testing and programming offer special challenges to communication.

COMMUNICATING WITH FAMILIES ABOUT TESTING AND PROGRAMMING

One of the most important and often most difficult instances of communication with families comes when the teacher must interpret test scores and specialized educational information for parents. Parents might have many questions about their child's testing and diagnosis, but they might not have the specialized educational and psychological background to understand the implications of testing and diagnoses without help. Just as each child is an individual, different from all others in significant ways, each child's family is also different from other families. The teacher must tailor communication strategies to the needs of each individual family, just as he or she must tailor instruction to each individual child. It is important to define terms and explain procedures that might be confusing to parents without talking down to them or appearing condescending or patronizing.

Interpreting tests and diagnostic results to parents can present special challenges. Parents often see numbers and percentages without understanding their significance. They hear diagnostic terms and labels without understanding what they mean. When reporting test results, it is important to briefly define each test or subtest in terms that the parent will understand. Telling parents that their child did well or poorly on the WRAML, for example, would not be helpful unless the teacher explains the relevant subtests briefly and outlines the implications of the child's score for instruction. It is best to be as specific as possible and to give concrete examples of how test results predict learning problems.

For instance, if the testing shows a child has poor auditory working memory, the teacher can point out that this could hamper the child's ability to remember lectured facts long enough to relate multiple facts to each other to draw conclusions. This has implications for both instruction (maybe using graphic organizers to outline relationships visually will be helpful for the student) and for testing accommodations (for example, allow the use of graphic organizers during a test).

Percentiles

Some numbers can also be confusing to parents. They might have no idea what a stanine is or what it means, so the term must be defined for them. There are two kinds of numbers that can be particularly confusing to parents: percentiles and grade equivalents. Percentiles can be confusing because parents are accustomed to looking at *percentage correct* for grading purposes. They might look at a score showing that their child is at the 50th percentile and think the child is failing, because 50% correct would be a failing grade. They need to be assured that a score at the 50th percentile merely indicates their child is solidly in the middle, having performed better than 50 percent of those taking the test. In addition, they might not understand how wide the range of "normal" percentiles is and this too must be explained to them.

Grade Equivalent Scores

Another problem area when discussing test scores with parents can be grade equivalent scores. These scores are so often misinterpreted by parents and teachers alike that the International Reading Association (IRA) issued a statement in 1981, which strongly urged teachers and schools NOT to use them. If they are used, the teacher must be *very* careful to explain what they do and **do not** mean. If, for example, 3rd grade Johnny's parents are told his grade equivalency on a reading test is 6.4, they are likely to think he is reading on a 6th grade level. The teacher will need to explain that the results mean that Johnny got a score similar to the score a typical 6th grader would get on this material. However, since the test material was NOT 6th grade material, this does not mean Johnny could read 6th grade material. It was 3rd grade material and Johnny did very well on it, as well as a 6th grader would do. This sort of confusion on the part of parents (and even some teachers) is why the IRA prefers the score not be used.

Finally, parents often want to know when their child will be "fixed," or "cured," or "at grade level." This is a very difficult question and most testing and diagnostic assessment simply will not answer it. The teacher needs to help the parents focus on what the results mean for instruction and accommodation. Of course, there will be implications for future planning, but it is unwise to try and make testing results into predictors of how long the child will need support.

EFFECTIVE COMMUNICATION SKILLS BETWEEN TEACHER AND STUDENT

Effective teaching depends on communication. By using good sending skills, the teacher can be assurance that he or she is getting the desired message across to the students as effectively as possible. By being a model of a good listener, a teacher can help students learn to listen and respond appropriately to others.

Attending Skills

Attending skills are used to receive a message. Some task-related attending skills that have been identified include:

1. Looking at the teacher when information is being presented (but be careful— some cultures consider looking directly at the teacher impolite)

2. Listening to assignment directions
3. Listening for answers to questions
4. Looking at the chalkboard
5. Listening to others speak when appropriate

For some students, special techniques must be employed to gain and hold their attention. For example, the teacher might first call the student by name when asking a question to assure that individual is paying attention, or the teacher might ask the question before calling the name of a student to create greater interest.

Selecting students at random to answer questions helps to keep them alert and listening. Being enthusiastic and keeping lessons short and interactive assists in maintaining the interest of those students who have shorter attention spans. Some students might be better able to focus their attention when environmental distractions are eliminated or at least reduced, and nonverbal signals can be used to draw students' attention to the task.

Clarity of Expression

Unclear communication between the teacher and special needs students sometimes contributes to problems in academic and behavioral situations because it adds to the student's confusion about certain processes or skills he or she is attempting to master.

There are many ways in which the teacher can improve the clarity of communication. Giving clear, precise directions is one way. Verbal directions can be simplified by using shorter sentences, familiar words, and relevant explanations. Asking a student to repeat directions or to demonstrate understanding of them by carrying out the instructions is another an effective way of monitoring the clarity of expression.

A teacher can also clarify his or her communication by using a variety of vocal inflections. The use of intonation can help make the message clearer, as can pauses at significant points in the communication. For example, verbal praise should be spoken with inflection that communicates sincerity. Pausing before speaking key words, or stressing the words that convey meanings, helps students learn concepts that are being taught.

Paraphrasing

Paraphrasing is restating what the student says using one's own words, and it can significantly improve communication. In restating what the student has communicated, the teacher is not judging the content, but is simply relating what he or she understands the message to be. If the message has been misinterpreted, the student can be asked to clarify it.

The act of paraphrasing sends the message that the teacher is trying to better understand the student and telegraphs a caring, attentive attitude on the part of the teacher. Restating the student's message as fairly and accurately as possible assists the teacher in seeing things from the student's perspective.

Paraphrasing is often a simple restatement of what has been said. Lead-ins, such as, "Your position is..." or "It seems to you that..." are helpful in paraphrasing a student's messages. A student's statement, "I am not going to do my math today," might be paraphrased by the teacher as, "Did I understand you to say that you are not going to do your math today?"

Descriptive Feedback

Descriptive feedback is a factual, objective (i.e., unemotional) recounting of a behavioral situation or message sent by a student. Descriptive feedback has the same effect as paraphrasing, in that: (1) when responding to a student's statement, the teacher restates (i.e., paraphrases) what the student has said or factually describes what has been seen, and (2) it allows the teacher to check the accuracy of his or her perceptions of the student and the message.

Evaluative Feedback

This type of feedback judges, evaluates, approves, or disapproves of the statements made by the student. Evaluative feedback occurs when the student makes a statement and the teacher responds openly with, "I think you're wrong," or "I agree with you entirely." The tendency to give evaluative responses is heightened in situations where feelings and emotions are deeply involved.

Since evaluative feedback intones a judgmental approval or disapproval of the student's remark or behavior, it can be a major barrier to mutual understanding and effective communication. However, it is a necessary mechanism for providing feedback of a quantitative (and sometimes qualitative) instructional nature (e.g., test scores, homework results, and classroom performance). In order to be effective, evaluative feedback must be offered in a factual, constructive manner. Descriptive feedback tends to reduce defensiveness because it communicates that the teacher is interested in the student as a person and has an accurate understanding of the student.

Skill 14.07   Demonstrating knowledge of ethical practices related to communication and collaboration with families, including confidentiality and informed consent

CONFIDENTIALITY

The Family Educational Rights and Privacy Act (1974), also known as the Buckley Amendment, assures confidentiality of student records. Parents are afforded the right to examine, review, and request changes in information deemed inaccurate and stipulate persons who might access their child's records. Please refer to Skill 5.08 for more on maintaining confidentiality in record keeping.

INFORMED CONSENT

Parents must give written consent prior to the first comprehensive evaluation of their child for eligibility for special services. They must also consent to re-evaluations. If services are to be initiated or eliminated outside of a formal IEP meeting, parental consent is required. If, however, a parent ignores requests for feedback, some changes in the child's services can be made without parental consent. For this reason, it is important that parents understand when their consent is required and when it is not required. Such issues are generally covered in a parents' rights brochure given to parents during the pre-referral or referral process.

DUE PROCESS

"Due process is a set of procedures designed to ensure the fairness of educational decisions and the accountability of both professionals and parents in making these decisions" (Kirk and Gallagher, 1986, p. 24). These procedures serve as a mechanism by which the child and his or her family can voice their opinions, concerns, or even dissents. Due process safeguards exist in all matters pertaining to identification, evaluation, and educational placement.

Please refer to Skill 16.03 for detailed information on due process.

COMPETENCY 0015   UNDERSTAND HOW TO ESTABLISH PARTNERSHIPS WITH EDUCATORS, ADMINISTRATORS, OTHER SCHOOL PROFESSIONALS, AND COMMUNITY MEMBERS TO ENHANCE LEARNING OPPORTUNITIES FOR STUDENTS WITH DISABILITIES

Skill 15.01   Demonstrating familiarity with a variety of collaborative, inclusive teaching models (e.g., co-teaching, push-in, consultant teaching (CT) and their implementation

Please refer to Skill 7.01 for a description of these models.

Special education teachers of students with mild to moderate disabilities are moving toward consultative and collaborative models of service delivery. This movement results in more team teaching in the regular classroom and a higher degree of mainstreaming of students. Education of students with more severe disabilities is now more like that of non-disabled peers. Technology enables a wide range of learners to participate meaningfully in learning and social interaction. Thus, the special education teacher must be able to identify student access needs and match technology resources, classroom management and transitions, and all aspects of service delivery with appropriate learning objectives and curricula.

COMPOSITE SCENARIO OF AN INCLUSIVE EDUCATIONAL SETTING

The following composite scenario provides a brief description of how regular and special education teachers work together to address the individual needs of all of their students (ERIC Clearinghouse on Disabilities and Gifted Education, 1993, pp. 4-5).

Jane Smith teaches 3rd grade at Lincoln Elementary School. Three days a week, she co-teaches the class with Lynn Vogel, a special education teacher. Their 25 students include four who have special needs due to disabilities and two others who currently need special help in specific curriculum areas. Each of the students with a disability has an IEP that was developed by a team that included both teachers. The teachers, paraprofessionals, and the school principal believe that these students have a great deal to contribute to the class and that they will achieve their best in the environment of a general education classroom.

All of the school personnel have attended in-service training designed to develop collaborative skills for teaming and problem solving. Ms. Smith and the two professionals who work in the classroom also received special training on disabilities and how to create an inclusive classroom environment. The school's principal, Ben Parks, had worked in special education many years ago and has received training on the impact of new special education developments and instructional arrangements on school administration.

Each year, Mr. Parks works with the building staff to identify areas in which new training is needed. For specific questions that might arise, technical assistance is available through a regional special education cooperative.

Ms. Smith and Ms. Vogel share responsibility for teaching and for supervising their paraprofessional. In addition to the time they spend together in the classroom, they spend two hours each week planning instruction, plus additional planning time with other teachers and support personnel who work with their students.

The teachers use their joint planning time to problem-solve and discuss the use of special instructional techniques for all students who need special assistance. Monitoring and adapting instruction for individual students is an ongoing activity. The teachers use curriculum-based measurement to systematically assess their students' learning progress. They adapt curricula so that lessons begin at the edge of the students' knowledge, add new material at the students' pace, and present it in a style consistent with the students' learning styles. For some students, pre-organizers or chapter previews are used to bring out the most important points of the material to be learned; for other students, new vocabulary words might need to be highlighted, or reduced reading levels might be required. Some students use special activity worksheets, while others learn best by using recorded materials.

In the classroom, the teachers group students differently for different activities. Sometimes the teachers and paraprofessionals divide the class, each teaching a small group or tutoring individuals. They use cooperative learning projects to help the students learn to work together and form social relationships. Peer tutors provide extra help to students who need it. Students without disabilities are more than willing to help their friends who have disabilities, and vice versa.

While the regular classroom might not be the best learning environment for every child with a disability, it is highly desirable for all who can benefit. It provides contact with age-peers and prepares all students for the diversity of the world beyond the classroom.

Skill 15.02 Demonstrating an understanding of effective communication (e.g., active listening, conflict resolution, building consensus, understanding verbal/nonverbal communication)

Please refer to Skill 14.06 for an overview of specific communication skills.

Effective communication must occur between teacher and students as well as among students. The special educator needs to be able to teach students who require varying techniques and approaches. He or she must be able to recognize specific needs, possess diagnostic capabilities, and make the necessary environmental and instructional adaptations, all on an individual basis.

Teachers must be able to diagnose individual learning styles because the way in which students learn differs, just as abilities vary. Learning can be affected by environmental elements (e.g., sound and room arrangement) or physical elements (e.g., time of day and mobility). The use of sensory channels such as visual, auditory, and haptic (touch) is also important. The special needs teacher must identify modality channels through which each student processes information most proficiently.

The teacher might need to respond to feelings as well as words. Not all communication is delivered verbally. Indeed, words spoken are not always true indicators of what a person means and feels. Nonverbal communication such as body language, facial expression, tone of voice, and speaking patterns are all clues to the underlying message the student is attempting to deliver.

To facilitate further communication, the teacher must become an active listener. This involves much more than just restating what the speaker has said (see the section on paraphrasing in Skill 14.06). Responses must reflect the student's feelings in addition to the spoken language. For example, a student who has failed a test might feel inadequate and have the need to blame the teacher for his failure. He might say to her, "You didn't tell me that you were including all the words from the last six weeks on the spelling test." The teacher, if she were to respond solely to the spoken message, might say, "I know I told you that you would be tested over the entire unit. You just weren't listening." The intuitive, sensitive teacher would look beyond the spoken words by saying, "You're telling me that it feels bad to fail a test." By responding to the child's feelings, the teacher lets him know that she understands his personal crisis, and the student is encouraged to communicate further

Using statements spoken in the present tense rather than questions and the use of personal pronouns that are reflective of current feelings about the situation also enhance communication. Offering self-disclosure of similar experiences or feelings may also be acceptable if the teacher feels inclined to do so.

Skill 15.03 **Apply collaborative strategies for working with general educators and other professionals in the school to solve problems and build consensus with regard to students with disabilities and the special education program**

Please also refer to Skills 6.02, 6.03, and 6.06 for more on techniques of collaboration.

PARAPROFESSIONALS AND GENERAL EDUCATION TEACHERS

Paraprofessionals and general education teachers are important collaborators with teachers of exceptional students. Although they might have daily exposure to exceptional students, they might not have the theoretical or educational experience to assure their effective interaction with such students. They do bring valuable perspective to and opportunities for breadth and variety in an exceptional child's educational experience. General education teachers also offer curriculum and subject matter expertise and a high level of professional support, and paraprofessionals can provide insights based on their particular familiarity with individual students. CEC suggests that teachers can best collaborate with general education teachers and paraprofessionals by:

- Offering information about the characteristics of children with exceptional learning needs
- Discussing and brainstorming ways to integrate children with exceptionalities into various settings within the school community
- Modeling best practices, instructional techniques, and accommodations, as well as coaching others in their use
- Keeping communication about children with exceptional learning needs and their families confidential
- Consulting with colleagues in the assessment of individuals with exceptional learning needs
- Engaging colleagues in group problem-solving and in developing, executing, and assessing collaborative activities
- Offering support to paraprofessionals by observing their work with students and offering feedback and suggestions

RELATED SERVICE PROVIDERS AND ADMINISTRATORS

Related service providers and administrators offer specialized skills and abilities that are critical to an exceptional education teacher's ability to advocate for his or her students and to meet a school's legal obligations to the students and their families. Related service providers—speech, occupational, and language therapists; psychologists; and physicians—offer expertise and resources unparalleled in meeting a child's developmental needs. Administrators are often experts in the resources available at the school and local education agency levels and the culture and politics of a school system. They can be powerful partners in meeting the needs of exceptional education teachers and students.

A teacher's most effective approach to collaborating with these professionals includes:

- Confirming mutual understanding of the accepted goals and objectives of the student with exceptional learning needs as documented in his or her IEP

- Soliciting input about ways to support related service goals in classroom settings
- Understanding the needs and motivations of each and offering support whenever possible
- Facilitating respectful and beneficial relationships between families and professionals
- Regularly and accurately communicating observations and data about the child's progress or challenges

SUPPORT AND PROFESSIONAL SERVICES

Teachers are involved in every aspect of the education of individual students, so they need to be knowledgeable not only about teaching and instructional techniques but also about support services. These services will need to be coordinated and teachers must be able to work in a collaborative manner.

Close contact and communication must be established and maintained among the teacher, the school district staff, each base school, and the various specialists (or consultants) providing ancillary services. These persons often serve special needs students in auxiliary (providing help outside the school setting) and supplementary (providing help in addition to that offered by the school) ways. Thus, the principles and methods of special education must be shared with regular educators and the tenets and practices of regular education must be conveyed to special educators. Job roles and unique responsibilities and duties of support specialists need to be known by all teachers.

Furthermore, the services that can be provided by community resources and the support that can be given by parents and professional organizations must be known to all in order to provide the maximum education for exceptional students. Professional services are offered on a local, state, and national level for most areas of disability. Teachers should stay abreast of the most current practices and changes by reading professional journals, attending professional conferences, and maintaining membership in professional organizations.

Skill 15.04 **Identifying principles and analyzing factors related to the coordination of efforts (e.g., information-sharing systems, scheduling) among professionals working with students with disabilities**

Please also refer to Skills 6.02, 6.03, and 6.06 for more on techniques of collaboration.

When professionals work together to provide services for students with disabilities, it is important that they work as a cohesive teaching unit, using information sharing systems and proper scheduling procedures.

A system should be put into place for sharing program materials, tracking students' mastery of goals and objectives, and supporting the various requirements of administrative and teaching staff. Because of the variety of learning objectives and the need to make the special education curriculum appropriate for each student, information sharing is critical. It is not uncommon for a teacher in one part of the school to be completely unaware of what another teacher is doing. Two teachers could have similar students with similar intensive needs, and by sharing information, lesson plans, and behavior modification strategies, the workload is shared and students benefit from a more cohesive program.

Professionals also need to work together to ensure that students with disabilities are receiving the services outlined in their IEPs. The speech teacher, the occupational therapist, the general education teacher, and the special education teacher might all be providing services to one student. In order to ensure that the proper amount of time is allotted for each service, the professionals involved will have to work together to develop a schedule for the student. This will ensure that nothing is left out and that all areas outlined in the IEP are addressed. This will also help by ensuring that students with disabilities that can be taught in groups are grouped with other students who might have the same requirements.

This kind of work can only be effectively done when professionals share schedules, student information, and student requirements. If they work together, they can accomplish a great deal more than when working independently. As mentioned in Competency 6, administrative support is critical for this sort of coordination of efforts.

Skill 15.05 Demonstrating an understanding of how to work effectively within school administrative structures to ensure that students with disabilities receive services as specified in their IEPs

Please refer to Skill 6.02 for an analysis of the roles of various educators and administrators.

The student's IEP must state the special education, related services, supplementary aids, and services to be provided to the student or on behalf of the student. A statement of the program modifications or supports for school personnel that will allow the student to become involved in and progress in the general curriculum should also be included in the IEP. In the past, students with disabilities were sometimes placed in the regular education classroom for the sake of inclusion without any help or support. This changed when IDEA 1997 required that supplementary aids and services, accommodations, modifications, and supports play a more important role in a student's education.

The IEP should specify supports for school personnel. The decisions as to which supplementary aids and services, accommodations, modifications, or supports are appropriate for a particular student are to be made on an individualized basis by the IEP team. However, the approach should be to create, from the beginning, a curriculum with built-in supports for diverse learners rather than to fit supplementary aids and services, accommodations, modifications, or supports into the curriculum after it is created. This means that the IEP must also reflect the nuances of administrative structure in the particular district and school the child attends. A representative of the administration should be at all IEP meetings as well as at meetings and consultations about the student's progress and whether or not the child is receiving services outlined in the IEP.

The IEP should include ways for the team and the teacher to objectively measure the student's progress or lack of progress (regression) in the special education program. If the student is not receiving the services specified in his or her IEP the student might not be able to meet the goals outlined in the IEP. This careful monitoring and reporting of goals and objectives every quarter should help ensure that students receive the services to which they are entitled.

If the student is entitled to additional services from a speech therapist, occupational therapist, or other specialist, the teachers should ensure that the specified services outlined in the IEP are being provided to that student. This can be done by working with the principal or other administrators and discussing how much time has been allotted for the additional services. It is important to ensure that each student receives the time allotted and spelled out in his or her IEP.

Skill 15.06 **Identify the roles of community personnel (e.g., social workers, case workers, psychiatrists/psychologists) in providing services to students with special needs, including transition services**

Please refer also to Skill 11.07 for additional information on transition issues.

Throughout their school years, the community personnel most involved with the student will be those assisting with medical, social, and counseling services. Since the ultimate goal for all students is transition to an adult world in which they can be as independent and productive as possible, later school life and transition will also include community personnel involved with such things as housing, transportation, recreation, and jobs. The specific community personnel who will be involved in providing services to students during their school years and throughout transition into the adult world will vary depending upon the specific needs, interests, and goals of the individual student, but many will fall into the following categories.

Medical Personnel: Outside physicians and specialists often provide testing and information about the child that educators can use in designing an IEP and providing necessary services to the student. If parental permission is obtained, it may be helpful for teachers to consult with them about medication and other medical issues.

Psychiatrists/Psychologists/Counselors: Like medical personnel, these specialists can be a valuable source of information and consultation about a child's needs and possible treatments.

Case workers/Social Workers: Family and other factors can result in the presence of a case worker or social worker in the child's life. This person possesses knowledge of available community and school services and makes these known to parents and teachers. He or she often visits the homes of students, conducts intake and assessment interviews, and assists in district enforcement policies.

Potential Employers: As the student approaches transition age (14 or older), it is helpful to maintain relationships with community businesses at which the student might one day find a job. These people can provide information on job and social skills necessary for work as well as sites for community-referenced and community-based Instruction (CRI and CBI; see Skill 11.03) during transition.

Housing Officials: Housing officials and landlords, as well as personnel from subsidized and sheltered housing resources, can be valuable during the transition period. They can provide lists of skills necessary for independent living as well as help in planning a student's move to a new location. Some communities have halfway houses that are appropriate for some students with disabilities after they leave school.

Municipal Recreation Personnel: During transition, these people can provide information on recreational resources in the community and help students learn how to take advantage of whatever interests them.

Transportation Personnel: These people are valuable resources during transition, both for designing CRI and CBI and for helping students access transportation services they might need after finishing school.

Rehabilitation Facilities and Sheltered Workshops: These are particularly appropriate for individuals with severe disabilities because they are geared toward slower-paced, intensive instruction in an effort to develop effective work habits, occupational skills, appropriate personal-social skills, and vocational interests. In addition, these facilities provide both treatment and training and generally have a variety of professionally trained counselors, evaluators, teachers, and supervisors.

It is important to plan ahead for student needs and establish partnerships with community personnel relevant to the student's needs early in the student's education. Long-term relationships will make eventual transition easier.

Skill 15.07 **Demonstrate an understanding of how to communicate and work effectively with community members (e.g., interagency collaboration, establishing relationships with advocacy groups)**

Please refer to Skills 11.07 and 15.06 for more information.

The purpose of interagency agreements is to provide the best services to a person with a disability so that this person can receive an education that prepares him or her for living and working in an integrated community setting of his or her choice and be prepared to move into that environment upon graduation.

When working with outside agencies and professionals on behalf of the students, close communication is critical and use of the specific communication techniques described in Skills 14.06 and 15.02 can be helpful.

It is important that these community interagency relationships be built over a period of time so the necessary foundation is there when transition to post-school life begins. Rather than waiting until the child is 14, begin establishing networks in the community early in the educational process. Keep in mind that non-governmental agencies can be useful resources for some services for students and their families.

New York has very specific regulations and procedures governing interagency collaboration on behalf of students with disabilities, and VESID is central to collaborations. VESID considers coordination with other state agencies to be critical to improving access to vocational training, employment opportunities, and other areas of post-school adult life, particularly for individuals with significant disabilities, who often have multiple needs requiring the intervention of more than one state agency.

VESID partners with:

- **Commission for the Blind and Visually Handicapped (CBVH)** to identify specialized services for the visually handicapped to complete employment objectives
- **Office of Mental Health (OMH) and Office of Mental Retardation and Developmental Disabilities (OMRDD)** to develop supported employment for persons with the most severe disabilities
- **Department of Health (DOH)** to deliver services to individuals with traumatic brain injuries (TBI) and access to health insurance for medically necessary physical and mental restoration during the rehabilitation process
- **Local Workforce Investment Boards** on local adult education and family literacy programs

- **New York State Financial Aid Administrators Association (NYSFAAA)** to help the disabled receive fair and equitable treatment in obtaining financial assistance for post-secondary education
- **Office of Alcoholism and Substance Abuse Services (OASAS)** to provide comprehensive and integrated services to alcohol and substance abusers
- **Office of Higher and Professional Education (OHPE)** to ensure necessary support services for qualified students with disabilities, academic learning and success for college students with disabilities, and successful transition from high school to college
- **State and federal veterans' agencies** to ensure that veterans with disabilities obtain the services necessary to return to work

VESID participates in such multiple-agency programs as:

- **Developmental Disabilities Planning Council (DDPC)** to review employment grants related to developing sector-based employment
- **Disability Program Navigator** to promote accessibility to the full range of "one stop" system employment services for people with disabilities
- **Model Transition Program** to support transition from school to employment or to post-secondary training
- **Most Integrated Setting Coordinating Council (MISCC)** to implement services for individuals with disabilities in the least restrictive community settings

For more information, see:
http://www.vesid.nysed.gov/partner_agencies/home.html

COMPETENCY 0016 UNDERSTAND THE HISTORICAL, SOCIAL, LEGAL, AND ETHICAL FOUNDATIONS OF EDUCATION FOR STUDENTS WITH DISABILITIES

Skill 16.01 Demonstrating an understanding of models, theories, and philosophies that provide the basis for special education practice and the beliefs, traditions, and values underlying them

HISTORICAL BACKGROUND

Special education as it is today is a relatively new approach to the perception and treatment of people with disabilities. Ancient Sparta practiced infanticide for any baby considered different or disabled. The ancient Greeks treated these children as outcasts, left to beg on the streets. Many religious groups assumed they were either being punished or were possessed by demons. Others revered them as otherworldly and still others employed them as court jesters and clowns.

It was not until the 17th century that hospitals began to provide any sort of treatment for people with emotional disturbances or mental retardation. The philosopher John Locke was the first to publicly differentiate between mental retardation and emotional disturbance. In many places, including America, people with mental or emotional disabilities were still treated as criminals at that time.

Special education is considered by many to have begun with the work of French physician Jean Marc Itard in the 19th century. His attempts to civilize a 12-year old boy who had been abandoned in the woods as an infant used many of the educational principles presently in use in the field of special education, including developmental and multi-sensory approaches, sequencing of tasks, individualized instruction, and a curriculum geared towards functional life skills.

Itard's work had an enormous impact upon public attitude toward individuals with disabilities, and they began to be seen as educable. During the late 1700s, rudimentary procedures were devised by which those with sensory impairments (i.e., deaf, blind) could be taught, closely followed in the early 1800s by attempts to teach students with mild intellectual disabilities and emotional disorders (who were at that time known as the "idiotic" or "insane").

Throughout Europe, schools for students with visual and hearing impairments were erected, paralleled by the founding of similar institutions in the United States. In 1817, Thomas Hopkins Gallaudet founded the first American school for students who were deaf. Known today as Gallaudet College in Washington, D.C., it is one of the world's best institutions of higher learning for those with deafness. Gallaudet's work was followed closely by that of Samuel Gridley who was instrumental in the founding of the Perkins Institute in 1829 for students who were blind.

The mid-1800s saw the further development of Itard's philosophy when his student, Edward Séguin, immigrated to the United States, where he wrote a publication entitled *Idiocy and Its Treatment by the Physiological Method* (Séguin, 1866). Seguin was instrumental in the establishment of the first residential school for individuals with retardation in the United States.

State legislatures began to assume the responsibility for housing people with physical and mental disabilities, but this institutional care was largely custodial. Institutions were often referred to as warehouses due to the deplorable conditions of many of them. Humanitarians like Dorothea Dix helped to relieve the anguish and suffering of persons with mental illnesses in institutions.

The early twentieth century saw the publication of the first standardized test of intelligence by Alfred Binet of France. This was later revised by an American, Louis Terman, and the concept of the intelligence quotient (IQ) was introduced. At approximately the same time, the Italian physician Maria Montessori was developing effective techniques for early childhood education. Her work included methods of education for children with mental retardation as well. The approach she developed is still used in preschool programs today.

In 1922, the Council for Exceptional Children (first called the International Council for Exceptional Children) was founded. During the 1920s, many comprehensive statewide programs were initiated. It wasn't until the Civil Rights Movement of the mid-1900s, however, that parents of children with disabilities discovered that the federal courts could be a powerful agent on behalf of their children. The 1954 decision in the *Brown v. the Topeka Board of Education* case not only struck down educational discrimination based on race, it also guaranteed equal opportunity rights to a free public education for all citizens, and the parents of children and youth with disabilities insisted that their children be included in that decision. From this point on, court cases and public laws too numerous to include here began to shape the field of Special Education.

LEGAL MANDATES IMPORTANT TO SPECIAL EDUCATION

The U.S. Constitution does not specify protection for education. However, all states provide education, and thus individuals are guaranteed protection and due process under the 14th Amendment. The 14th Amendment guarantees that, regardless of the state in which they reside, all U.S. citizens are entitled to certain rights and equal protection under the law and no state may do anything that deprives citizens of their equal rights. If a state provides education to any of its citizens, it must provide it equally for all of them.

The basic source of law for special education is the Individuals with Disabilities Education Act (IDEA) and its accompanying regulations (see below). IDEA represents the latest phase of legislation governing the education of children with disabilities. By the time this legislation began, about half of the estimated 8 million children with disabilities in the U.S. were either not being appropriately served in school or were excluded from schooling altogether. Data also showed a disproportionate number of minority children placed in special programs. Identification and placement procedures were inconsistent and parental involvement was generally not encouraged.

After *Brown v. Board of Education* (1954) declared segregation on the basis of race unconstitutional, parents and other advocates began filing similar lawsuits on behalf of children with disabilities, and the resulting body of law and Supreme Court decisions are known as the Doctrine of Selective Incorporation, under which the states are compelled to honor various substantive rights under procedural authority of the 14th Amendment. This section is a brief summary of that law and other major legislation affecting special education.

Diana v. the State Board of Education, 1970. This case resulted in the decision that all children must be tested in their native language.

Wyatt v. Stickney, 1971. This case established the right to adequate treatment (education) for institutionalized persons with mental retardation.

Pennsylvania Association for Retarded Citizens (PARC) v. Commonwealth of Pennsylvania, 1972. Special education was guaranteed to children with mental retardation. The victory in this case sparked additional court cases for children with other disabilities.

Mills v. Board of Education of the District of Columbia, 1972. The right to special education was extended to all children with disabilities, not just children with mental retardation. Judgments in PARC and Mills paved the way for *The Education for All Handicapped Children Act.*

Rehabilitation Amendments of 1973 (Public Law 93-112). The first comprehensive federal statute to address specifically the rights of youth with disabilities. It prohibited illegal discrimination in education, employment, or housing on the basis of a disability.

Section 504, Rehabilitation Act of 1973. Section 504 expands an older law by extending its protection to other areas that receive federal assistance, such as education. Protected individuals must (a) have a physical or mental impairment that substantially limits one or more major life activities, such as self-care, walking, seeing, breathing, working, and or *learning*; (b) have a record of such an impairment; or (c) be regarded as having such an impairment. A disability in itself is not sufficient grounds for a complaint of discrimination. The person must be otherwise qualified, or able to meet, the requirements of the program in question.

- This Section is important because it assists with several categories of children not comprehensively covered under IDEA. Children in these categories might meet the definition for disabled, but don't fit IDEA eligibility definitions (e.g., a child with a medical condition such as AIDS, which is not listed specifically in Other Health Impaired).

Education Amendments of 1974. (Public Law 93-380 and Public Law 94-142 is the funding portion of this act). These amendments required the states to provide full educational opportunities for children with disabilities. It addressed identification, fair evaluation, alternative placements, due process procedures, and free, appropriate public education.

Education for all Handicapped Children Act (EHA; Public Law 94-142), 1975. This law provided for a free, appropriate public education for all children with disabilities, defined special education and related services, and imposed rigid guidelines on the provisions of those services. Subsequent revisions in this law in 1983 and 1986 included the provision for a free and appropriate public education that extended these services to preschool children with disabilities (ages 3-5) and included incentives to locate children at risk from birth to 3 years old.

The philosophy behind these pieces of legislation and their subsequent reauthorization and renaming as IDEA in 1990 is that education is to be provided to all children ages 3-18 who meet age eligibility requirements. All children are assumed capable of benefiting from education. For children with severe or profound handicaps, "education" may be interpreted to include training in basic self-help skills and vocational training as well as academics.

The principles of IDEA also incorporate the concept of "normalization." Within this concept, persons with disabilities are allowed access to everyday patterns and conditions of life that are as close as possible or equal to those of their non-disabled peers. There are seven fundamental provisions of IDEA (see Skill 16.02 for details):

1. Free Appropriate Public Education (FAPE)
2. Notification and procedural rights for parents
3. Identification and services to all children
4. Necessary related services

5. Individualized assessments
6. Individualized Education Plans
7. Least Restrictive Environment (LRE)

Goss v. Lopez, 1975. This case ruled that the state could not deny a student: education without following *due process.* Although this decision is not based on a special education issue, the process of school suspension and expulsion is obviously critical in assuring an appropriate public education to children with disabilities.

Gifted and Talented Children's Act (Public Law 95-56), 1978. This case defined the gifted and talented population and focused upon this exceptionality category, which was not included in EHA (*Public Law 94-142*).

Larry P. v. Riles, 1979. This case ordered the reevaluation of black students enrolled in classes for educable mental retardation (EMR) and enjoined the California State Department of Education from the use of biased intelligence tests in subsequent EMR placement decisions.

Parents in Action on Special Education (PASE) v. Hannon, 1980. This case ruled that IQ tests are necessarily biased against ethnic and racial subcultures.

Board of Education v. Rowley, 1982. Amy Rowley was an elementary school student with deafness whose parents rejected their school district's proposal to provide a tutor and speech therapist services to supplement their daughter's instruction in the regular classroom. Her parents insisted on an interpreter, even though Amy was making satisfactory social, academic, and educational progress without one. In deciding in favor of the school district, the Supreme Court ruled that school districts must provide those services that permit a student with disabilities to benefit from instruction. Essentially, the court ruled that the states are obligated to provide a "basic floor of opportunity" "that is reasonable to allow the child to benefit from social education."

Irving Independent School District v. Tatro, 1984. EHA and IDEA list health services as one of the "related services" that schools are mandated to provide to exceptional students. Amber Tatro, who had spina bifida, required the insertion of a catheter on a regular schedule in order to empty her bladder. The issue, specifically, was the classification of clean, intermittent catheterization (CIC) as a "medical service" (which would not be covered under IDEA) or a "related health service," which would be covered. In this instance, the catheterization was not declared a medical service, but a "related service" necessary for the student to have in order to benefit from special education. The school district was obliged to provide the service. The Tatro case has implications for students with other medical impairments who might need services to allow them to attend classes at the school.

Smith v. Robinson, 1984. This case concerned reimbursement of attorney's fees for parents who win litigation under IDEA. At the time of this case, IDEA did not provide for such reimbursement. Following this ruling, Congress passed a law awarding attorney's fees to parents who win their litigation.

Handicapped Children's Protection Act of 1985 (Public Law 99-372). This law allowed parents who are unsuccessful in due process hearings or reviews to seek recovery of attorney's fees.

School Board of Nassau County v. Arline, 1987. This case established that a contagious disease can be a disability under Section 504 of the Rehabilitation Act and that people with such diseases are protected from discrimination if otherwise qualified (actual risk to health and safety to others make persons unqualified).

Honig v. Doe, 1988. Essentially, students may not be denied education or exclusion from school when their misbehavior is related to their handicap. The "stay put" provision of IDEA allows students to remain in their current educational setting pending the outcome of administrative or judicial hearings. In the case of behavior that is a danger to the student or to others, the court allows school districts to apply their normal procedures for dealing with dangerous behavior. Where the student has presented an immediate threat to others, that student may be temporarily suspended for up to 10 school days to give the school and the parent's time to review the IEP and discuss possible alternatives to the current placement. Refer to Skill 13.06 for Manifest Determination Hearing.

American with Disabilities Act-ADA (Public Law 101-336), 1990. This law was patterned after Section 504 of the Rehabilitation Act of 1973 and gives civil rights protection to individuals with disabilities (or contagious diseases) in private sector employment, all public services, public accommodations, transportation, and telecommunications in all aspects of life, not just those receiving federal funding. Title II and Title III are applicable to special education because they cover the private sector (such as private schools) and require access to public accommodations.

Individuals with Disabilities Education Act/IDEA (Public Law 101-476), 1990. Reauthorized and renamed existing EHA. This amendment to EHA changed the term "handicapped" to "disability," expanded related services, and required individual education programs (IEPs) to contain transitional goals and objectives for adolescents (students ages 16 and above).

Florence County School District Four v. Shannon Carter, 1993. This case established the parents' right to seek reimbursement for private schooling when a school district does not provide FAPE for a student with a disability. This decision has encouraged districts to be more inclusive of students with disabilities.

IDEA 97 Reauthorization. This amendment retains the major provisions of previous federal laws and also includes major changes in the areas of the evaluation procedures, parental rights, transitions, and discipline. Some changes included:

- Participation of students with disabilities in statewide assessment programs with accommodations when required
- Increased IEP emphasis on students with disabilities participating in the general curriculum and regular education teachers taking part in developing the IEP
- Lowering the age to begin focusing on transition service from 16 to 14
- The guarantee that no student with a disability is deprived of continuing educational services because of disability-related behavior
- Amendments to the evaluation process requiring examination and use of previously collected data, tests, and information where appropriate. Previous to IDEA 97, an entire reevaluation had to be conducted every three years to determine if the child continued to be a "child with a disability." This was changed to allow existing information and evaluations to be considered, preventing the unnecessary assessment of students and reducing the cost of evaluations.
- Parents were specifically included as members of the group making the eligibility decision (a requirement not present in earlier IDEA law).

No Child Left Behind Act (NCLB, Public Law 107-110), 2002. This law was signed on January 8, 2002. It addresses accountability of school personnel for student achievement with the expectation that *every* child will demonstrate proficiency in reading, math, and science.

Educators are affected as follows: Teachers of grades K-3 are responsible for teaching reading and using varied, research-based approaches with measurable outcomes. Elementary teachers of upper grades will teach reading, math and science. Middle and high school teachers will teach to new, higher standards. Special educators are responsible for teaching students to a level of proficiency comparable to that of their non-disabled peers. This raises the bar of academic expectations throughout the grades. It requires special education teachers to be *highly qualified*, that is, certified or licensed in their area of special education, and to show proof of a specific level of professional development in the core subjects that they teach

M. L. v. Federal Way School District (WA) in the Ninth Circuit Court of Appeals, 2004. This case ruled that absence of a regular education teacher on an IEP team was a serious procedural error.

IDEA 2004 Reauthorization, 2004. IDEA was reauthorized as the Individuals with Disabilities Education Improvement Act of 2004 (IDEIA 2004), but is commonly referred to as IDEA 2004. It became effective July 1, 2005. This added language recognizing the need to prepare special education students for study beyond the high school setting by teaching compensatory methods. Accordingly, IDEA 2004 provided a close tie to the Elementary and Special Education Act of 1965, and stated that students with special needs should have maximum access to the general curriculum. This was defined as the amount or access needed for an individual student to reach his or her fullest potential. Full inclusion was stated not to be the only option by which to achieve this, and the Act specified that skills should be taught to help students compensate later in life in cases where inclusion was not the best setting.

- IDEA 2004 added a new requirement for special education teachers on the secondary level, enforcing NCLBs "highly qualified" requirements in the subject area of their curriculum. The rewording in this part of IDEA states that they shall be "no less qualified" than teachers in the core areas.
- IDEA 2004 suggested that the continuing disproportionate number of minority students classified as needing special education services resulted from improper evaluations of students with limited English language proficiency.
- The definition of *assistive technology devices* was amended to exclude devices that are surgically implanted (i.e., cochlear implants), and clarified that students with assistive technology devices shall not be prevented from having special education services. Assistive technology devices may need to be monitored by school personnel, but schools are not responsible for the surgical implantation or replacement of such devices surgically. An example of this would be a cochlear implant.
- The definition of *Child with a disability* is the term used for children ages 3-9 with a developmental delay. This definition was changed to allow for the inclusion of Tourette's Syndrome.
- IDEA 2004 recognized that all states must follow the National Instructional Materials Accessibility Standards, which state that students who need materials in a certain form will receive those at the same time their non-disabled peers receive their materials. Teacher recognition of this standard is important.

Keep up to date on the law and special education by subscribing to the free email service at: *http://wrightslaw.com*

MODELS AND THEORIES UNDERLYING SPECIAL EDUCATION

Services for students with disabilities may employ a variety of educational approaches. Because each student represents a unique combination of needs, the combination of services provided to the child per his or her IEP is also unique. There are many models and approaches that can be used in designing programs to meet student needs.

The cognitive approach to special education emphasizes measurable outcomes of a student's learning. It is often associated with Bloom's taxonomy of higher level thinking (knowledge, comprehension, application, analysis, and synthesis) and Haladyna's learning processes of understanding, problem solving, critical thinking, and creativity. Cognitive approaches to teaching often emphasize teaching metacognitive strategies through which the student becomes an active participant in the conceptual and cognitive learning process as the teacher facilitates.

The constructivist approach to special education is based heavily upon observations by Piaget and Vygotsky and uses student experience and experimentation to gain new knowledge rather than a presentation by the teacher. Many exceptional students learn well from a participatory, hands-on approach and might benefit from a constructivist component in the classroom.

Social and behavioral approaches look at the social interactions of students in the classroom that instruct or have an impact on learning opportunities. The psychological approaches behind both theories are subject to individual variables that are learned and applied either proactively or negatively in the classroom. The stimulus of the classroom can promote effective learning or evoke behavior that is counterproductive for both students and teachers. Cooperative and group exploratory activities are important components of this approach.

The sociological approach to special education takes into account the value of education in different cultures. If a child's sociological background is different from the prevailing culture where he lives, he may be perceived (inappropriately) as needing special education.

The ecological approach to special education emphasizes understanding the child in his or her life context. It recognizes that the effect of a disability is influenced by the child's family, background, culture, and the entire environment surrounding the child throughout life. It is important to take this background into consideration when making the determination of special education needs.

The therapeutic approach to special education addresses delays and disabilities using techniques such as:

- Speech and language therapy
- Physical therapy (gross motor function such as walking, climbing, running, jumping)
- Occupational therapy (fine motor function such as handwriting, using buttons and zippers, and manipulating objects such as puzzle pieces)
- Vision therapy (such as visual tracking)
- Art therapy

Learning Theories and Research explores how learning is affected by factors such as student learning style, how material is presented, and student background knowledge or experiences. Several educational learning theories have implications for classroom practices.

Some of the most prominent learning theories in education today have been influenced by brain-based learning research and the emergence of Multiple Intelligence Testing. Supported by recent brain research, these approaches suggest that knowledge about the way the brain retains information enables educators to design the most effective learning environments. Caine, et al (2005) cites twelve principles that relate knowledge about the brain to teaching practices. These twelve principles are

- The brain is a complex adaptive system.
- The brain is social.
- The search for meaning is innate.
- We use patterns to learn more effectively.
- Emotions are crucial to developing patterns.
- Each brain perceives and creates parts and whole simultaneously.
- Learning involves focused and peripheral attention.
- Learning involves conscious and unconscious processes.
- We have at least two ways of organizing memory.
- Learning is developmental.
- Complex learning is enhanced by challenge (and inhibited by threat).
- Every brain is unique (this is particularly relevant to teachers of students with special needs).

The Multiple Intelligences Theory, developed by Howard Gardner (1999), suggests that students learn in (at least) seven different ways. These include visually/spatially, musically, verbally, logically/mathematically, interpersonally, intrapersonally, and bodily/kinesthetically. Many students with disabilities find it particularly difficult to learn in a non-preferred style, so identifying the student's preferred style can be crucial to the accommodations needed for a student with disabilities.

THE INCLUSION MOVEMENT

The inclusion model has had enormous impact on special education. In its purest form, this movement is based on the philosophy that **all** children with disabilities belong in a general education classes, and that all must be accommodated and taught in that setting. This movement attracted many supporters who are both vocal and insistent about their beliefs. In many cases, the need for social integration of students with and without disabilities is at the heart of their concerns. Kirk, et al (2003) list six beliefs central to this movement:

- ALL students belong in general education class—NO exceptions whatsoever
- General education teachers can and should teach **all** students, including those with disabilities
- General education teachers will have all necessary supports to do this
- Quality education is a right, not a privilege
- Success, literacy, and graduation are a must for all students
- Alternative channels will be created for students who cannot otherwise succeed

Modifying Inclusion for Individual Needs

Although most educators today accept at least parts of this model as desirable, there are those who feel that there are problems inherent is assuming that **all** children benefit from this approach. They point out that to be successful, this approach requires either that general education teachers are also highly qualified in special education, or that every class has two teachers, one of whom is highly qualified in special education. It also requires a great deal of support from outside specialists and additional support staff in each classroom, supports that are not always available.

More importantly, opponents of full inclusion for **every** child without exception contend that each child's individual needs should determine the best placement. Forcing all children into one model of service conflicts with the modern movement to *individualize* each child's program and assumes that all children need the same approach. They contend that some children need alternative placement and are better served by a different model. They cite particularly students who need highly specialized instruction that cannot be delivered in a large classroom full of children, even when a small group is pulled to one side, as well as children who have demonstrated that they cannot learn in a large group because they need a smaller, quieter, more self-contained environment in which to function effectively.

See Skill 4.03 for an overview of a continuum of services to suit varying student needs.

Skill 16.02   Demonstrating knowledge of the rights and responsibilities of students, parents/guardians, teachers, other professionals, and schools as they relate to individual learning needs

SCHOOL AND EDUCATOR RESPONSIBILITIES

IDEA legislation is legally binding on all educators and schools and, in its current form, requires the following:

1. **Free Appropriate Public Education (FAPE)**
   This includes special education and related services which: (1) are provided at public expense; (2) meet the standards of the state educational agency; (3) include preschool, elementary, and/or secondary education in the state involved, and (4) are provided in conformity with each student's individualized education program, if the program is developed to meet requirements of the law.
   IDEA 2004 revised the definition of FAPE by mandating that students have maximum access to appropriate general education. Additionally, LRE placement for those students with disabilities must have the same school placement rights as those students who are not disabled. IDEA 2004 recognizes that due to the nature of some disabilities, appropriate education might vary in the amount of participation in the general education setting. For some students, FAPE will mean a choice of the type of educational institution they attend (for example, a public or a private school), any of which must provide the special education services deemed necessary for the student through the IEP.

2. **Notification and procedural rights for parents**
   These include:
   - The right to examine records and obtain independent evaluations
   - The right to receive a clearly written notice (in their native language) that states the results of the school's evaluation of their child and whether the child meets eligibility requirements for placement or continuation of special services, as well as advance notices of CSE meetings
   - Parents who disagree with the school's decision may request a *due process* hearing and a *judicial hearing* if they do not receive satisfaction through due process (see Skill 16.03).

3. **Identification and services to all children**
   States must conduct public outreach programs to seek out and identify children who might need services. Often referred to as *Zero Reject*, this requirement means schools cannot reject students regardless of the type (e.g., retardation, contagious disease) or severity of a disability, but must serve ALL. Efforts to find and serve all must be reported annually.

4. **Necessary related services**
   Developmental, corrective, and other support services that make it possible for a student to benefit from special education services must be

provided. These might include speech, recreation, or physical therapy.

5. **Individualized assessments**

    Evaluations and tests must be nondiscriminatory, individualized, and in the student's native language. IDEA 97 also placed an additional requirement of a definitive reason why a standard general education assessment would not be deemed appropriate for a child and how the child should then be assessed.

6. **Individualized Education Plans**

    Each student receiving special education services must have an *Individualized Education Plan* developed at a meeting that is attended by a qualified representative of the local education agency (LEA). Others who should attend include the proposed special education teachers, mainstream teachers, parents, and, when appropriate, the student. See Skill 5.02 for IEP details.

7. **Least Restrictive Environment (LRE)**

    There is no simple definition of LRE. LRE differs with the child's needs. LRE means that the student is placed in an environment that is not dangerous, overly controlling, or intrusive but that is as close to the general education setting as is consistent with the child's needs. The student should be given opportunities to experience what peers of similar mental or chronological age are doing. IDEA recognizes that LRE for one child might be a regular classroom with support services, while LRE for another might be a self-contained classroom in a special school. (See Skill 4.01 for a cascade of placements relevant to LRE.)

IDEA requires schools to establish performance goals and indicators for children with disabilities—consistent to the maximum extent appropriate with other goals and standards for all children established by the state—and to report on progress toward meeting those goals.

In summary, all schools, teachers, and other school personnel providing services to students with disabilities are required by law to abide by the provisions of each child's IEP.

Consequences for Violating IDEA (and IEP) Provisions

Any school system, school, or teacher violating IDEA law can be held legally accountable. "Violating IDEA" can mean many different things. School systems can be found in violation if they fail to adequately search for students with disabilities, if they take too long to identify and provide services to a child, or if they fail to provide services listed in the IEP, among other things. When teachers are found in violation, it is usually because they have failed to provide the modifications and accommodations required by a student's IEP. All such "violations" mean, basically, that a student's rights have been violated, that something a school or teacher did or did NOT do deprived a student of the right to FAPE or LRE.

Katsyannis and Maag (1997) found that "Courts have consistently upheld the right of parents to receive relief for violations that inhibit a student's right to FAPE" (p. 452). This usually involves compensatory education at the expense of the school, reimbursement to the family of educational costs and legal fees, paying for alternative schools and services, and, increasingly, awarding monetary damages to students and their families. These damages have been assessed against schools and *against individual teachers*. In Doe v. Withers (1992), for instance, the school was assessed a large fine and the teacher involved was required to pay $35,000.00 in restitution to the parents.

Such legal requirements and the potential consequences for violations can pose a challenge to the teachers who must be familiar with each child's IEP and provide the modifications and accommodations outlined in it. The teacher who is listed as the liaison on the IEP is also responsible for keeping an eye on everyone *else* providing services to the student to be sure *they* are following the IEP. If the IEP says, for example, that the student may dictate answers to tests, the teacher cannot say that there is no time for this or no aide to help. If the IEP says to enlarge printed materials and place information on four separate panels with a frame around each, the teacher cannot plead a lack of ink or paper. If the IEP says the child gets a ten minute break every hour, the teacher must find a way to deliver the lessons in the remaining fifty minutes.

These requirements can be challenging, but teachers must understand that they are legally required to follow them. IDEA is the blueprint for special education today and it is the teacher's responsibility to be familiar with it in its most current form and to abide by its provisions. It may not always be easy, but it's part of the job.

Additional Educator Responsibilities

In New York State, teachers, like all school officials, are "mandated reporters" and are required by law to report suspected child abuse or neglect to the New York State Central Register (SCR) of Child Abuse and Maltreatment. Such reports do NOT require parental permission. Failure to carry out this responsibility carries both civil and criminal consequences. Teachers are also required to abide by New York State "conflict of interest" regulations.

Additional Parental Rights

Parents and students have certain rights under the No Child Left Behind (NCLB) Act of 2002. The purpose of the NCLB is to ensure that all children have a fair, equal, and significant opportunity to obtain a high-quality education. The act has several parental involvement provisions that reflect shared accountability between schools and parents for high student achievement, including expanded public school choice and supplemental educational services for eligible children in low performing schools, local development of parental involvement plans with sufficient flexibility to address local needs, and the building of parents' capacities for using effective practices to improve their own children's academic achievement.

Great Resource: Printable Parents' Rights Guides:
http://www.specialednews.com/behavior/behavnews/CECbehavassess021900.html

The NYS Parents' Rights Guide:
http://www.vesid.nysed.gov/specialed/publications/policy/parentguide.htm

Skill 16.03   Recognizing and analyzing due process rights related to assessment, eligibility, and placement

Please refer to Skill 16.02 for more information on this topic.

Due process occurs in two realms: substantive and procedural. Substantive due process is the content of the law (e.g., appropriate placement for special education students). Procedural due process is the form through which substantive due process is carried out (e.g., parental permission for testing). IDEA contains many items of both substantive and procedural due process, such as:

1. A due process hearing may be initiated by parents or the Local Education Agency (LEA) as an impartial forum for challenging decisions about identification, evaluation, or placement. Either party may present evidence, cross-examine witnesses, obtain a record of the hearing, and be advised by counsel or by individuals having expertise in the education of individuals with disabilities. Findings may be appealed to the state education agency (SEA), and, if still dissatisfied, either party may bring civil action in a state or federal district court. Hearing timelines are set by legislation.

2. Parents may obtain an independent evaluation if there is disagreement about the education evaluation performed by the LEA. The results of such an evaluation: (1) must be considered in any decision made with respect to the provision of a free, appropriate public education for the child and (2) may be presented as evidence at a hearing. Further, the parents may request this evaluation at public expense: (1) if a hearing officer requests an independent educational evaluation or (2) if the decision from a due process hearing is that the LEA's evaluation was inappropriate. If the final decision holds that the evaluation performed is appropriate, the parent still has the right to an independent educational evaluation, but not at public expense.

3. Written notice must be provided to parents prior to a proposal or refusal to initiate or make a change in the child's identification, evaluation, or educational placement and must include the following:

a. A listing of parental due process safeguards
b. A description and a rationale for the chosen action
c. A detailed listing of the components (e.g., tests, records, reports) that were the basis for the decision
d. Assurance that the language and content of notices were understood by the parents

4. Parental consent must be obtained before evaluation procedures can occur unless parents or guardians cannot be identified to function in the due process role. When this occurs, a suitable person must be assigned to act as a surrogate. This is done by the LEA in full accordance with legislation.

Learn more about due process here:
http://www.wrightslaw.com/info/dp.index.htm

Skill 16.04 Demonstrating knowledge of health and safety issues related to the definition and provision of special education services

HEALTH ISSUES

In addition to having a disability that affects learning, students might also have medical conditions and other health impairments that affect the school day. Such medical complications must be considered when developing schedules and curricular plans. Students might miss school due to medical conditions that require extensive rest or hospital-based intervention. Cooperative programs with home and hospital teachers can decrease the impact of such absences.

Also of considerable concern is the tendency to overcompensate. Teachers should try not to focus too much on the medical implications of a student's handicap. Interruptions for suctioning, medication, or other medical interventions should not be disruptive to the classroom and the learning atmosphere. Focus should be on maximizing opportunities for educational success and social interaction, not on limitations and isolation. For example, class parties can include food treats that meet a student's dietary restrictions, or medical intervention can be completed during individual work times rather than during group-learning activity periods.

Students with seizures will require considerable medical support. A seizure is an abnormal electrical discharge in the brain. Incidences and behaviors range from experiencing odd tastes or smells to jerking and spasms throughout the body. The individual may experience altered consciousness or the loss of consciousness, muscle control, or bladder control. All staff must be familiar with the particular child's seizure pattern and possible triggers, and be trained to respond appropriately.

Asthma is another condition that can require intervention during the school day. Asthma is a condition in which the person's airway becomes inflamed, often followed by airway constriction. The inflammation may cause coughing, wheezing, tightness of chest, and shortness of breath. Students might have inhalers or medication at school and staff should be trained to recognize symptoms and respond appropriately.

Juvenile diabetes, a condition in which the pancreas cannot produce insulin, or insulin is produced in extremely small amounts, can require students to take insulin injections at school. A student with diabetes should have a plan worked out with the child's doctor and the school nurse. This plan may include such things as allowing the child to eat snacks during the day, monitor blood sugar levels, and take insulin shots.

Some students might also require tube feeding. Tube feeding is a method of providing nutrition to people who cannot sufficiently obtain calories by eating, or to those who cannot eat because they have difficulty swallowing. Staff will require special training for tube feeding. Tube feeding is common among students with dysphagia, a condition that hampers swallowing.

Other students might need to use catheters. A catheter is a thin, flexible, hollow plastic tube that can be used to perform various diagnostic and/or therapeutic procedures. They are designed to gain access to the body with as little trauma as possible.

See Skill 2.04 for information on common medications.

Several laws and court cases have had a direct impact on handling medical conditions in the school setting, so these cases are mentioned again here, though they can be found earlier in this guide:

School Board of Nassau County v. Arline, 1987: This case established that contagious diseases are a disability under Section 504 of the Rehabilitation Act and that people with contagious diseases are protected from discrimination if otherwise qualified (actual risk to the health and safety to others make persons unqualified).

Irving Independent School District v. Tatro 1984: IDEA lists health services as one of the "related services" that schools are mandated to provide to exceptional students. Amber Tatro, who had spina bifida, required the insertion of a catheter on a regular schedule in order to empty her bladder. The issue was specifically over whether clean, intermittent catheterization (CIC) is categorized as a "medical service" (not covered under IDEA) or as a "related health service," which would be covered. In this instance, the catheterization was not declared a medical service, but a related service necessary for the student to benefit from special education. The school district was obliged to provide the service. The

Tatro case has implications for students with other medical impairments who may need services to allow them to attend classes at the school.

OTHER SAFETY ISSUES

Children need to feel safe from dangers while at school and during transit to and from school. Educators must respond to this basic need by providing adequate supervision and by developing appropriate safety procedures.
Functional reading skills

Attention to functional reading skills is even more important for the child or adult with a disability than for a person who has no identified disability. It is incorrect to assume that there will always be a caretaker available to the person with a disability to read for him or her, especially in times of danger and personal necessity. If reading skills are too poor for safety, visual symbols must be used as accommodations.

Examples of reading requirements on the most basic level are STOP, DO NOT TOUCH, HOT, and OFF/ON signs; directions for use with most appliances, conveyances, and facilities; and warnings in many social settings. The individual with a disability will need some reading skills in order to deal successfully with the pedestrian crossing lane at a busy intersection, the tramway at the airport, the taxicab, the stairs in a public building, a revolving door, an escalator, and a fire exit.

Physical Arrangements

The special education classroom, as well as regular classroom and support areas that are utilized by all students, should be set up and maintained so that students can move about freely without incurring physical harm. Avoiding physical barriers and formulating appropriate procedures for emergencies are also necessary conditions for students with disabilities. Children with sensory impairments who are not able to hear audible alarms or see danger signals, or those with limited intellectual capabilities who may not respond well in atypical situations, need to be protected with pre-established, well-thought-out procedural regulations. Furthermore, school personnel need to be trained in handling and positioning students with physical impairments so that risk of further physical disability is minimized.

Vocational training programs: These may involve the use of specialized machines and equipment and presenting modifications and teaching techniques can be of benefit, such as (1) ensuring a stable and predictable training environment; (2) outlining concrete, step-by-step procedures; (3) posting a list of classroom and laboratory safety rules; and (4) reacting calmly to inappropriate behavior, while firmly enforcing set procedures and regulations.

Skill 16.05   Demonstrating knowledge of ethical practices in instruction and other professional activities (e.g., interactions with students, use of copyrighted educational materials, use of information technology) related to the education of students with disabilities

Please refer to Skills 5.08 (confidentiality), 14.07 (communication and collaboration), 16.02 (rights and responsibilities), and 17.02 (CEC Code of Ethics).

The special educator is expected to demonstrate ethical practice in all areas of his or her teaching responsibilities. With regards to interaction with students, teaching and discipline practices should reflect practices that are respectful of the student as a person and follow IDEA law. Researched-based methods should be employed that will provide measurable outcomes.

The ethics of special education go beyond methods to materials. With students of a variety of age and/or ability levels, and often limited funding, appropriate materials can be difficult to obtain. If possible, students should be included in the headcount for ordering general education materials. When alternative materials are needed, it is important to secure those through special education funding sources in the school. Teaching materials that are copyrighted may not be photocopied unless they are specifically intended for such use (as printed on the materials). The same is true for musical materials that have a copyright. If materials are intended for reproduction, it will be stated.

Information technology brings a world of information to the classroom. Careful consideration should be given, however, to the validity of the information before it is incorporated into practice or curricular material. Reputable sources for education practices will have connections to recognized organizations for special educators, such as the Council for Exceptional Children, or to teacher training programs.

Likewise, students should be guided in finding and using valid websites for research and learning. It is important to teach the philosophy that not everything on the internet is true.

Ethical practice in communication is an additional expectation of all educators— especially of those teaching students with disabilities. Confidentiality is crucial. Specific information regarding a student's disability and IEP should be discussed only with the team of professionals working with the student and the student's family. When an exchange of information is needed with another school district, physician, therapist, or other professional outside of the school district, it is necessary to get written permission from the student's parent. Often, forms for this are available from the school district.

COMPETENCY 0017 UNDERSTAND THE PROFESSIONAL FOUNDATIONS OF EDUCATION FOR STUDENTS WITH DISABILITIES

Skill 17.01 Demonstrating knowledge of how to advocate effectively for students with disabilities and for the special education program

Because of the unique needs of each student with disabilities, special education teachers are frequently advocates for their students and for the special education program in general.

In order to be an effective advocate, the teacher must be knowledgeable in a number of areas. First, the special educator must understand the general education program that is the counterpart to the special education program. Factors such as student expectations (learning standards), materials used, teacher training, and in-service provide a starting point. If the special educator is familiar with the goals and standards for all students at a specific grade level, he or she will have a clear picture of the direction in which to be working.

The special educator should also have a clear understanding of each student's strengths and needs. The teacher must be intimately familiar with the provisions of each child's IEP and the implications of those provisions for all aspects of the student's education. He or she must consider how each student can participate in the general education curriculum to the extent that it is beneficial for that student (IDEA 2004). For example, the teacher should know when services and instruction take place outside of the general education classroom.

In addition, special educators should have an understanding of alternate materials that can be useful or necessary for students as well as what resources for these materials are available.

Knowledge of the Individuals with Disabilities Education Act (IDEA 2004) and NCLB (No Child Left Behind) provides an outline of legislative mandates for special education.

Often advocacy happens between regular and special education teachers. A special educator might see modification or accommodation possibilities that could take place in the general education classroom. It is his or her responsibility to advocate for those practices, particularly if they are mandated in the student's IEP. The special education teacher may also offer to make supplementary materials or to work with a group of students in the general education setting to achieve that goal (see skills in Subarea II on collaboration).

There might even be cases where the special education teacher needs to advocate and educate others (parents, administrators, general education teachers) about the need for the special education program and the resources it uses. They might need to field questions about why certain students get particular accommodations and others don't, why some classes have aides and others don't, why a small subset program has so few students and several teachers, why so much of the budget is spent on special education, or even why a proposed field trip must include an expensive special bus for a child in a wheelchair. Teachers who are knowledgeable about the law and the principles behind special education rights and responsibilities will be well equipped to advocate for the program when these questions arise.

Such advocacy is sometimes necessary with the administration as well. It is the responsibility of the teacher to explain the need for comparable materials written at a different reading level, the need for assistance in the classroom, or the need to offer specific classes or therapies.

Occasionally, the local school district cannot provide an appropriate educational setting. The special educator may then wish to advocate with the school district for appropriate placement of the child in another, more suitable, environment. However, the teacher should be familiar with school policies on this matter and whether such recommendations can be made in meetings or must be delivered through the teacher's superior. A list of groups that can help advocate for students with disabilities is included at the end of this document.

Learn more about advocating for the special education child in an inclusive setting here: *http://www.ldonline.org/article/5690*

Skill 17.02 Demonstrating knowledge of the standards and policies of the profession (e.g., the codes of ethics of the Council for Exceptional Children [CEC] and other organizations)

New York State has a Code of Ethics for Educators that is binding on all educators in New York (see below).

The Council for Exceptional Children (CEC) is a national professional organization concerned specifically with teaching students with disabilities. The CEC has established the *Ethical Principles for Special Education Professionals* (CEC, Updated in January, 2010). This code follows the New York Code.

New York State Code of Ethics for Educators:
http://www.highered.nysed.gov/tcert/resteachers/codeofethics.html#statement17.02

Statement of Purpose

The Code of Ethics is a public statement by educators that sets clear expectations and principles to guide practice and inspire professional excellence. Educators believe a commonly-held set of principles can assist in the individual exercise of professional judgment. This Code speaks to the core values of the profession. "Educator," as used throughout, means all educators serving New York schools in positions requiring a certificate, including classroom teachers, school leaders, and pupil personnel service providers.

Principle 1: Educators nurture the intellectual, physical, emotional, social, and civic potential of each student.

Educators promote growth in all students through the integration of intellectual, physical, emotional, social, and civic learning. They respect the inherent dignity and worth of each individual. Educators help students to value their own identities, learn more about their cultural heritage, and practice social and civic responsibilities. They help students to reflect on their own learning and connect it to their life experiences. They engage students in activities that encourage diverse approaches and solutions to issues while providing a range of ways for students to demonstrate their abilities and learning. They foster the development of students who can analyze, synthesize, evaluate, and communicate information effectively.

Principle 2: Educators create, support, and maintain challenging learning environments for all.

Educators apply their professional knowledge to promote student learning. They know the curriculum and utilize a range of strategies and assessments to address differences. Educators develop and implement programs based on a strong understanding of human development and learning theory. They support a challenging learning environment. They advocate for necessary resources to teach to higher levels of learning. They establish and maintain clear standards of behavior and civility. Educators are role models, displaying the habits of mind and work necessary to develop and apply knowledge while simultaneously displaying a curiosity and enthusiasm for learning. They invite students to become active, inquisitive, and discerning individuals who reflect upon and monitor their own learning.

Principle 3: Educators commit to their own learning in order to develop their practice.

Educators recognize that professional knowledge and development are the foundations of their practice. They know their subject matter and they understand how students learn. Educators respect the reciprocal nature of learning between educators and students. They engage in a variety of individual and collaborative learning experiences essential to develop professionally and to promote student learning. They draw on and contribute to various forms of educational research to improve their own practice.

Principle 4: Educators collaborate with colleagues and other professionals in the interest of student learning.

Educators encourage and support their colleagues to build and maintain high standards. They participate in decisions regarding curriculum, instruction, and assessment designs, and they share responsibility for the governance of schools. They cooperate with community agencies in using resources and building comprehensive services in support of students. Educators respect fellow professionals and believe that all have the right to teach and learn in a professional and supportive environment. They participate in the preparation and induction of new educators and in professional development for all staff.

Principle 5: Educators collaborate with parents and community, building trust and respecting confidentiality.

Educators partner with parents and other members of the community to enhance school programs and to promote student learning. They also recognize how cultural and linguistic heritage, gender, family, and community shape experiences and learning. Educators respect the private nature of the special knowledge they have about students and their families and use that knowledge only in the students' best interests. They advocate for fair opportunity for all children.

Principle 6: Educators advance the intellectual and ethical foundation of the learning community.

Educators recognize the obligations of the trust placed in them. They share the responsibility for understanding what is known, pursuing further knowledge, contributing to the generation of knowledge, and translating knowledge into comprehensible forms. They help students understand that knowledge is often complex and sometimes paradoxical. Educators are confidantes, mentors, and advocates for their students' growth and development. As models for youth and the public, they embody intellectual honesty, diplomacy, tact, and fairness.

CEC Ethical Principles for Special Education Professionals

Professional special educators are guided by the CEC professional ethical principles and practice standards in ways that respect the diverse characteristics and needs of individuals with exceptionalities and their families. They are committed to upholding and advancing the following principles:

1. Maintaining challenging expectations for individuals with exceptionalities to develop the highest possible learning outcomes and quality of life potential in ways that respect their dignity, culture, language, and background

2. Maintaining a high level of professional competence and integrity and exercising professional judgment to benefit individuals with exceptionalities and their families

3. Promoting meaningful and inclusive participation of individuals with exceptionalities in their schools and communities

4. Practicing collegially with others who are providing services to individuals with exceptionalities

5. Developing relationships with families based on mutual respect and actively involving families and individuals with exceptionalities in educational decision making

6. Using evidence, instructional data, research, and professional knowledge to inform practice

7. Protecting and supporting the physical and psychological safety of individuals with exceptionalities

8. Neither engaging in nor tolerating any practice that harms individuals with exceptionalities

9. Practicing within the professional ethics, standards, and policies of CEC; upholding laws, regulations, and policies that influence professional practice; and advocating for improvements in laws, regulations, and policies

10. Advocating for professional conditions and resources that will improve learning outcomes of individuals with exceptionalities

11. Engaging in the improvement of the profession through active participation in professional organizations

12. Participating in the growth and dissemination of professional knowledge and skills

Adopted by the CEC Board of Directors, January 2010.

Skill 17.03   Demonstrating the ability to exercise objective professional judgment

The special education teacher comes to the job with past experiences as well as personal opinions and beliefs. It is vital that he or she not let those personal persuasions guide professional actions. Objective professional judgment is important in all areas of the teacher's role.

Objective professional judgment should be exercised when considering the cultural, religious, and sexual orientations of the special educator's students and families. An unbiased approach to communication maintains positive interaction and increased cooperation between home and school. The result is a better educational program that will meet the individual student's needs. (See Skill 13.08 for information on self-assessment in this regard.)

Objectivity should also be exercised when considering assessment of a possible disability. An educator's preference for a particular assessment should be secondary to matching the needs of the child with the best assessment instrument. Assessment tools should be research-based and determined to be appropriate for the needs of the specific student.

When establishing the special education program, the specific student's IEP must be followed. If the special educator determines that the goals and objectives of the IEP no longer fit the child's needs, an IEP meeting should be called to review and possibly revise the document. Again, the revision of the IEP should be based on the needs of the child as determined objectively and not on the personal preference of the teacher for a particular type of program or schedule. This objectivity should include materials, scheduling, activities, and evaluation.

The student's IEP should also be focused on the learning standards established by the state. In particular, learning activities should be employed that provide measurable outcomes. Such data provides objective evaluation of student progress and mastery of the targeted standards.

Professional objectivity is crucial in communication with administration for the representation of students' needs for placement, programming, materials, scheduling, and staffing. When documented, data-driven information is presented, optimum decisions are made for students with disabilities and for the school community in general.

Skill 17.04 Identifying ways to address one's own cultural biases and differences to ensure positive regard for the culture, religion, gender, and sexual orientation of individual students

Refer also to Skill 13.08.

The role of the special education teacher is to advocate for the most appropriate education for students and to guide them in discovering new knowledge and developing new skills to the best of their potential. According to IDEA 2004, the teacher is to prepare them for future purposeful work in society with the possibility of post-secondary education or training.

Although each special educator is also a person with a set of experiences, opinions, and beliefs, it is important to remain unbiased and positive in a professional role with students, parents, administration, and the community. Differences in culture, religion, gender, or sexual orientation should not influence the teacher's approach to instruction, student goals or expectations, or advocacy.

In order to remain unbiased, the special educator should avail him or herself of opportunities to learn about various cultures, religions, genders, and sexual orientations. This can be accomplished through reading, classroom awareness activities, and teacher in-service.

- Reading to increase awareness and acceptance of cultural differences can be done through professional, adult literature, as well as through books to be read with the class.
- Cultural activities in the classroom are especially well-received. This includes foods, dress, and games, which are easily added to curriculum and often address learning standards.

The special educator is charged with academic, social, communicative, and independent skills instruction. Education or influence in other areas (e.g., political or religious views) is a violation of ethics. In addition, teachers must be careful that their actions both inside and outside the school setting do not violate state conflict of interest regulations.

When the special educator remains unbiased, he or she is better able to meet the needs of students without reacting to additional, irrelevant factors. The students and their families are also more open to school-related suggestions.

The teacher's reaction to differences models the commonly taught character trait of respect in education. When the teacher demonstrates respect for all individuals in a program, it is likely that respect will also be practiced by students, parents, and administration.

Learn more about cultural competence for teachers here:
http://www.opb.org/education/minisites/culturalcompetence/teachers.html

Skill 17.05   Identifying professional activities, including self-reflection and self-assessment, to improve one's own effectiveness in providing services to individuals with disabilities and their families

When providing services to students with disabilities and their families, teachers need to be involved in a wide range of professional activities that will help improve their instruction and their effectiveness in the classroom. This should include self-reflection and self-assessment. (See Skill 13.08 for more on this topic.)

Self-reflection involves considering one's practice to improve instruction and to guide professional growth. In the area of special education, this entails evaluating how successful one is at ensuring that students are meeting their short- and long-term goals in the classroom. When teachers reflect on their own performance, they can evaluate what they are doing right and where they can make improvements.

The teacher should participate in professional activities and organizations that benefit individuals with exceptional needs, their families, and their colleagues. This will ensure that they are on the cutting edge of any new legislation that applies to special education teachers; it will also ensure that they are aware of the research-based best practices that are being implemented in teaching students with disabilities. They should incorporate the newly discovered research into their daily teaching practices.

Other activities that improve teacher effectiveness include using available and innovative resources and technologies to enhance personal productivity and efficiency; using methods to remain current regarding evidence-based practices; and maintaining student, familial, and collegial confidentiality.

Special education teachers need to be aware of how personal cultural biases and differences impact teaching and learning. They should also be aware of professional organizations relevant to their practice.

The self-assessment and reflection process should form the basis for decisions about programs and instructional strategies. After the teacher has reflected and assessed his or her own performance in the classroom, he or she should work to improve teaching practice because professional growth is the practitioner's responsibility.

Skill 17.06 Recognizing strategies for establishing and maintaining ongoing communication and collaboration with other professionals in the field

Please refer to Subarea III for information on collaboration with other professionals in the school setting.

In their efforts to continually improve their own knowledge and skills and to remain current on relevant research and practices that might be helpful to their students, teachers need to go beyond their own schools and establish collaborative relationships with other professionals in the field. There are a variety of strategies for doing this, including such practices as:

- Joining professional associations such as the National Association of Special Education Teachers or the Council for Exceptional Children
- Reading relevant professional journals
- Contributing to relevant professional journals
- Attending professional workshops, seminars, and conferences
- Participating in professionally relevant interactive websites and list serves that allow professionals to consult on common issues
- Visiting and observing other professionals in the field

SUBAREA IV.   **PROMOTING STUDENT LEARNING AND DEVELOPMENT IN A COLLABORATIVE LEARNING COMMUNITY: CONSTRUCTED RESPONSE**

The content to be addressed by the constructed-response assignment is described in Subarea II, Competencies 06–13.

Sample Test

1. **Which is an educational characteristic common to students with mild intellectual learning and behavioral disabilities?** *(Skill 1.01) (Easy)*

   A. Show interest in schoolwork
   B. Have intact listening skills
   C. Require modification in classroom instruction
   D. Respond better to passive than to active learning tasks

2. **Which of the following statements about children with an emotional/behavioral disorder is true?** *(Skill 1.01) (Average)*

   A. They have very high IQs
   B. They display poor social skills
   C. They are academic achievers
   D. They have a mature understanding of concepts

3. **Which of these is not true for most children with behavior disorders?** *(Skill 1.01) (Average)*

   A. Many score in the "slow learner" or "mildly retarded" range on IQ tests
   B. They are frequently behind their classmates in academic achievement
   C. They are bright but bored with their surroundings
   D. They spend a large amount of time in nonproductive, nonacademic behaviors

4. **Echolalia is a characteristic of what?** *(Skill 1.01) (Average)*

   A. Autism
   B. Mental retardation
   C. Social Pragmatic Disorder
   D. ADHD

5. **The social skills of students in mental retardation programs are likely to be appropriate for children of their mental age, rather than chronological age. This means that the teacher will need to do all of the following except:** *(Skill 1.01) (Easy)*

   A. Model desired behavior
   B. Provide clear instructions
   C. Expect age appropriate behaviors
   D. Adjust the physical environment when necessary

6. **Jonathan has attention deficit hyperactivity disorder (ADHD). He is in a regular classroom and appears to be doing okay. However, his teacher does not want Jonathan in her class because he will not obey her when she asks him to stop doing a repetitive action such as tapping his foot. The teacher sees this as distractive during tests. Jonathan needs:** *(Skill 1.02) (Easy)*

   A. An IEP
   B. A 504 Plan
   C. A VESID evaluation
   D. A more restrictive environment

7. Five-year-old Tom continues to substitute the "w" sound for the "r" sound when pronouncing words; therefore, he often distorts words (e.g., "wabbit" for "rabbit" and "wat" for "rat"). His articulation disorder is basically a problem in: *(Skill 1.04) (Easy)*

   A. Phonology
   B. Morphology
   C. Syntax
   D. Semantics

8. Mark is a 6th grader. You have noticed that he doesn't respond to simple requests like the other students in your class. If you ask him to erase the board, he might look at you, shake his head, and say "no," but then he will clean the board. When the children gather together for recess, he joins them. However, you observe that it takes him much longer to understand the rules to a game. Mark retains what he reads. Mark most likely has: *(Skill 1.04) (Rigorous)*

   A. Oppositional-Defiant Disorder
   B. Tourette's syndrome
   C. Mental retardation
   D. A pragmatic language disability

9. Which of the following is an example of cross-modal perception involving integrating visual stimuli to an auditory verbal process? *(Skill 2.01) (Average)*

   A. Following spoken directions
   B. Describing a picture
   C. Finding certain objects in pictures
   D. Both B and C

10. Justin is diagnosed with autism and is in an inclusive setting. You were called down to "stop him from turning off the lights and remove him." When you arrive, you learn that today a movie was supposed to be finished, but the VCR broke, so the teacher planned another activity. What is the best way to explain to the teacher why Justin was turning off the lights? *(Skill 2.02) (Easy)*

   A. He is perseverating and will stop shortly.
   B. He is telling you the lights bother him.
   C. He needs forewarning before a transition. Next time you have an unexpected change in classroom schedule, please let him know.
   D. Please understand, this is part of who Justin is. He will leave the lights alone after I talk to him.

11. Which of these characteristics is NOT included in the IDEA definition of emotional disturbance? *(Skill 2.02) (Average)*

A. General pervasive mood of unhappiness or depression
B. Social maladjustment such as gang activity or truancy manifested in a number of settings
C. Tendency to develop physical symptoms, pains, or fear associated with school or personal problems
D. Inability to learn that is not attributed to intellectual, sensory, or health factors

12. Children with visual-spatial difficulties might struggle with tasks such as: *(Skills 2.03 and 10.05) (Rigorous)*

A. Writing fractions and before/after concepts in math
B. Differentiating the characteristics of a certain letter in print
C. A delay in achieving the "th" sound
D. Both A and B

13. A developmental delay may be indicated by a: *(Skill 2.03) (Rigorous)*

A. Second grader having difficulty buttoning clothing
B. Stuttered response
C. Kindergartner not having complete bladder control
D. Withdrawn behavior

14. For which of the following purposes is a norm-referenced test least appropriate? *(Skill 3.01) (Average)*

A. Screening
B. Individual program planning
C. Program evaluation
D. Making placement decisions

15. Marcie is often not in her seat when the bell rings. She can be found at the pencil sharpener, throwing paper away, or fumbling through her notebook. Which of these descriptions of her behavior can be described as a pinpoint? *(Skill 3.01 and 13.07) (Easy)*

A. Is tardy
B. Is out of seat
C. Is not in seat when late bell rings
D. Is disorganized

16. The purpose of error analysis of a test is to: *(Skill 3.01) (Easy)*

A. Determine which events were labeled in error
B. Determine if the test length was the cause of error
C. Evaluate the types of errors made by categorizing incorrect answers
D. Establish a baseline

17. **Behaviors for which frequency is an appropriate measure include all but those that:** *(Skill 3.01) (Average)*

    A. Have an observable beginning
    B. Last a long time
    C. Last only a short time
    D. Occur often

18. **The extent to which a test measures what it claims to measure is called:** *(Skill 3.01) (Rigorous)*

    A. Reliability
    B. Validity
    C. Factor analysis
    D. Chi square

19. **Which would not be an advantage of using a criterion-referenced test?** *(Skill 3.02) (Rigorous)*

    A. Information is obtained about an individual's mastery of specific objectives.
    B. It can pinpoint exact areas of weaknesses and strengths
    C. You can design this type of test yourself
    D. You get comparative information

20. **Michael's teacher complains that he is constantly out of his seat. She also reports that he has trouble paying attention to what is going on in class for more than a couple of minutes at a time. He appears to be trying, but his writing is often illegible and contains many reversals. Although he seems to want to please, he is very impulsive and is constantly in trouble with his teacher. He is failing reading, and his math grades, though somewhat better, are still below average. Michael's psychometric evaluation should include assessment for:** *(Skill 3.02) (Average)*

    A. Mild mental retardation
    B. Specific learning disabilities
    C. Mild behavior disorders
    D. Hearing impairment

21. **Which of the following examples would be considered the highest priority when determining the need for the delivery of appropriate special education and related services?** *(Skill 4.01) (Rigorous)*

    A. A ten-year-old girl with profound mental retardation is receiving education services in a state institution.
    B. A six-year-old girl who has been diagnosed as autistic is placed in a special education class within the local school. Her mother wants her to attend a residential school next year, even though the girl is showing progress.

C. An eight-year-old boy is repeating first grade for the second time and exhibits problems with toileting, gross motor functions, and remembering number and letter symbols. His regular classroom teacher claims the referral forms are too time-consuming and refuses to complete them. He also refuses to make accommodations because he feels every child should be treated alike.

D. A twelve-year-old boy with mild disabilities was placed in a behavior disorders program, but displays obvious perceptual deficits (e.g., reversal of letters and symbols, inability to discriminate sounds). He was originally thought to have a learning disability, but did not meet state criteria for this exceptionality category based on results of standard scores. He has always had problems with attending to a task, and is now beginning to get into trouble during seatwork time. His teacher feels that he will eventually become a real behavior problem. He receives social skills training in the resource room one period a day.

22. **Acculturation refers to the individual's:**
    (Skill 4.07) (Rigorous)

    A. Gender
    B. Experiential background
    C. Social class
    D. Ethnic background

23. **Which components of the IEP are required by law?**
    (Skill 5.02) (Average)

    A. Present level of academic and functional performance; statement of how the disability affects the student's involvement and progress; evaluation criteria and timelines for instructional objective achievement; modifications and accommodations
    B. Projected dates for services initiation with anticipated frequency, location, and duration; statement of when parent will be notified; statement of annual goals
    C. Extent to which child will not participate in regular education program; transitional needs for students age 14 and older
    D. All of the above

24. **Shyquan is in your inclusive class, and she exhibits a slower comprehension of assigned tasks and concepts. Her first two grades were Bs but she is now receiving failing marks. She has seen the resource teacher. You should:**
    (Skill 5.04 and 5.05) (Rigorous)

    A. Ask for a review of current placement
    B. Tell Shyquan to seek extra help
    C. Ask Shyquan if she is frustrated
    D. Ask the regular education teacher to slow instruction

25. Taiquan's parents are divorced and have joint custody. They have both requested to be present at the CSE. You call to make sure that they received the letter informing them of the upcoming CSE. Taiquan's father did not receive the notification and is upset. You should: *(Skill 5.04 and 16.02)* *(Rigorous)*

    A. Tell him that you could review the meeting with him later
    B. Ask him if he can adjust his schedule
    C. Tell him you can reschedule the meeting
    D. Ask him to coordinate a time for the CSE to meet with his ex-wife

26. Teachers must keep meticulous records. They are required to share all of them with the student's parent/guardian EXCEPT: *(Skill 5.08) (Rigorous)*

    A. Daily attendance record
    B. Grade reports
    C. Teacher's personal notes
    D. Discipline notice placed in cumulative record

27. Kareem's father sounds upset and is in the office demanding to see his son's cumulative record. You should: *(Skill 5.08) (Average)*

    A. Tell him that he will have to make an appointment
    B. Bring the record to a private room for him to review with either an administrator or yourself
    C. Take the record to the principal's office for review
    D. Give the record to the parent

28. Students with autistic tendencies can be more successful academically when the teacher: *(Skill 6.01) (Average)*

    A. Ignores inappropriate behaviors
    B. Allows them to go out of the room during instruction
    C. Keeps a calendar on the board of expected transitions
    D. Asks the CSE for a 1:1 aide

29. Charise comes into your room and seems to know every button to push to make you upset with her. What would be a good intervention? *(Skill 6.01) (Rigorous)*

    A. Nonverbal Interactions
    B. Self-monitoring
    C. Proximity control
    D. Planned ignoring

30. In a positive classroom environment, errors are viewed as: *(Skill 6.01) (Average)*

    A. Symptoms of deficiencies
    B. The result of lack of attention or ability
    C. A natural part of the learning process
    D. The result of going too quickly

31. Which of the following is a responsibility that cannot be delegated to a classroom aide? *(Skill 6.08) (Average)*

    A. Small group instruction
    B. Small group planning
    C. Designing a lesson plan
    D. Assisting in BIP implementation

32. The greatest number of students receiving special services are enrolled primarily in: *(Skill 7.01) (Average)*

    A. The regular classroom
    B. The resource room
    C. Self-contained classrooms
    D. Special schools

33. Which is a less-than-ideal example of collaboration in successful inclusion? *(Skill 7.01) (Rigorous)*

    A. Special education teachers are part of the instructional team in a regular classroom
    B. Special education teachers are informed of the lesson beforehand and assist regular education teachers in the classroom
    C. Teaming approaches are used for problem solving and program implementation
    D. Regular teachers, special education teachers, and other specialists or support teachers co-teach

34. Which of the following is/are critically important determinant(s) of success for the exceptional student placed in a regular classroom? *(Skill 7.01) (Average)*

    A. Receipt of necessary accommodations and adaptations
    B. The student's perception that he or she is an accepted part of the class
    C. The mainstream teacher's belief that the student will profit from the placement
    D. All of the above

35. A consultant teacher should be meeting the needs of his or her students by: *(Skill 7.01) (Easy)*

  A. Pushing in to do small group instruction with regular education students

  B. Reviewing lesson plan content for accuracy

  (C.) Meeting with the teacher before class to discuss adaptations and modifications

  D. Accompanying the student to class

36. Jane is a third grader. Mrs. Smith, her teacher, noted that Jane was having difficulty with math and reading assignments. The results from recent diagnostic tests showed a strong sight vocabulary, strength in computational skills, but a weakness in comprehending what she read. This weakness was apparent in mathematical word problems as well. The multi-disciplinary team recommended placement in a special education resource room for learning disabilities two periods each school day. For the remainder of the school day, her placement will be: *(Skill 7.01) (Easy)*

  (A) In the regular classroom

  B. At a special school

  C. In a self-contained classroom

  D. In a resource room for mental retardation

37. Teaching techniques that stimulate active participation and understanding in the mathematics class include all but which of the following? *(Skill 7.02) (Easy)*

  (A.) Having students copy computation facts for a set number of times

  B. Allowing students extensive exploration and practice with manipulatives at a concrete level

  C. Giving students highlighters or post-it arrows for marking relevant information in problems

  D. Having both students and teacher model and talk aloud as they work through problems

38. Which of the following teaching activities is *least* likely to enhance learning in students with special needs? *(Skill 7.02) (Rigorous)*

    A. A verbal description of the task to be performed, followed by having the children immediately attempt to perform the instructed behavior

    B. A demonstration of the behavior, followed by an immediate opportunity for the children to imitate the behavior

    C. A simultaneous demonstration and explanation of the behavior, followed by ample opportunity for the children to rehearse the instructed behavior

    D. Physically guiding the children through the behavior to be imitated while verbally explaining the behavior

39. Which of the following is a good example of a generalization? *(Skill 7.05) (Average)*

    A. Jim has learned to add and is now ready to subtract

    B. Sarah adds sets of units to obtain a product

    C. Bill recognizes a vocabulary word on a billboard when traveling

    D. Jane can spell the word "net" backwards to get the word "ten"

40. All of the following are suggestions for *pacing* or altering the presentation of tasks to match the student's rate of learning except: *(Skill 7.06) (Average)*

    A. Teach in several shorter segments of time rather than a single lengthy session

    B. Continue to teach a task until the lesson is completed in order to provide more time on task

    C. Watch for nonverbal cues that indicate students are becoming confused, bored, or restless

    D. Avoid giving students an inappropriate amount of written work

41. Alan has failed repeatedly in his academic work. He needs continuous feedback in order to experience small, incremental achievements. What type of instructional material would best meet this need? *(Skill 8.06) (Rigorous)*

    A. Programmed materials
    B. Audiotapes
    C. Materials with no writing required
    D. Worksheets

42. **What criteria must be considered when choosing assistive technology (AT) to help a particular student?** *(Skill 8.07) (Easy)*

   A. Whether there is a specific need the AT can meet (e.g., a goal on the IEP that requires it)
   B. The degree of independence with which the student can use the device
   C. The need for collaborative planning for the device to be used across all relevant settings and transfer between settings
   D. All of the above

43. **Bobby can give accurate, detailed oral answers to prompts and content area questions. His oral answers are well thought out and organized. When he tries to write down his ideas, however, he struggles and his poor spelling makes his writing unreadable. His punctuation and capitalization are erratic, too. You decide:** *(Skill 9.01) (Rigorous)*

   A. Bobby needs help with writing expression so he can organize his ideas into good paragraphs.
   B. Bobby needs help with writing mechanics and phonics.
   C. Bobby would benefit from an accommodation allowing him to dictate his compositions first, then write them down from the recording.
   D. Both B and C

44. **In 2000, the National Reading Panel reviewed research on reading instruction showing that:** *(Skill 9.02) (Average)*

   A. Top-down approaches that emphasize meaning, like the whole language approach, are the most effective reading programs.
   B. Bottom-up or code-emphasis approaches, like phonics, are the most effective for reading programs.
   C. There are five critical components of an effective reading program: phonemic awareness, phonics, fluency, vocabulary, and comprehension.
   D. Approaches that emphasize sight word vocabulary and fluency are the most effective reading programs.

45. **Teachers in grades K-3 are mandated (by NCLB, 2002) to teach reading using what?** *(Skill 9.02 and 16.01) (Average)*

   A. Whole language and language experience approaches
   B. Varied scientifically based methods with measurable outcomes
   C. Code-emphasis and phonics-based methods
   D. federally developed basal reader programs

46. Ryan is working on a report about dogs. He uses scissors and tape to cut and rearrange sections and paragraphs. He then photocopies the paper so he can continue writing. In which stage of the writing process is Ryan?
(Skill 9.03) (Easy)

A. Final draft
B. Prewriting
C. Revision
D. Drafting

47. Mrs. Smith's students are engaged in activities such as saying rhyming words and words that begin with the same sound or finding pictures in a list that start with the same or different sound, changing the sounds in words (e.g., if 'dog' started with the same sound as 'cat' it would be 'cog'). There are no printed words or letters in the exercises. You can tell Mrs. Smith is trying to improve her students':
(Skill 9.03) (Rigorous)

A. Sight word recognition
B. Phoneme awareness
C. Vocabulary understanding
D. Reading comprehension

48. Which of the following sentences will NOT test recall?
(Skill 9.05) (Average)

A. What words in the story describe Goldilocks?
B. Why did Goldilocks go into the three bears' house?
C. Name in order the things that belonged to the three bears that Goldilocks tried.
D. What did the three bears learn about leaving their house unlocked?

49. In what order does the National Council of Teachers of Mathematics (NCTM) say new math concepts and operations should be taught?
(Skill 10.02) (Rigorous)

A. Teach the meaning of symbols first, then pictures, then concrete manipulatives.
B. Teach with concrete manipulatives, then pictorial representations, then symbols.
C. Start with pictures, move to concrete manipulatives, then symbols and words.
D. Teach in any order as long as you do it consistently in all areas.

50. **Kenny is a 9th grader enrolled in Wood Shop; he is having difficulty grasping fractions. You know that Kenny has difficulty with abstract concepts. What would be a good method to teach this concept?**
(Skill 10.04) (Rigorous)

   A. Pie blocks that proportionately measure whole, half, 1/4, 1/8, etc.
   B. Strips of paper that proportionately measure whole, half, 1/4, 1/8, etc.
   C. One-on-one review of the worksheet
   D. Working in the wood shop, privately showing him how to measure

51. **Mr. Ward notes that Jennifer, a 9th grade student, understands the concept for three-step equations but seems unable to do problems successfully. When he reviews Jennifer's work, he notes that her addition and subtraction are not correct. What strategy would be most appropriate?**
(Skill 10.05) (Average)

   A. Basic multiplication and addition charts
   B. Checks for understanding
   C. Private instruction on adding and subtracting
   D. Calculator usage

52. **Although there are many strategies that can help students with disabilities learn new math concepts, what one strategy is almost universally necessary and helpful?**
(Skill 10.05) (Rigorous)

   A. More repetition of skills and practice problems
   B. More detailed teacher demonstrations of the concept
   C. More student time spent at the concrete level interacting with manipulatives
   D. More homework practice on new concepts

53. **Functional curriculum focuses on all of the following EXCEPT:**
(Skill 11.03) (Rigorous)

   A. Skills needed for social living
   B. Occupational readiness
   C. Use of community resources
   D. Remedial academic skills

54. Bob shows behavior problems like lack of attention, out of seat, and talking out. His teacher has kept data on these behaviors and has found that Bob is showing much better self-control since he has been self-managing himself through a behavior modification program. The most appropriate placement recommendation for Bob at this time is probably: *(Skill 11.04) (Average)*

A. Any available part-time special education program
B. The regular classroom, solely
C. A behavior disorders resource room for one period per day
D. A specific learning disabilities resource room for one period per day

55. Marisol has been mainstreamed into a 9th grade language arts class. Although her behavior is satisfactory and she likes the class, Marisol's reading level is about two years below grade level. The class has been assigned to read *Great Expectations* and write a report. What intervention would be LEAST successful in helping Marisol complete this assignment? *(Skill 11.04) (Average)*

A. Having Marisol listen to a taped recording while following the story in the regular text
B. Giving her a modified version of the story at her reading level
C. Telling her to choose a different book that she can read
D. Providing an abbreviated story outline at her reading level

56. Sam is working to earn half an hour of basketball time with his favorite P.E. teacher. At the end of each half hour, Sam marks his point sheet with an X if he reached his goal of no call-outs. When he has received 25 marks, he will receive his basketball free time. This behavior management strategy is an example of: *(Skill 11.04) (Average)*

A. Self-recording
B. Self-evaluation
C. Self-reinforcement
D. Self-regulation

57. David is a 16 year old in your class who recently came from another country. The girls in your class have come to you to complain about the way he treats them in a sexist manner. When they complain, you realize that this is also the way he treats adult females. You have talked to David before about appropriate behavior. You should first?
(Skill 11.05) (Rigorous)

A. Complain to the principal
B. Ask for a parent-teacher conference
C. Check to see if this is a cultural norm in his country
D. Create a behavior contract for him to follow

58. Teacher modeling, templates and lists of problem solving steps, student-teacher dialogues, and other individualized aids that are gradually faded out are part of which teaching technique designed to provide support during the initial stages of instruction?
(Skill 11.05) (Rigorous)

A. Reciprocal teaching
B. Scaffolding
C. Peer tutoring
D. Cooperative learning

59. You are working with a functional program and have placed a student in a vocational position in the kitchen of a coffee house. A waiter takes orders and relays them to the student, whose job is to make the coffee as ordered. You need to perform a task analysis of making a cup of coffee. Which task should be first in the analysis?
(Skill 11.06) (Average)

A. Filling the pot with water
B. Taking the order
C. Measuring the coffee
D. Picking the correct coffee

60. Transition planning for post-school life requires which of the following?
(Skill 11.07) (Average)

A. School-based instruction tailored to meet the student's goals,
B. Community-based experiences for independent living or job skills
C. Development of objectives related to specific employment and other post-school areas
D. All of the above

61. **Social maturity can be evidenced by the student's:** *(Skill 12.01) (Easy)*

    A. Recognition of rights and responsibilities (his or her own and those of others)
    B. Display of respect for legitimate authority figures
    C. Formulation of a valid moral judgment
    D. Demonstration of all of the above

62. **In establishing a classroom behavior management plan with the students, it is best to:** *(Skill 13.01) (Average)*

    A. Have rules written and in place on day one
    B. Hand out a copy of the rules to the students on day one
    C. Have separate rules for each class on day one
    D. Have students involved in creating the rules on day one

63. **A Life Space Interview is used for:** *(Skill 13.01) (Rigorous)*

    A. Transition to exit interview
    B. Analysis of proficiency levels
    C. Maintenance of acceptable behavior
    D. Creating awareness of distorted perceptions

64. **Laura is beginning to raise her hand first instead of talking out. An effective schedule of reinforcement should be:** *(Skill 13.01) (Average)*

    A. Continuous
    B. Variable
    C. Intermittent
    D. Fixed

65. **Janelle is just as "antsy" as Jaquan, who has ADHD. You want to keep a good eye on them, so you put them in the same corner. Later you suspect Amanda also has ADHD, so you move her to the same area. You are creating a:** *(Skill 13.04) (Average)*

    A. Self-fulfilling prophecy
    B. Cooperative learning circle
    C. Disordered support group
    D. Buffer zone to observe and direct behavior centrally

66. **Mr. Smith is on a field trip with a group of high school EH students. On the way, they stop at a fast-food restaurant for lunch, and Warren and Raul get into an argument. After some heated words, Warren stalks out of the restaurant and refuses to return to the group. He leaves the parking lot, continues walking away from the group, and ignores Mr. Smith's directions to come back. What would be the best course of action for Mr. Smith?** *(Skill 13.05) (Rigorous)*

    A. Leave the group with the class aide and follow Warren to try to talk him into coming back
    B. Wait a little while and see if Warren cools off and returns
    C. Telephone the school and let the crisis teacher notify the police in accordance with school policy
    D. Call the police himself

67. Hector is a 10th grader in a program for the severely emotionally handicapped. After a classmate taunted him about his mother, Hector threw a desk at the other boy and attacked him. A crisis intervention team tried to break up the fight, and one teacher hurt his knee. The other boy received a concussion. Hector now faces disciplinary measures. How long can he be suspended without a meeting to review a possible "change of placement"?
(Skill 13.06) (Rigorous)

A. 5 days
B. 10 days
C. 10 - 30 days
D. 60 days

68. Statements like "Darren is lazy" are not helpful in describing his behavior for all but which of these reasons?
(Skill 13.07) (Average)

A. There is no way to determine if any change occurs from the information given
B. The student—not the behavior—becomes labeled
C. Darren's behavior will manifest itself clearly enough without any written description
D. Constructs are open to various interpretations among the people who are asked to define them

69. The first step in writing a Functional Behavioral Assessment (FBA) is:
(Skill 13.07) (Rigorous)

A. Establish a replacement behavior
B. Establish levels of interventions
C. Clearly define the behavior in need of modification
D. Establish assessment periods of FBA effectiveness

70. To reinforce Audrey each time she is on task and in her seat, Ms. Wright delivers specific praise and stickers, which Audrey may collect and redeem for a reward. The data collected during the time Ms. Wright is using this reward system is called:
(Skill 13.07) (Average)

A. Referral phase
B. Intervention phase
C. Baseline phase
D. Observation phase

71. Lotzie is not labeled as needing special education services, but he appears to be unable to function at his grade level both academically and socially. He is in 9th grade, but reads picture books and consistently displays immature behavior that can be misinterpreted. You have already observed these behaviors. What should be done first?
(Skill 14.01) (Rigorous)

A. Establish a rapport with the parents
B. Write a CSE referral
C. Plan and discuss possible interventions with the teacher
D. Address the class about acceptance

72. Parent contact should first begin when:
(Skill 14.02) (Average)

A. You are informed the child will be your student
B. The student fails a test
C. The student exceeds others on a task
D. A CSE is coming and you have had no previous replies to letters

73. You should prepare for a parent-teacher conference by:
(Skill 14.02) (Average)

A. Memorizing student progress/grades
B. Anticipating questions
C. Scheduling the meetings during your lunch time
D. Planning a tour of the school

74. You note that a child in your class is expressing discomfort when placing his back against a chair. You ask him if he is okay, and he says it's nothing. You notice what appears to be a belt mark on his shoulder. What is the first thing you should do?
(Skill 14.04) (Rigorous)

A. Send the child to the nurse
B. Contact an administrator
C. Call Child Protective Services
D. Follow the school policy and report it

75. Janiay requires occupational therapy and speech therapy services. She is your student. What must you do to insure that her services are met?
(Skill 15.04) (Rigorous)

A. Watch the services being rendered
B. Schedule collaboratively
C. Ask for services to be given in a push-in model
D. Ask school administration to train you to give the service

76. An individual with disabilities in need of employability training, as well as a job, should be referred to what governmental agency for assistance? *(Skill 15.07)*
(Average)

A. OMRDD
B. VESID
C. Social Services
D. ARC

77. Which two student behaviors are indicative of a possible crisis? *(Skill 15.07) (Average)*

A. Bullying and being socially active
B. Intermittent periods of laughter and rage
C. High academic performance and gang activity
D. Detailed threats of lethal violence and severe rage for minor reasons

78. Which of these groups is not comprehensively covered by IDEA? *(Skill 16.01) (Easy)*

A. Gifted and talented
B. Mentally retarded
C. Specific learning disabilities
D. Speech and language impaired

79. Educators who advocate educating all children, without exception, in their neighborhood classrooms and schools, who propose the end of labeling and segregation of special needs students in special classes, and who call for the delivery of special supports and services directly in the classroom may be said to support the:
(Skill 16.01) (Easy)

A. Full service model
B. Regular education initiative
C. Full inclusion model
D. Mainstream model

80. Which of the following would constitute violation of IDEA law? *(Skill 16.01) (Rigorous)*

A. A school takes too long to identify or provide services to a child.
B. A school does not provide all the services specified in a child's IEP.
C. A teacher does not provide an accommodation listed in a child's IEP because she does not think it is necessary.
D. All of the above

81. IDEA 2004 stated that there was a disproportionate number of minority students classified in need of special education services. The reason for this that IDEA 2004 suggests is: *(Skill 16.01) (Average)*

A. Socioeconomic status where disproportionate numbers exist
B. Improper evaluations; not making allowances for students who speak English as a second language
C. Growing population of minorities
D. Percentage of drug abuse per ethnicity

82. **Cheryl is a 15-year old student receiving educational services in a full-time substantially separate classroom. The date for her IEP review is planned for two months before her 16th birthday. According to the requirements of IDEA, what must ADDITIONALLY be included in this review?** *(Skill 16.01) (Average)*

    A. Graduation plan
    B. Individualized transition plan
    C. Vocational assessment
    D. Transportation planning

83. **How do the 10th and 14th Amendments to the U.S. Constitution affect education?** *(Skill 16.01) (Rigorous)*

    A. The federal government determines the content of education.
    B. Education is an unstated power vested in the states.
    C. States that provide services like education must provide them to ALL children.
    D. Both B and C

84. **What determines whether a person is entitled to protection under Section 504?** *(Skill 16.01) (Average)*

    A. The individual must meet the definition of a person with a disability
    B. The person must be able to meet the requirements of a particular program in spite of his or her disability
    C. The school, business, or other facility must be the recipient of federal funding assistance
    D. All of the above

85. **How was the training of special education teachers changed by the No Child Left Behind Act of 2002?** *(Skill 16.01) (Average)*

    A. The act required all special education teachers to be certified in reading and math
    B. The act required all special education teachers to take the same coursework as general education teachers
    C. The act required that if a special education teacher is teaching a core subject, he or she must meet the standard of a highly qualified teacher in that subject
    D. All of the above

86. **What is true about IDEA? In order to be eligible, a student must:** *(Skill 16.01) (Easy)*

    A. Have a medical disability
    B. Have a disability that fits into one of the categories listed in the law
    C. Have a disability that actually affects school performance
    D. Both B and C

87. **The definition of assistive technology devices was amended in the IDEA reauthorization of 2004 to exclude what?** *(Skill 16.01) (Average)*

    A. iPods and other hand-held devices
    B. Computer-enhanced technology
    C. Surgically implanted devices
    D. Braille and/or special learning aids

88. **Which of the following must be completed first, before comprehensive testing occurs?** *(Skill 16.02) (Average)*

   A. Teacher consult on student needs
   B. Pre-CSE conference
   C. Parental permission for each test
   D. All of the above

89. **What does Zero Reject require for all children with disabilities?** *(Skill 16.02) (Average)*

   A. Full inclusion of ALL students with disabilities in regular education classrooms and reporting annually
   B. Seeking out and providing services to ALL students with disabilities regardless of type or severity and reporting annually
   C. Free, appropriate public education provided to ALL students
   D. Both B and C

90. **According to IDEA 2004, students with disabilities are to do what?** *(Skill 16.02) (Average)*

   A. Participate in the general education program to the fullest extent that it is beneficial for them
   B. Participate in a vocational training program within the general education setting
   C. Participate in a general education program for physical education
   D. Participate in a Full Inclusion program that meets their needs

Answer Key

1.	C	31.	C	61.	D
2.	B	32.	A	62.	D
3.	C	33.	B	63.	D
4.	A	34.	D	64.	A
5.	C	35.	C	65.	A
6.	B	36.	A	66.	C
7.	A	37.	A	67.	B
8.	D	38.	A	68.	C
9.	B	39.	C	69.	C
10.	C	40.	B	70.	B
11.	B	41.	A	71.	A
12.	D	42.	D	72.	A
13.	A	43.	D	73.	B
14.	B	44.	C	74.	D
15.	C	45.	B	75.	B
16.	C	46.	C	76.	B
17.	B	47.	B	77.	D
18.	B	48.	D	78.	A
19.	D	49.	B	79.	C
20.	B	50.	B	80.	D
21.	C	51.	D	81.	B
22.	B	52.	C	82.	B
23.	D	53.	D	83.	D
24.	A	54.	B	84.	D
25.	C	55.	C	85.	C
26.	C	56.	A	86.	D
27.	B	57.	C	87.	C
28.	C	58.	B	88.	C
29.	D	59.	D	89.	D
30.	C	60.	D	90.	A

Rationales with Sample Questions

1. **Which is an educational characteristic common to students with mild intellectual learning and behavioral disabilities?** *(Skill 1.01) (Easy)*

   A. Show interest in schoolwork
   B. Have intact listening skills
   C. Require modification in classroom instruction
   D. Respond better to passive than to active learning tasks

   Answer: C. Require modification in classroom instruction

   Some of the characteristics of students with mild learning and behavioral disabilities are as follows: Lack of interest in schoolwork; preferring concrete rather than abstract lessons; weak listening skills; low achievement; limited verbal and/or writing skills; responding better to active rather than passive learning tasks; areas of talent or ability often overlooked by teachers; preferring to receive special help in regular classroom; higher dropout rate than regular education students; achievement in accordance with teacher expectations; requiring modification in classroom instruction; and being easily distracted.

2. **Which of the following statements about children with an emotional/behavioral disorder is true?** *(Skill 1.01) (Average)*

   A. They have very high IQs
   B. They display poor social skills
   C. They are academic achievers
   D. They have a mature understanding of concepts

   Answer: B. They display poor social skills

   Children who exhibit mild behavioral disorders are also characterized by:

   - Average or above average scores on intelligence tests
   - Poor academic achievement; learned helplessness
   - Unsatisfactory interpersonal relationships
   - Immaturity; attention seeking behaviors
   - Aggressive, acting-out behavior OR
   - Anxious, withdrawn behavior

3. **Which of these is not true for most children with behavior disorders?** *(Skill 1.01) (Average)*

    A. Many score in the "slow learner" or "mildly retarded" range on IQ tests
    B. They are frequently behind their classmates in academic achievement
    C. They are bright but bored with their surroundings
    D. They spend a large amount of time in nonproductive, nonacademic behaviors

    Answer: C. They are bright but bored with their surroundings

    Most children with behavior disorders display the traits found in A, B, or D. A child who is simply bored may misbehave briefly and periodically, but the overall rate, duration, persistence over time, and intensity of the problem would not be high.

4. **Echolalia is a characteristic of what?** *(Skill 1.01) (Average)*

    A. Autism
    B. Mental retardation
    C. Social Pragmatic Disorder
    D. ADHD

    Answer: A. Autism

    Echolalia is echoing/repeating the speech of others, which is a characteristic of autism. In IDEA, the 1990 Amendment to the Education for All Handicapped Children Act, autism was classified as a separate exceptionality category. It is thought to be caused by a neurological or biochemical dysfunction, and generally becomes evident before age three. The condition occurs in about 4 out of every 10,000 persons. Smith and Luckasson (1992) describe it as a severe language disorder that affects thinking, communication, and behavior. They list the following characteristics: Absent or distorted relationships with people; extreme or peculiar problems in communication (such as echolalia); self-stimulation that can lead to self-injury; perceptual anomalies.

5.   The social skills of students in mental retardation programs are likely to be appropriate for children of their mental age, rather than chronological age. This means that the teacher will need to do all of the following except: *(Skill 1.01) (Easy)*

A. Model desired behavior
B. Provide clear instructions
C. Expect age appropriate behaviors
D. Adjust the physical environment when necessary

Answer: C. Expect age appropriate behaviors

Because their mental age is not equivalent to their chronological age, it is unrealistic to expect age appropriate behavior. The teacher should assess their mental age and expect behaviors appropriate to that age.

6.   Jonathan has attention deficit hyperactivity disorder (ADHD). He is in a regular classroom and appears to be doing okay. However, his teacher does not want Jonathan in her class because he will not obey her when she asks him to stop doing a repetitive action such as tapping his foot. The teacher sees this as distractive during tests. Jonathan needs: *(Skill 1.02) (Easy)*

A. An IEP
B. A 504 Plan
C. A VESID evaluation
D. A more restrictive environment

Answer: B. A 504 Plan

Jonathan is exhibiting normal grade-level behavior with the exception of the ADHD behaviors, which might need some acceptance or accommodations for his academic success. Jonathan has not shown any academic deficiencies. He needs a 504 Plan to provide small adaptations to meet his needs. Such a 504 Plan might, for example, state that he have frequent breaks, be allowed to work standing at a counter or lying on the floor, be provided with "fiddle objects" when required to listen, and so forth.

7.   Five-year-old Tom continues to substitute the "w" sound for the "r" sound when pronouncing words; therefore, he often distorts words (e.g., "wabbit" for "rabbit" and "wat" for "rat"). His articulation disorder is basically a problem in: *(Skill 1.04) (Easy)*

A. Phonology
B. Morphology
C. Syntax
D. Semantics

Answer: A. Phonology

Phonology refers to the study of the basic, individual sounds (phonemes) used in a language and the manner in which those individual sounds can be combined into words. Tom is substituting sounds, which is a problem in phonology. It might be related to a physiologically based articulation problem or to a hearing problem.

8.   Mark is a 6th grader. You have noticed that he doesn't respond to simple requests like the other students in your class. If you ask him to erase the board, he might look at you, shake his head, and say "no," but then he will clean the board. When the children gather together for recess, he joins them. However, you observe that it takes him much longer to understand the rules to a game. Mark retains what he reads. Mark most likely has: *(Skill 1.04) (Rigorous)*

A. Oppositional-Defiant Disorder
B. Tourette's syndrome
C. Mental retardation
D. A pragmatic language disability

Answer: D. A pragmatic language disability

Pragmatics is the basic understanding of a communicator's intent, including nonverbal cues. Mark is not oppositional or defiant because he complies with the request, though he uses incorrect body language as he does so. The issue here is Mark's ability to respond correctly to other people.

9. **Which of the following is an example of cross-modal perception involving integrating visual stimuli to an auditory verbal process?** *(Skill 2.01) (Average)*

   A. Following spoken directions
   B. Describing a picture
   C. Finding certain objects in pictures
   D. Both B and C

   Answer: B. Describing a picture

   When describing a picture, we see (visual modality) the picture and use words (auditory modality) to describe it.

10. **Justin is diagnosed with autism and is in an inclusive setting. You were called down to "stop him from turning off the lights and remove him." When you arrive, you learn that today a movie was supposed to be finished, but the VCR broke, so the teacher planned another activity. What is the best way to explain to the teacher why Justin was turning off the lights?** *(Skill 2.02) (Easy)*

    A. He is perseverating and will stop shortly.
    B. He is telling you the lights bother him.
    C. He needs forewarning before a transition. Next time you have an unexpected change in classroom schedule, please let him know.
    D. Please understand, this is part of who Justin is. He will leave the lights alone after I talk to him.

    Answer: C. He needs forewarning before a transition. Next time you have a unexpected change in classroom schedule, please let him know.

    The teacher already knows that Justin will stop after you talk to him. That is why she called you. She needs to know what to do if this happens again. Explaining the problem with transition might enable the teacher to see a problem before it occurs or to prevent a possible problem.

11. **Which of these characteristics is NOT included in the IDEA definition of emotional disturbance?** *(Skill 2.02) (Average)*

    A. General pervasive mood of unhappiness or depression
    B. Social maladjustment such as gang activity or truancy manifested in a number of settings
    C. Tendency to develop physical symptoms, pains, or fear associated with school or personal problems
    D. Inability to learn that is not attributed to intellectual, sensory, or health factors

    Answer: B. Social maladjustment such as gang activity or truancy manifested in a number of settings

    Social maladjustment in itself is not considered a disability. Certainly, some emotional disturbances can *cause* maladjusted social behavior, but if the cause of the behavior is not an emotional disability it would not qualify a student for special services under IDEA.

12. **Children with visual-spatial difficulties might struggle with tasks such as:** *(Skills 2.03 and 10.05) (Rigorous)*

    A. Writing fractions and before/after concepts in math
    B. Differentiating the characteristics of a certain letter in print
    C. A delay in achieving the "th" sound
    D. Both A and B

    Answer: D. Both A (Writing fractions and before/after concepts in math) and B (Differentiating characteristics of a certain letter in print)

    Visual-spatial difficulties can lead a student to misinterpret direct compositions of objects and symbols. The lines of a letter are visual stimuli arranged in a specific spatial formation that could be misperceived. For the same reasons, writing fractions requires proper perception and placement of digits above and below a line. Before and after concepts in math are usually related to placement on a number line—a primarily visual-spatial stimulus.

13. **A developmental delay may be indicated by a:** *(Skill 2.03) (Rigorous)*

A. Second grader having difficulty buttoning clothing
B. Stuttered response
C. Kindergartner not having complete bladder control
D. Withdrawn behavior

Answer: A. Second grader having difficulty buttoning clothing

Buttoning of clothing is generally mastered by the age of four. While many children have full bladder control by age four, it is not unusual for "embarrassing accidents" to occur. Stuttering is an articulation disability, not a developmental delay, and withdrawn behavior would fall into the emotional disturbance category.

14. **For which of the following purposes is a norm-referenced test least appropriate?** *(Skill 3.01) (Average)*

A. Screening
B. Individual program planning
C. Program evaluation
D. Making placement decisions

Answer: B. Individual program planning

Norm-referenced tests are useful for screening and placement because they yield scores that allow comparison of the student with age or grade peers and can demonstrate needs that would make a student eligible for special services. Although some norm-referenced tests such as Intelligence tests might provide subtests that can pinpoint weaknesses relevant to instructional programming, criterion-referenced tests are usually more appropriate for planning instruction because they pinpoint the degree to which a student meets certain criteria or has mastered specific skills. An example of this is assessing a new student to figure out in which reading group he or she would be a good fit.

15. **Marcie is often not in her seat when the bell rings. She can be found at the pencil sharpener, throwing paper away, or fumbling through her notebook. Which of these descriptions of her behavior can be described as a pinpoint?** *(Skill 3.01and 13.07) (Easy)*

    A. Is tardy
    B. Is out of seat
    C. Is not in seat when late bell rings
    D. Is disorganized

    Answer: C. Is not in seat when late bell rings

    Even though A, B, and D describe the behavior, C is the most precise. It is very objective (anyone can take the measurement) and pinpoints the exact behavior so it can be measured and altered. Once the behavior is pinpointed, it can be measured for the baseline phase of a behavior modification plan.

16. **The purpose of error analysis of a test is to: (Skill 3.01) (Easy)**

    A. Determine which events were labeled in error
    B. Determine if the test length was the cause of error
    C. Evaluate the types of errors made by categorizing incorrect answers
    D. Establish a baseline

    Answer: C. Evaluate the types of errors made by categorizing incorrect answers

    Error analysis examines how and why a person makes a mistake. In an informal reading inventory, for example, questions are given to specifically address possible errors. A math assessment might provide a selection of answers on a multiple choice test that pinpoint whether the error is due to a failure to understand place value, a failure to regroup, or a failure to remember basic addition facts, etc. Other tests that utilize error analysis provide specific possible answers to denote which error was made. The purpose of both is to see where problems lie and to provide clues to assist the learning process.

17. **Behaviors for which frequency is an appropriate measure include all but those that:** *(Skill 3.01) (Average)*

    A. Have an observable beginning
    B. Last a long time
    C. Last only a short time
    D. Occur often

    Answer: B. Last a long time

    We use frequency to measure behaviors that do not last a long time, but that occur repeatedly and have a discrete beginning and end. We use duration to measure behaviors that might last a long time. We are measuring the varying length of time (from shorter to longer) during which the behavior occurs. If it always occurs for only a short time, we would not need to measure its duration.

18. **The extent to which a test measures what it claims to measure is called:** *(Skill 3.01) (Rigorous)*

    A. Reliability
    B. Validity
    C. Factor analysis
    D. Chi square

    Answer: B. Validity

    Validity is defined as the degree to which a test measures is what it claims to measure. There are several kids of validity, such as content validity, construct validity, and predictive validity.

19. **Which would not be an advantage of using a criterion-referenced test?** *(Skill 3.02) (Rigorous)*

    A. Information is obtained about an individual's mastery of specific objectives.
    B. It can pinpoint exact areas of weakness and strength
    C. You can design this type of test yourself
    D. You get comparative information

    Answer: D. You get comparative information

    Criterion-referenced tests measure mastery of content or specific goals rather than performance compared to others (which would require a norm-referenced test). Test items are usually prepared from specific educational objectives or IEP goals and may be teacher-made or commercially-prepared. Scores are measured by the percentage of correct items for a skill (e.g., adding and subtracting fractions with like denominators).

20. **Michael's teacher complains that he is constantly out of his seat. She also reports that he has trouble paying attention to what is going on in class for more than a couple of minutes at a time. He appears to be trying, but his writing is often illegible and contains many reversals. Although he seems to want to please, he is very impulsive and is constantly in trouble with his teacher. He is failing reading, and his math grades, though somewhat better, are still below average. Michael's psychometric evaluation should include assessment for:** *(Skill 3.02) (Average)*

A. Mild mental retardation
B. Specific learning disabilities
C. Mild behavior disorders
D. Hearing impairment

Answer: B. Specific learning disabilities

The definition of "learning disability" is "a disorder in one or more of the basic psychological processes involved in understanding or in using language, spoken or written." Tests need to show a discrepancy between potential and performance in order to indicate a specific learning disability. Classroom observations and samples of student work (such as those demonstrating impaired reading ability) also provide indicators of possible learning disabilities. Here are some of the characteristics of persons with learning disabilities:

- Hyperactivity: A rate of motor activity higher than normal
- Perceptual difficulties: Visual, auditory, and haptic perceptual problems
- Perceptual-motor impairments: Poor integration of visual and motor systems, often affecting fine motor coordination
- Disorders of memory and thinking: Memory deficits, trouble with problem-solving, poor concept formation and association, poor awareness of own metacognitive skills (learning strategies)
- Impulsiveness: Acts before considering consequences, poor impulse control often followed by remorselessness
- Academic problems in reading, math, writing, or spelling; significant discrepancies in ability levels

21. **Which of the following examples would be considered the highest priority when determining the need for the delivery of appropriate special education and related services?** *(Skill 4.01) (Rigorous)*

A. A ten-year-old girl with profound mental retardation is receiving education services in a state institution.

B. A six-year-old girl who has been diagnosed as autistic is placed in a special education class within the local school. Her mother wants her to attend a residential school next year, even though the girl is showing progress.

C. An eight-year-old boy is repeating first grade for the second time and exhibits problems with toileting, gross motor functions, and remembering number and letter symbols. His regular classroom teacher claims the referral forms are too time-consuming and refuses to complete them. He also refuses to make accommodations because he feels every child should be treated alike.

D. A twelve-year-old boy with mild disabilities was placed in a behavior disorders program, but displays obvious perceptual deficits (e.g., reversal of letters and symbols, inability to discriminate sounds). He was originally thought to have a learning disability, but did not meet state criteria for this exceptionality category based on results of standard scores. He has always had problems with attending to a task, and is now beginning to get into trouble during seatwork time. His teacher feels that he will eventually become a real behavior problem. He receives social skills training in the resource room one period a day.

Answer: C. An eight-year-old boy is repeating first grade for the second time and exhibits problems with toileting, gross motor functions, and remembering number and letter symbols. His regular classroom teacher claims the referral forms are too time-consuming and refuses to complete them. He also refuses to make accommodations because he feels every child should be treated alike.

No modifications are being made, so the child is not receiving any services whatsoever. This is the situation in greatest need of change. The other situations might also need consideration, but in those situations at least there are some services in place. This child is getting no services at all and is not being served by his teacher either.

22. **Acculturation refers to the individual's:** *(Skill 4.07) (Rigorous)*

    A. Gender
    B. Experiential background
    C. Social class
    D. Ethnic background

    Answer: B. Experiential background

    Acculturation is differences in experiential background. A person's culture has little to do with gender, social class, or ethnicity. A person is the product of his or her experiences.

23. **Which components of the IEP are required by law?**
    (Skill 5.02) (Average)

    A. Present level of academic and functional performance; statement of how the disability affects the student's involvement and progress; evaluation criteria and timelines for instructional objective achievement; modifications and accommodations
    B. Projected dates for services initiation with anticipated frequency, location, and duration; statement of when parent will be notified; statement of annual goals
    C. Extent to which child will not participate in regular education program; transitional needs for students age 14 and older
    D. All of the above

    Answer: D. All of the above

    IEPs must contain many elements and these are sometimes altered when legislation is updated or reauthorized, so educators must keep themselves apprised of the changes and amendments to laws.

24. **Shyquan is in your inclusive class, and she exhibits a slower comprehension of assigned tasks and concepts. Her first two grades were Bs but she is now receiving failing marks. She has seen the resource teacher. You should:** *(Skills 5.04 and 5.05) (Rigorous)*

    A. Ask for a review of current placement
    B. Tell Shyquan to seek extra help
    C. Ask Shyquan if she is frustrated
    D. Ask the regular education teacher to slow instruction

    Answer: A. Ask for a review of current placement

    All of the responses listed above might be useful at one time or another, but you are responsible for reviewing Shyquan's ability to function in the inclusive environment. Shyquan may or may not know she is not grasping the work, and she has sought out extra help with the resource teacher. If the regular education class students are successful, the class should not be slowed to adjust to Shyquan's learning rate. It is more likely that she may require a more modified curriculum to stay on task and to succeed academically. This might require a more restrictive environment, or at least more significant modifications and accommodations.

25. **Taiquan's parents are divorced and have joint custody. They have both requested to be present at the CSE. You call to make sure that they received the letter informing them of the upcoming CSE. Taiquan's father did not receive the notification and is upset. You should:** *(Skills 5.04 and 16.02) (Rigorous)*

    A. Tell him that you could review the meeting with him later
    B. Ask him if he can adjust his schedule
    C. Tell him you can reschedule the meeting
    D. Ask him to coordinate a time for the CSE to meet with his ex-wife

    Answer: C. Tell him you can reschedule the meeting

    A parent should be informed if he or she is divorced, if both have joint custody, and if he or she has expressed a desire to be present at the CSE. The law requires that both parents in this situation be notified. In this case, if one of the parents wants to be at the meeting but did not receive the notice, the meeting cannot be held. The school should review its procedures to be sure the father receives future notifications as well.

26. **Teachers must keep meticulous records. They are required to share all of them with the student's parent/guardian EXCEPT:** *(Skill 5.08) (Rigorous)*

   A. Daily attendance record
   B. Grade reports
   C. Teacher's personal notes
   D. Discipline notice placed in cumulative record

   Answer: C. Teacher's personal notes

   Information about students that a teacher writes down for his or her own reference does not have to be shared with parents. However, the teacher may choose to share these notes with the parent/guardian.

27. **Kareem's father sounds upset and is in the office demanding to see his son's cumulative record. You should:** *(Skill 5.08) (Average)*

   A. Tell him that he will have to make an appointment
   B. Bring the record to a private room for him to review with either an administrator or yourself
   C. Take the record to the principal's office for review
   D. Give the record to the parent

   Answer: B. Bring the record to a private room for him to review with either an administrator or yourself

   Parents have the right to see their children's cumulative records. You do not have the right to remove something so that the parent may not see it. However, it is important to remember that the documents should remain in the folder and that the parent may need information explained or interpreted; therefore, someone should be present.

28. **Students with autistic tendencies can be more successful academically when the teacher:** *(Skill 6.01) (Average)*

   A. Ignores inappropriate behaviors
   B. Allows them to go out of the room during instruction
   C. Keeps a calendar on the board of expected transitions
   D. Asks the CSE for a 1:1 aide

   Answer: C. Keeps a calendar on the board of expected transitions

   Students with autism tend to demonstrate an inability to transition unless that transition is expected. Placing calendars and a schedule where they can be seen are important.

29. **Charise comes into your room and seems to know every button to push to make you upset with her. What would be a good intervention?** *(Skill 6.01) (Rigorous)*

   A. Nonverbal Interactions
   B. Self-monitoring
   C. Proximity control
   D. Planned ignoring

   Answer: D. Planned ignoring

   Planned ignoring takes control from the student and tends to reduce the irritating behaviors, because they do not draw the attention they were employed to receive.

30. **In a positive classroom environment, errors are viewed as:** *(Skill 6.01) (Average)*

   A. Symptoms of deficiencies
   B. The result of lack of attention or ability
   C. A natural part of the learning process
   D. The result of going too quickly

   Answer: C. A natural part of the learning process

   We often learn a great deal from our mistakes and shortcomings. It is normal. Where it is not normal, fear develops. This fear of failure inhibits children from working and achieving. Copying and other types of cheating result from this fear of failure. It is particularly important for students with disabilities to learn this principle. They probably have a history of feeling as though the emphasis has been on their errors rather than on their learning.

31. **Which of the following is a responsibility that cannot be delegated to a classroom aide?** *(Skill 6.08) (Average)*

   A. Small group instruction
   B. Small group planning
   C. Designing a lesson plan
   D. Assisting in BIP implementation

   Answer: C. Designing a lesson plan

   Teachers are responsible for all lesson planning. However, It can be helpful to encourage input from a good classroom aide who might notice something that would be useful to you in designing the plans.

32. **The greatest number of students receiving special services are enrolled primarily in:** *(Skill 7.01) (Average)*

   A. The regular classroom
   B. The resource room
   C. Self-contained classrooms
   D. Special schools

   Answer: A. The regular classroom

   The majority of students receiving special services are enrolled primarily in regular classes. Those with mild learning and behavior problems exhibit academic and/or social interpersonal deficits that are often evident only in a school-related setting. These students appear no different from their peers physically. Well-chosen modifications can help them succeed in the regular classroom.

33. **Which is a less-than-ideal example of collaboration in successful inclusion?** *(Skill 7.01) (Rigorous)*

   A. Special education teachers are part of the instructional team in a regular classroom
   B. Special education teachers are informed of the lesson beforehand and assist regular education teachers in the classroom
   C. Teaming approaches are used for problem solving and program implementation
   D. Regular teachers, special education teachers, and other specialists or support teachers co-teach

   Answer: B. Special education teachers are informed of the lesson beforehand and assist regular education teachers in the classroom

   In an inclusive classroom, all students need to see both teachers as equals. This situation places the special education teacher in the role of a paraprofessional/ teacher aide. Both teachers should be co-teaching in some way.

34. **Which of the following is/are critically important determinant(s) of success for the exceptional student placed in a regular classroom?** *(Skill 7.01) (Average)*

A. Receipt of necessary accommodations and adaptations
B. The student's perception that he or she is an accepted part of the class
C. The mainstream teacher's belief that the student will profit from the placement
D. All of the above

Answer: D. All of the above

If either the teacher or the student feels that success is impossible, the result could be a self-fulfilling prophecy. In addition, without the regular teacher's belief that the student can benefit, it is likely that the student will not receive adequate accommodations. In addition, the teacher's negative attitude will likely be communicated to the student, making the student feel unworthy and unwelcome. No special accommodations will be provided. The IEP evaluation has already determined that the student needs the accommodations in order to be successful, so it is critical that they are available to the student.

35. **A consultant teacher should be meeting the needs of his or her students by:** *(Skill 7.01) (Easy)*

A. Pushing in to do small group instruction with regular education students
B. Reviewing lesson plan content for accuracy
C. Meeting with the teacher before class to discuss adaptations and modifications
D. Accompanying the student to class

Answer: C. Meeting with the teacher before class to discuss adaptations and expectations

Students who receive consult services are receiving minimal services. They might require some modification to their educational programs, and a consultant teacher can help the mainstream teacher to determine ways to differentiate instruction to meet the needs of the student, or to apply whatever accommodations are in the IEP. The regular education teacher is responsible for the content, not the consultant teacher. In a push-in model, the special education teacher comes into the classroom and teaches one or more students with special needs a differentiated form of the lesson that the general education teacher is teaching the rest of the class.

36. **Jane is a third grader. Mrs. Smith, her teacher, noted that Jane was having difficulty with math and reading assignments. The results from recent diagnostic tests showed a strong sight vocabulary, strength in computational skills, but a weakness in comprehending what she read. This weakness was apparent in mathematical word problems as well. The multi-disciplinary team recommended placement in a special education resource room for learning disabilities two periods each school day. For the remainder of the school day, her placement will be:** *(Skill 7.01) (Easy)*

   A. In the regular classroom
   B. At a special school
   C. In a self-contained classroom
   D. In a resource room for mental retardation

   Answer: A. In the regular classroom

   An emphasis on instructional remediation and individualized instruction in problem areas, as well as a focus on mainstreaming, is characteristic of the resource room, a special room inside the school environment where the child goes to be taught by a teacher who is certified in the area of disability. It is hoped that the accommodations and services provided in the resource room will help her to catch up and perform with her peers in the regular classroom.

37. **Teaching techniques that stimulate active participation and understanding in the mathematics class include all but which of the following?** *(Skill 7.02) (Easy)*

   A. Having students copy computation facts for a set number of times
   B. Allowing students extensive exploration and practice with manipulatives at a concrete level
   C. Giving students highlighters or sticky arrows for marking relevant information in problems
   D. Having both students and teacher model and talk aloud as they work through problems

   Answer: A. Having students copy computation facts for a set number of times

   Copying does not stimulate participation or understanding. All the other methods are proven to help students with disabilities participate in and master math concepts.

38. **Which of the following teaching activities is least likely to enhance learning in students with special needs?** *(Skill 7.02) (Rigorous)*

   A. A verbal description of the task to be performed, followed by having the children immediately attempt to perform the instructed behavior
   B. A demonstration of the behavior, followed by an immediate opportunity for the children to imitate the behavior
   C. A simultaneous demonstration and explanation of the behavior, followed by ample opportunity for the children to rehearse the instructed behavior
   D. Physically guiding the children through the behavior to be imitated while verbally explaining the behavior

   Answer: A. A verbal description of the task to be performed, followed by having the children immediately attempt to perform the instructed behavior

   A verbal description alone does not give the students a chance to observe the behavior so that they can imitate it. Some of the students might have hearing deficiencies. In addition, students with special needs often benefit from hands-on, multi-modal activities.

39. **Which of the following is a good example of a generalization? (Skill 7.05) (Average)**

    A. Jim has learned to add and is now ready to subtract.
    B. Sarah adds sets of units to obtain a product.
    C. Bill recognizes a vocabulary word on a billboard when traveling.
    D. Jane can spell the word "net" backwards to get the word "ten."

    Answer: C. Bill recognizes a vocabulary word on a billboard when traveling.

    Generalization is the occurrence of a learned behavior in the presence of a stimulus other than the one that produced the initial response. Students must be able to expand or transfer what is learned to other settings (e.g., reading to math word problems, resource room to regular classroom). Transfer of learning can be positive or negative. Positive transfer occurs when elements of what is learned on one task are also applicable to a new task, making the second task is easier to learn. Negative transfer occurs when elements of what was learned on one task interfere with what needs to be learned on a new task. Generalization can be enhanced by the following:

    - Using many examples in teaching to deepen application of learned skills
    - Using consistency in initial teaching situations, later introducing variety in format, procedure, and examples
    - Having the same information presented by different teachers, in different settings, and under varying conditions
    - Including a continuous reinforcement schedule at first, and later changing to delayed and intermittent schedules as instruction progresses
    - Teaching students to record instances of generalization and to reward themselves when they do
    - Associating naturally occurring stimuli when possible

40. **All of the following are suggestions for** *pacing* **or altering the presentation of tasks to match the student's rate of learning except:** *(Skill 7.06) (Average)*

   A. Teach in several shorter segments of time rather than a single lengthy session
   B. Continue to teach a task until the lesson is completed in order to provide more time on task
   C. Watch for nonverbal cues that indicate students are becoming confused, bored, or restless
   D. Avoid giving students an inappropriate amount of written work

   Answer: B. Continue to teach a task until the lesson is completed in order to provide more time on task

   This action does not alter the subject content; nor does it alter the rate at which tasks are presented. Pacing is the term used for altering tasks to match the student's rate of learning. This can be done in two ways: altering the subject content and the rate at which tasks are presented. However, both methods require adjusting presentation based on the child's performance along the way, and introducing a new task only when the student has demonstrated mastery of the previous task in the learning hierarchy.

41. **Alan has failed repeatedly in his academic work. He needs continuous feedback in order to experience small, incremental achievements. What type of instructional material would best meet this need?** *(Skill 8.06) (Rigorous)*

   A. Programmed materials
   B. Audiotapes
   C. Materials with no writing required
   D. Worksheets

   Answer: A. Programmed materials

   Programmed materials are best suited to Alan, because he would be able to chart his progress as he achieves each goal. He can monitor himself and take responsibility for his successes.

42. **What criteria must be considered when choosing assistive technology (AT) to help a particular student?** *(Skill 8.07) (Easy)*

    A. Whether there is a specific need the AT can meet (e.g., a goal on the IEP that requires it)
    B. The degree of independence with which the student can use the device
    C. The need for collaborative planning for the device to be used across all relevant settings and transfer between settings
    D. All of the above

    Answer: D. All of the above

    In addition to the above, it is also necessary to consider the amount of training the student and staff will need with the device, the specific contexts in which the device will be used (e.g., a language board might be used in all settings, but a computer program might only be used in writing), the plan for transitions, and storage of the device.

43. **Bobby can give accurate, detailed oral answers to prompts and content area questions. His oral answers are well thought out and organized. When he tries to write down his ideas, however, he struggles and his poor spelling makes his writing unreadable. His punctuation and capitalization are erratic, too. You decide:** *(Skill 9.01) (Rigorous)*

    A. Bobby needs help with writing expression so he can organize his ideas into good paragraphs.
    B. Bobby needs help with writing mechanics and phonics.
    C. Bobby would benefit from an accommodation allowing him to dictate his compositions first, then write them down from the recording.
    D. Both B and C

    Answer: D. Both B (Bobby needs help with writing mechanics and encoding phonics) and C (Bobby would benefit from an accommodation allowing him to dictate his compositions first, then write them down from the recording)

    Bobby's difficulty is not with expression. When the act of encoding (spelling out his words on paper) is removed, as in oral answers, he provides well thought out answers. His problem is that he does not have the phonic knowledge to properly encode or spell his words and he is also weak on conventions like capitals and punctuation. He should be allowed to dictate his ideas so his strengths in composition and knowledge are used, then practice his weaker skills (phonics and spelling) afterward. This way his weakness in one area will not slow down his progress in another.

44. **In 2000, the National Reading Panel reviewed research on reading instruction showing that:** *(Skill 9.02) (Average)*

    A. Top-down approaches that emphasize meaning, like the whole language approach, are the most effective reading programs.
    B. Bottom-up or code-emphasis approaches, like phonics, are the most effective for reading programs.
    C. There are five critical components of an effective reading program: phonemic awareness, phonics, fluency, vocabulary, and comprehension.
    D. Approaches that emphasize sight word vocabulary and fluency are the most effective reading programs.

    Answer: C. There are five critical components of an effective reading program: phonemic awareness, phonics, fluency, vocabulary, and comprehension.

    According to the National Reading Panel, research clearly shows that all five components are necessary for a successful program. They recommend that all components be present in a balanced fashion, and that educators evaluate their proposed approach to ensure it covers all areas. Approaches that lack an emphasis on one of the five critical areas should be modified to ensure all areas are well integrated into the instruction.

45. **Teachers in grades K-3 are mandated (by NCLB, 2002) to teach reading using what?** *(Skills 9.02 and 16.01) (Average)*

    A. Whole language and language experience approaches
    B. Varied scientifically based methods with measurable outcomes
    C. Code-emphasis and phonics-based methods
    D. Federally developed basal reader programs

    Answer: B. Varied scientifically based methods with measurable outcomes

    NCLB clearly made teachers accountable for locating and using the most effective research-based methods and programs suitable for their students. Teachers are held accountable for updating their own knowledge and being familiar with current research in the field.

46. **Ryan is working on a report about dogs. He uses scissors and tape to cut and rearrange sections and paragraphs. He then photocopies the paper so he can continue writing. In which stage of the writing process is Ryan?** *(Skill 9.03) (Easy)*

A. Final draft
B. Prewriting
C. Revision
D. Drafting

Answer: C. Revision

Ryan is revising and reordering before final editing. Using scissors and glue to physically separate and reorganize the text is a particularly effective technique for students with many disabilities. Sometimes this physical act is even more effective than using a word processor, though it may lead to better use of a word processor in the long run. Prewriting would involve generating ideas and organizing them, often using a web or graphic organizer. Final drafting would involve "publication" as a finished piece.

47. **Mrs. Smith's students are engaged in activities such as saying rhyming words and words that begin with the same sound or finding pictures in a list that start with the same or different sound, changing the sounds in words (e.g., if 'dog' started with the same sound as 'cat' it would be 'cog'). There are no printed words or letters in the exercises. You can tell Mrs. Smith is trying to improve her students':** *(Skill 9.03) (Rigorous)*

A. Sight word recognition
B. Phoneme awareness
C. Vocabulary understanding
D. Reading comprehension.

Answer: B. Phoneme awareness

These tasks help the student hear and understand that words are made up of distinct sounds (phonemes) that must be blended together. Unlike phonics exercises, which involve attaching sounds to letter symbols, phoneme awareness can be done orally, with no letters or text at all. It is a manipulation of sounds, not letters. It is one of the five critical components of an effective reading program.

48. **Which of the following sentences will NOT test recall?** *(Skill 9.05) (Average)*

   A. What words in the story describe Goldilocks?
   B. Why did Goldilocks go into the three bears' house?
   C Name in order the things that belonged to the three bears that Goldilocks tried.
   D. What did the three bears learn about leaving their house unlocked?

   Answer: D. What did the three bears learn about leaving their house unlocked?

   Recall requires the student to produce from memory ideas and information explicitly stated in the story. Answer D requires an inference (unless the "moral" that they learned was clearly stated in the story).

49. **In what order does the National Council of Teachers of Mathematics (NCTM) say new math concepts and operations should be taught?** *(Skill 10.02) (Rigorous)*

   A. Teach the meaning of symbols first, then pictures, then concrete manipulatives.
   B. Teach with concrete manipulatives, then pictorial representations, then symbols.
   C. Start with pictures, move to concrete manipulatives, then symbols and words.
   D. Teach in any order as long as you do it consistently in all areas.

   Answer: B. Teach with concrete manipulatives, then pictorial representations, then symbols.

   NCTM's review of the research and of the developmental order of math concepts clearly shows the effectiveness of teaching math concepts and operations in this order:

   - Concrete representations: The extensive exploration and use of objects and manipulatives to discover and then demonstrate operations and relationships
   - Pictorial representations (semi-abstract): The use of concrete pictures of objects and actions, often in the presence of the objects, as discoveries and demonstrations are made
   - Symbolic representations (abstract): The use of symbols exclusively to conduct operations, explorations, and discoveries about math concepts

50. **Kenny is a 9th grader enrolled in Wood Shop; he is having difficulty grasping fractions. You know that Kenny has difficulty with abstract concepts. What would be a good method to teach this concept?** *(Skill 10.04) (Rigorous)*

    A. Pie blocks that proportionately measure whole, half, 1/4, 1/8, etc.
    B. Strips of paper that proportionately measure whole, half, 1/4, 1/8, etc.
    C. One-on-one review of the worksheet
    D. Working in the wood shop, privately showing him how to measure

    Answer: B. Strips of paper that proportionately measure whole, half, 1/4, 1/8, etc.

    Strips of paper can be used to teach the concept by tearing a whole sheet into proportionate pieces. They can also be used like a tape measure to measure a length of wood. Although other methods might help him learn the concept, this method of using a linear form will make generalization to the wood shop most likely.

51. **Mr. Ward notes that Jennifer, a 9th grade student, understands the concept for three-step equations but seems unable to do problems successfully. When he reviews Jennifer's work, he notes that her addition and subtraction are not correct. What strategy would be most appropriate?** *(Skill 10.05) (Average)*

    A. Basic multiplication and addition charts
    B. Checks for understanding
    C. Private instruction on adding and subtracting
    D. Calculator usage

    Answer: D. Calculator usage

    If Jennifer is in 9th grade and still has difficulty adding and subtracting correctly, it is likely that this is part of her disability. The correct compensatory intervention would be a calculator and brief tutoring on how to correctly use it. This will allow her to progress in the mastery of the conceptual use of math without being held back by a computational disability.

52. **Although there are many strategies that can help students with disabilities learn new math concepts, what one strategy is almost universally necessary and helpful?** *(Skill 10.05) (Rigorous)*

A. More repetition of skills and practice problems
B. More detailed teacher demonstrations of the concept
C. More student time spent at the concrete level interacting with manipulatives
D. More homework practice on new concepts

Answer: C. More student time spent at the concrete level interacting with manipulatives

Although specific strategies will depend upon the individual child's strengths and disability, more time spent allowing the student to interact with and carry out operations with manipulatives and more time using manipulatives to illustrate concepts will almost universally be helpful. In addition, when moving to the next level (pictorial representations), it might also be helpful to keep manipulatives near the pictures for longer. See Skill 10.05 for more strategies for teaching math to students with disabilities.

53. **Functional curriculum focuses on all of the following EXCEPT:** *(Skill 11.03) (Rigorous)*

A. Skills needed for social living
B. Occupational readiness
C. Use of community resources
D. Remedial academic skills

Answer: D. Remedial academic skills

Remedial academics may be applied but are not a focus. The primary goal is to achieve skills for functioning in society on an independent basis, where possible.

54. **Bob shows behavior problems like lack of attention, out of seat, and talking out. His teacher has kept data on these behaviors and has found that Bob is showing much better self-control since he has been self-managing himself through a behavior modification program. The most appropriate placement recommendation for Bob at this time is probably:** *(Skill 11.04) (Average)*

   A. Any available part-time special education program
   B. The regular classroom, solely
   C. A behavior disorders resource room for one period per day
   D. A specific learning disabilities resource room for one period per day

   Answer: B. The regular classroom, solely

   Bob is able to self-manage himself and is very likely to behave like the other children in the regular classroom. The regular classroom is the least restrictive environment.

55. **Marisol has been mainstreamed into a 9th grade language arts class. Although her behavior is satisfactory and she likes the class, Marisol's reading level is about two years below grade level. The class has been assigned to read *Great Expectations* and write a report. What intervention would be LEAST successful in helping Marisol complete this assignment?** *(Skill 11.04) (Average)*

   A. Having Marisol listen to a taped recording while following the story in the regular text
   B. Giving her a modified version of the story at her reading level
   C. Telling her to choose a different book that she can read
   D. Providing an abbreviated story outline at her reading level

   Answer: C. Telling her to choose a different book that she can read

   A, B, and D are positive accommodations that allow her to access the same curriculum as her classmates. C denies Marisol access to the same curriculum accessed by the other students and violates her rights to FAPE. It would de facto separate her from the class when she is supposed to be a part of it. It is also unnecessary. With any of the other accommodations, she could participate in discussions, and this would contribute to her independence as well.

56. Sam is working to earn half an hour of basketball time with his favorite P.E. teacher. At the end of each half hour, Sam marks his point sheet with an X if he reached his goal of no call-outs. When he has received 25 marks, he will receive his basketball free time. This behavior management strategy is an example of:
(Skill 11.04) (Average)

A. Self-recording
B. Self-evaluation
C. Self-reinforcement
D. Self-regulation

Answer: A. Self-recording

Self-management is an important part of social skills and independence training, especially for older students preparing for employment. Components of self-management include:

- **Self-monitoring and recording**: Choosing behaviors and alternatives and monitoring those actions, like Sam does in the example
- **Self-evaluation:** Deciding the effectiveness of the behavior in solving the problem. For example, a student whose goal is to finish his math work records, on a scale of 0 to 3, how well he has done this each day.
- **Self-reinforcement:** Telling oneself that one is capable of achieving success and planning personal rewards.

In this case, Sam is simply recording his behavior, but this is a first step for further evaluation and monitoring.

57. **David is a 16 year old in your class who recently came from another country. The girls in your class have come to you to complain about the way he treats them in a sexist manner. When they complain, you realize that this is also the way he treats adult females. You have talked to David before about appropriate behavior. You should first:** *(Skill 11.05) (Rigorous)*

    A. Complain to the principal
    B. Ask for a parent-teacher conference
    C. Check to see if this is a cultural norm in his country
    D. Create a behavior contract for him to follow

    Answer: C. Check to see if this is a cultural norm in his country

    Although A, B, and D are good actions, it is important to remember that David might come from a culture where woman are treated differently than they are in America. Learning this information will enable the school as a whole to address this behavior. At that point, it may be useful to talk to parents or involve a counselor in helping David learn how to adjust his behavior to meet new cultural norms. It might also involve class study of aspects of his culture that will be viewed as positive by his peers in order to improve his acceptance.

58. **Teacher modeling, templates and lists of problem solving steps, student-teacher dialogues, and other individualized aids that are gradually faded out are part of which teaching technique designed to provide support during the initial stages of instruction?** *(Skill 11.05) (Rigorous)*

    A. Reciprocal teaching
    B. Scaffolding
    C. Peer tutoring
    D. Cooperative learning

    Answer: B. Scaffolding

    Scaffolding provides support by building of new knowledge on previous knowledge, much like one layer is placed on another. It provides instructional "training wheels" for the student until the student can complete the task independently.

59. **You are working with a functional program and have placed a student in a vocational position in the kitchen of a coffee house. A waiter takes orders and relays them to the student, whose job is to make the coffee as ordered. You need to perform a task analysis of making a cup of coffee. Which task should be first in the analysis?** *(Skill 11.06) (Average)*

   A. Filling the pot with water
   B. Taking the order
   C. Measuring the coffee
   D. Picking the correct coffee

   Answer: D. Picking the correct coffee

   While the student is in a coffee house, the task was to make coffee, not to wait on customers. There are different kinds of coffee (decaffeinated, regular, etc.) and they all have their appropriate canisters. The student must be able to choose the correct coffee before measuring it.

60. **Transition planning for post-school life requires which of the following?** *(Skill 11.07) (Average)*

   A. School-based instruction tailored to meet the student's goals
   B. Community-based experiences for independent living or job skills
   C. Development of objectives related to specific employment and other post-school areas
   D. All of the above

   Answer: D. All of the above

   All of these are mandated by IDEA unless the CSE can provide evidence that they are unnecessary. Community-referenced instruction refers to instruction that takes place in the classroom but is designed to generalize to life outside the classroom. To do this, instruction will be designed to be as similar to the real-life community or home situation as possible (e.g., using checkbook registers obtained from banks to learn to balance a checkbook in class or watching a video on how to get on and off a city bus). Alternatively, community-*based* instruction is instruction that takes place outside the classroom in the natural community setting (e.g., on-the-job training, riding actual city busses). Whether community-referenced instruction based in the school or community-based instruction in the natural setting is used, these areas of career education should be included:

   - Career awareness: Diversity of available jobs
   - Career exploration: Skills needed for occupational groups
   - Career preparation: Specific training and preparation required for the world of work

61. **Social maturity can be evidenced by the student's:** *(Skill 12.01)*
    (Easy)

    A. Recognition of rights and responsibilities (his or her own and those of others)
    B. Display of respect for legitimate authority figures
    C. Formulation of a valid moral judgment
    D. Demonstration of all of the above

    Answer: D. Demonstration of all of the above

    Some additional evidence of social maturity includes:

    - The ability to cooperate
    - Following procedures formulated by an outside party
    - Achieving appropriate levels of independence

62. **In establishing a classroom behavior management plan with the students, it is best to:** *(Skill 13.01) (Average)*

    A. Have rules written and in place on day one
    B. Hand out a copy of the rules to the students on day one
    C. Have separate rules for each class on day one
    D. Have students involved in creating the rules on day one

    Answer: D. Have students involved in creating the rules on day one

    Rules are easier to follow when students not only know the reason they are in place, but also took part in creating them. It may be good to already have a few rules pre-written and then to discuss if these cover all the rules the students have created. If not, it is possible you may want to modify your set of pre-written rules.

63. **A Life Space Interview is used for:** *(Skill 13.01) (Rigorous)*

    A. Transition to exit interview
    B. Analysis of proficiency levels
    C. Maintenance of acceptable behavior
    D. Creating awareness of distorted perceptions

    Answer: D. Creating awareness of distorted perceptions

    Life Space Interviews are given in a here-and-now fashion. They often employ role-playing to increase awareness of misunderstandings, and can be used to prepare a student for mediation.

64. **Laura is beginning to raise her hand first instead of talking out. An effective schedule of reinforcement should be:** *(Skill 13.01) (Average)*

    A. Continuous
    B. Variable
    C. Intermittent
    D. Fixed

    Answer: A. Continuous

    Note that the behavior is new. The pattern of reinforcement should not be variable, intermittent, or fixed. Continuous reinforcement is most effective for establishing new behaviors.

65. **Janelle is just as "antsy" as Jaquan, who has ADHD. You want to keep a good eye on them, so you put them in the same corner. Later you suspect Amanda also has ADHD, so you move her to the same area. You are creating a:** *(Skill 13.04) (Average)*

    A. Self-fulfilling prophecy
    B. Cooperative learning circle
    C. Disordered support group
    D. Buffer zone to observe and direct behavior centrally

    Answer: A. Self-fulfilling prophecy

    When you treat students like they have a disability, you could be creating the appearance of a disability. Amanda and Janelle might not have ADHD, but you are placing them in a group where ADHD behavior is rewarded with attention. You are then creating a self-fulfilling prophecy.

66. **Mr. Smith is on a field trip with a group of high school EH students. On the way, they stop at a fast-food restaurant for lunch, and Warren and Raul get into an argument. After some heated words, Warren stalks out of the restaurant and refuses to return to the group. He leaves the parking lot, continues walking away from the group, and ignores Mr. Smith's directions to come back. What would be the best course of action for Mr. Smith?** *(Skill 13.05) (Rigorous)*

A. Leave the group with the class aide and follow Warren to try to talk him into coming back
B. Wait a little while and see if Warren cools off and returns
C. Telephone the school and let the crisis teacher notify the police in accordance with school policy
D. Call the police himself

Answer: C. Telephone the school and let the crisis teacher notify the police in accordance with school policy

Mr. Smith is still responsible for his class. He cannot leave the entire class with the aide. His school should have a policy in place for such situations. This is his best option.

67. Hector is a 10th grader in a program for the severely emotionally handicapped. After a classmate taunted him about his mother, Hector threw a desk at the other boy and attacked him. A crisis intervention team tried to break up the fight, and one teacher hurt his knee. The other boy received a concussion. Hector now faces disciplinary measures. How long can he be suspended without a meeting to review a possible "change of placement"?
(Skill 13.06) (Rigorous)

A. 5 days
B. 10 days
C. 10 - 30 days
D. 60 days

Answer: B. 10 days

According to Honig versus Doe (1988), in cases where the student has presented an immediate threat to others, that student may be temporarily suspended for up to 10 school days to give the school and the parents time to review the IEP and discuss possible alternatives to the current placement. A Manifest Determination meeting should be held to evaluate the behavior in light of the student's disability. IDEA 2004 states that if the disability was not related to the behavior, the student should be given the same punishment/result as a "regular education" student. However, if the behavior resulting in suspension was a result of the student's disability, then such punishment is not allowed and the team must decide whether the current placement and accommodations meet the child's needs. If not, then the placement can be changed.

A temporary (less than 10 days) change in placement for non-disciplinary reasons does not require a CSE; however, it does require a parental/guardian signature. The temporary placement of services should be reviewed at a CSE to discuss permanent placement.

68. **Statements like "Darren is lazy" are not helpful in describing his behavior for all but which of these reasons?** *(Skill 13.07) (Average)*

    A. There is no way to determine if any change occurs from the information given
    B. The student—not the behavior—becomes labeled
    C. Darren's behavior will manifest itself clearly enough without any written description
    D. Constructs are open to various interpretations among the people who are asked to define them

    Answer: C. Darren's behavior will manifest itself clearly enough without any written description

    "Darren is lazy" is a pejorative label. The word "lazy" can be interpreted in a variety of ways, and there is no way to measure this description for change. A behavioral description should be objective and measurable. Darren's behavior manifesting itself is hardly the point. It *has* manifested itself and it needs to be measured and steps taken to change it.

69. **The first step in writing a Functional Behavioral Assessment (FBA) is:** *(Skill 13.07) (Rigorous)*

    A. Establish a replacement behavior
    B. Establish levels of interventions
    C. Clearly define the behavior in need of modification
    D. Establish assessment periods of FBA effectiveness

    Answer: C. Clearly define the behavior in need of modification

    An FBA will only be successful if the behavior in question is defined in a specific, observable, measurable way in order for it to be possible to set up a program to alter it and measure the success of that program. Following that, it is critical to determine antecedents for as well as consequences of or purposes for the behavior. Only then can effective replacement behavior be identified and intervention be planned. FBAs must be written and reviewed by the whole team.

70. To reinforce Audrey each time she is on task and in her seat, Ms. Wright delivers specific praise and stickers, which Audrey may collect and redeem for a reward. The data collected during the time Ms. Wright is using this reward system is called: *(Skill 13.07) (Average)*

   A. Referral phase
   B. Intervention phase
   C. Baseline phase
   D. Observation phase

   Answer: B. Intervention phase

   Ms Wright is involved in behavior modification. This is the intervention phase.

71. Lotzie is not labeled as needing special education services, but he appears to be unable to function at his grade level both academically and socially. He is in 9th grade, but reads picture books and consistently displays immature behavior that can be misinterpreted. You have already observed these behaviors. What should be done first? *(Skill 14.01) (Rigorous)*

   A. Establish a rapport with the parents
   B. Write a CSE referral
   C. Plan and discuss possible interventions with the teacher
   D. Address the class about acceptance

   Answer: A. Establish a rapport with the parents

   When a student enters 9th grade in a poor placement such as this, it is not unusual for the parents to have been opposed to special education. The best way to help the student is to establish a rapport with the parents. You need to find out why he has not been referred, and if possible, help them see why their child would benefit from special education services.

72. Parent contact should first begin when: *(Skill 14.02) (Average)*

   A. You are informed the child will be your student
   B. The student fails a test
   C. The student exceeds others on a task
   D. A CSE is coming and you have had no previous replies to letters

   Answer: A. You are informed the child will be your student

   Student contact should start as a getting to know you piece, which allows you to begin on a non-judgmental platform. It also allows the parent to see that you are a professional who is willing to work with them.

73. **You should prepare for a parent-teacher conference by:** *(Skill 14.02)* *(Average)*

    A. Memorizing student progress/grades
    B. Anticipating questions
    C. Scheduling the meetings during your lunch time
    D. Planning a tour of the school

    Answer: B. Anticipating questions

    It pays to anticipate parent questions. It makes you more likely to be able to answer them. If you anticipate these questions, it is likely that you can plan some of the discussion in the conference.

74. **You note that a child in your class is expressing discomfort when placing his back against a chair. You ask him if he is okay, and he says it's nothing. You notice what appears to be a belt mark on his shoulder. What is the first thing you should do?**
    (Skill 14.04) (Rigorous)

    A. Send the child to the nurse
    B. Contact an administrator
    C. Call Child Protective Services
    D. Follow the school policy and report it

    Answer: D. Follow the school policy and report it.

    In New York State, all educators are mandated reporters and all instances of suspected abuse must be reported to New York Office of Children and Family Services. However, your school should have a policy about whom you should first report suspected abuse; it could be the nurse or an administrator or counselor who will investigate further. You will need to use sensitivity in your interactions with the child in this matter.

75. **Janiay requires occupational therapy and speech therapy services. She is your student. What must you do to insure that her services are met?** *(Skill 15.04) (Rigorous)*

    A. Watch the services being rendered
    B. Schedule collaboratively
    C. Ask for services to be given in a push-in model
    D. Ask school administration to train you to give the service

    Answer: B. Schedule collaboratively

    Collaborative scheduling of students to receive services is both your responsibility and that of the service provider. Scheduling together is convenient for you and the service provider. It also provides you with an opportunity to make sure the student does not miss important information.

76. **An individual with disabilities in need of employability training, as well as a job, should be referred to what governmental agency for assistance?** *(Skill 15.07) (Average)*

   A. OMRDD
   B. VESID
   C. Social Services
   D. ARC

   Answer: B. VESID

   VESID stands for Vocational and Educational Services for Individuals with Disabilities, and is New York State's body for coordinating post-school services for students with disabilities. VESID works with a number of community agencies to meet these needs.

77. **Which two student behaviors are indicative of a possible crisis?** *(Skill 15.07) (Average)*

   A. Bullying and being socially active
   B. Intermittent periods of laughter and rage
   C. High academic performance and gang activity
   D. Detailed threats of lethal violence and severe rage for minor reasons

   Answer: D. Detailed threats of lethal violence and severe rage for minor reasons

   While a student might display one behavior indicating that he or she might be entering a crisis state that the school should be concerned about, often two or more signs are displayed. Students who display uncontrolled rage and verbalize violent threats may be seen as a crisis waiting to happen. This is particularly true if the student is him- or herself a victim of violence.

78. **Which of these groups is not comprehensively covered by IDEA?** *(Skill 16.01) (Easy)*

   A. Gifted and talented
   B. Mentally retarded
   C. Specific learning disabilities
   D. Speech and language impaired

   Answer: A. Gifted and talented

   IDEA did not cover all exceptional children; it covered children with disabilities. The *Gifted and Talented Children's Act (Public Law 95-56) of 1978* established guidelines for services to students who are gifted or talented.

79. **Educators who advocate educating all children, without exception, in their neighborhood classrooms and schools, who propose the end of labeling and segregation of special needs students in special classes, and who call for the delivery of special supports and services directly in the classroom may be said to support the: (Skill 16.01) (Easy)**

    A. Full service model
    B. Regular education initiative
    C. Full inclusion model
    D. Mainstream model

Answer: C. Full inclusion model

Advocates of full inclusion believe that all students must be included in the regular classroom, without exception.

80. **Which of the following would constitute violation of IDEA law? (Skill 16.01) (Rigorous)**

    A. A school takes too long to identify or provide services to a child.
    B. A school does not provide all the services specified in a child's IEP.
    C. A teacher does not provide an accommodation listed in a child's IEP because she does not think it is necessary.
    D. All of the above

Answer: D. All of the above

An IEP is a legally binding document and ALL provisions in it must be provided to the student. Both schools and teachers have been held by the courts to be legally (and financially) liable if they fail to follow the requirements of the IEP. If a teacher feels an accommodation is inappropriate for a child, or another would be better, it is necessary to alert the IEP team and consider an amendment. FAPE and IDEA, along with the 14th Amendment, all guarantee every child equal access to education. IDEA requires that it be in the least restrictive environment.

81. **IDEA 2004 stated that there was a disproportionate number of minority students classified in need of special education services. The reason for this that IDEA 2004 suggests is:** *(Skill 16.01) (Average)*

   A. Socioeconomic status where disproportionate numbers exist
   B. Improper evaluations; not making allowances for students who speak English as a second language
   C. Growing population of minorities
   D. Percentage of drug abuse per ethnicity

   Answer: B. Improper evaluations; not making allowances for students who speak English as a second language

   IDEA 2004 questioned the overrepresentation of students who speak English as a second language and cautioned schools to abide by guidelines for working with students with limited English proficiency. The 2004 revisions in NCLB provided allowances for schools not to require students with LEP to take and pass state reading exams if the students were enrolled in U.S. schools for less than a year. States may substitute an English language proficiency exam for students who have been in this country for less than a year, and may include scores of those who have become proficient in English in their annual reporting. After the one-year grace period, however, students must take the reading exam.

82. **Cheryl is a 15-year old student receiving educational services in a full-time, substantially separate, classroom. The date for her IEP review is planned for two months before her 16th birthday. According to the requirements of IDEA, what must ADDITIONALLY be included in this review?** *(Skill 16.01) (Average)*

   A. Graduation plan
   B. Individualized transition plan
   C. Vocational assessment
   D. Transportation planning

   Answer: B. Individualized transition plan

   This is necessary, because the student should be receiving services aimed at helping her to transition to the world of work and more independent living.

83. **How do the 10th and 14th Amendments to the U.S. Constitution affect education?** *(Skill 16.01) (Rigorous)*

    A. The federal government determines the content of education.
    B. Education is an unstated power vested in the states.
    C. States that provide services like education must provide them to ALL children.
    D. Both B and C

    Answer: D. both B and C

    The 10th Amendment states that all powers not already described as controlled by the U.S. government (this includes education because it is not listed as a federal power) belong to the "states or to the people." Because education is not mentioned specifically, it is an "unstated power." The 14th Amendment mandates that any service a state provides to any citizen must be provided to all citizens and the provision of these services cannot violate any federal laws forbidding discrimination. This is the source of special education law.

84. **What determines whether a person is entitled to protection under Section 504?** *(Skill 16.01) (Average)*

    A. The individual must meet the definition of a person with a disability.
    B. The person must be able to meet the requirements of a particular program in spite of his or her disability.
    C. The school, business, or other facility must be the recipient of federal funding assistance.
    D. All of the above

    Answer: D. All of the above

    To be entitled to protection under Section 504, an individual must meet the definition of a person with a disability, which is: any person who (i) "has a physical or mental impairment which substantially limits one or more of that person's major life activities, such as self-care, walking, seeing, breathing, working, and or *learning*," (ii) has a record of such impairment; or (iii) is regarded as having such an impairment. This phrase led to the establishment of the right of all to a Free and Appropriate Education. IDEA expanded the definition of FAPE to include an individualized educational program. In addition, the person must also be "otherwise qualified," which means that the person must be able to meet the requirements of a particular program in spite of the disability. The person must also be afforded "reasonable accommodations" by recipients of federal financial assistance.

85. **How was the training of special education teachers changed by the No Child Left Behind Act of 2002?** *(Skill 16.01) (Average)*

   A. The act required all special education teachers to be certified in reading and math.
   B. The act required all special education teachers to take the same coursework as general education teachers.
   C. The act required that if a special education teacher is teaching a core subject, he or she must meet the standard of a highly qualified teacher in that subject.
   D. All of the above

   Answer: C. The act required that if a special education teacher is teaching a core subject, he or she must meet the standard of a highly qualified teacher in that subject

   In order for special education teachers to be a student's sole teacher of a core subject, he or she must meet the professional criteria of NCLB. Teachers must be *highly qualified*—that is, certified or licensed in their area of special education—and show proof of a specific level of professional development in the core subjects that they teach. When special education teachers receive specific education in the core subjects they teach, they will be better prepared to teach to the same level of learning standards as general education teachers.

86. **What is true about IDEA? In order to be eligible, a student must:** *(Skill 16.01) (Easy)*

   A. Have a medical disability
   B. Have a disability that fits into one of the categories listed in the law
   C. Have a disability that actually affects school performance
   D. Both B and C

   Answer: D. Both B. (Have a disability that fits into one of the categories listed in the law) and C. (Have a disability that actually affects school performance)

   Having a disability is not enough to warrant eligibility for special services. The disability must be shown to negatively impact school performance. In other words, it must be preventing the student from accessing the curriculum all other students can access in some way.

87. **The definition of assistive technology devices was amended in the IDEA reauthorization of 2004 to exclude what?** *(Skill 16.01) (Average)*

    A. iPods and other hand-held devices
    B. Computer-enhanced technology
    C. Surgically implanted devices
    D. Braille and/or special learning aids

    Answer: C. Surgically implanted devices

    The definition of assistive technology devices was amended to exclude devices that are surgically implanted (e.g., cochlear implants), and clarified that students with assistive technology devices shall not be prevented from having special education services. Assistive technology devices might need to be monitored by school personnel, but schools are not responsible for the implantation or replacement of such devices surgically.

88. **Which of the following must be completed before comprehensive testing occurs?** *(Skill 16.02) (Average)*

    A. Teacher consult on student needs
    B. Pre-CSE conference
    C. Parental permission for each test
    D. All of the above

    Answer: C. Parental permission for each test

    The only piece required by both Part 200 and IDEA 2004 is parental permission for each test.

89. **What does Zero Reject require for all children with disabilities?**
(Skill 16.02) (Average)

A. Full inclusion of ALL students with disabilities in regular education classrooms and reporting annually
B. Seeking out and providing services to ALL students with disabilities regardless of type or severity and reporting annually
C. Free, appropriate public education provided to ALL students
D. Both B and C

Answer: D. Both B and C

The principle of Zero Reject requires that all children with disabilities be provided with a free, appropriate public education regardless of the type or severity of the disability. It also requires that states have procedures to *seek out* and identify students in need of services through effective outreach programs. The LEA reporting procedure locates, identifies, and evaluates children with disabilities within a given jurisdiction to ensure their attendance in public school and reports on these efforts annually. Zero Reject does NOT mean all will be served in full inclusion.

90. **According to IDEA 2004, students with disabilities are to do what?**
(Skill 16.02) (Average)

A. Participate in the general education program to the fullest extent that it is beneficial for them
B. Participate in a vocational training program within the general education setting
C. Participate in a general education program for physical education
D. Participate in a Full Inclusion program that meets their needs

Answer: A. Participate in the general education program to the fullest extent that it is beneficial for them

The term "full inclusion" is not used in IDEA or federal statutes. IDEA requires that students be included in the least restrictive environment that meets their needs. It states that this environment should be as close to that experienced by students without disabilities as is practical, but also states that not all students can benefit from full participation in general education classrooms, and school systems must provide for all levels of placement. This can mean that a particular student's LRE may restrict him or her to a substantially separate program for the entire school day, but it should be possible to meet most students' needs in a less restrictive setting. Choices B, C, and D are all examples of possible settings related to participating in the general education setting to the fullest extent possible.

WRITTEN ASSIGNMENT

Sample Question

You are teaching a resource class of intermediate-aged students with mild to moderate disabilities listed as learning disabled, autistic, and other health impaired. Patrick is a ten year old student diagnosed with PDD. His parents are opposed to Patrick taking medication, which has impacted his ability to concentrate on the presentation of lessons, particularly in larger classroom environments. Patrick receives instruction for Reading, Spelling, and English in your program. Although he is a fourth grader, his reading level is 2.0. The resource program includes instruction in Reading as well as study skills and provides special education services (including modifications and accommodations) for the same students in a grade-level inclusion class for Social Studies.

In Social Studies, Patrick sits in a pod of desks with three other students, facing the teacher's desk, which is in front of the windows to the playground. Patrick is distracted by the activity outside the classroom. He is also distracted by Jack, his best friend from the resource program, who sits across from him. The students are sitting in the same pod for ease of providing support services. Patrick's class is studying the Midwest region of the United States. The regular education students will read and discuss a five-page lesson from the fourth grade textbook, which includes key vocabulary, text, charts, graphs, pictures, and questions. They will then complete a three-page, fill-in-the-blank study guide for the lesson. This lesson/assignment pattern will continue for four lessons in every chapter. Patrick often shuts down or goes into meltdown when presented with the assignments given in this inclusion classroom. Describe how you would address the curriculum and materials needs for Patrick in his Social Studies class. Include THREE curriculum and instructional considerations and describe the implementation of your ideas.

Sample Response A
Score: 3

Due to Patrick's PDD (Pervasive Developmental Disorder) he is easily distracted in his learning environment. This is compounded by the fact that he is not taking medication to help him stay focused. Before curriculum considerations can be met, Patrick should be sitting where he is least distracted in the classroom (facing the teacher, but away from the window). This may be addressed by discussing Patrick's distractibility with the teacher and asking that she move his desk and reposition herself for instruction. In addition, Patrick should be sitting away from Jack. They could sit in separate pods, facing the teacher, but not facing each other, and still be easily reached for support services in the classroom.

Patrick's ability to work with the regular education Social Studies curriculum is impacted by the reading level of the text and the length and format of the written assignments. Begin by reviewing the state standards in the social sciences for students in the fourth grade. Patrick may not be able to master all of the information covered in his Social Studies book. Trimming the learning expectations to match the state standards is one option.

Because Patrick reads 2.0 years below his grade level, he is overwhelmed by the fourth grade Social Studies textbook. He will have difficulty following the text as it is read in class and even more difficulty reading it independently. Patrick would benefit from materials and strategies to bridge the gap between his functional level of reading and the reading level of the material. Plan for speakers, field trips, or videos to present information in an alternate or additional fashion. While Patrick's class would not be able to travel out of the region to learn about the Midwest, they could watch a videotape that would present the information through auditory and visual modes. When using the textbook, Patrick would benefit from preview strategies: looking through the lesson for titles, subtitles, bold faced words, definitions, pictures and charts, and their captions. He should be instructed in how to predict what the lesson will include as well as in forming questions that he hopes will be answered. Discuss the main points and review questions for the lesson. Patrick would also benefit from hearing the text read on tape to become familiar with the lesson before he hears the presentation in class.

Because Patrick's reading level is two grades below his textbook, it may be necessary to modify the text to make it more readable to him, or to find the same material written at a simpler reading level. Nonfiction leveled readers aligned with curriculum standards are becoming more widely available. The teacher should investigate such resources. IDEA (Individuals with Disabilities Education Act) legislation specifies equal access to content area curriculum, and a text that is too far above reading level is not accessible to the student. The teacher can also rewrite certain sections to include the same concepts presented in simpler language (e.g., avoiding passive case, simpler vocabulary, simple, declarative sentences conveying one concept at a time, etc.). The material can also be modified to present more of it in diagrams or labeled pictures, etc. Presenting the Social Studies material at a reading level closer to Patrick's reading level will reduce his frustration and help keep him on task while ensuring he gets the same curriculum as his fellow students.

When Patrick is completing the written work for the lesson, he should be able to identify the section (based on subheadings) where the information will likely be found. This would be easier to do in a text selection that has been modified as described above, or one that is written closer to his reading level. Then a teacher or aide can read the section as Patrick follows to find the needed answer. Patrick should be encouraged to reread his answers to make sure they make sense in context.

The format of the written work could be modified. Matching activities could be rewritten with A-B-C-D etc. assigned to each answer choice so that Patrick does not have to write each answer. Instead of writing definitions, he could be given a page with the definitions provided and a list of vocabulary words choices to be filled in. Fill-in-the-blanks could be written with a word box of choices or two choices typed under each blank. The page numbers of where to look for the answers could be written in for each response. Short response questions could provide answer prompts (*give three examples, use first-then, include the name of the person*, etc.). Patrick might be assigned alternate activities to demonstrate his knowledge of a lesson. These could include verbally answering questions or creating a map or other hands-on project. If studying the crops of the Midwest, Patrick could make a poster that contains a cut-out map of the region and hand-drawn pictures of wheat, corn, and soybeans.

Long matching activities could be broken into smaller sets. The length of the written work could be modified. Lengthy fill-in-the-blank paragraphs could be written into shorter paragraphs or even single sentence cloze responses. Items that repeat information (such as vocabulary) could be removed so that Patrick is completing information only once. Patrick could be given the written work in smaller chunks (one part to be done at school, another small section to be completed for homework).

Score Rationale
This response thoroughly addresses curriculum and instructional considerations to meet Patrick's needs (minimizing distractions, modifying the presentation of materials, modifying readability of text, providing alternate instruction types, modifying the format of student work, and offering alternate assignments).

Sample Response B
Score: 2

Patrick should be given recorded books to help address the discrepancy between his reading level and the level of the Social Studies book. Having him listen to the chapters on a CD should make up for the reading problem. A videotape on the topic being studied (the Midwest) could also provide Patrick with information.

Patrick could answer the questions on the worksheets out loud for a teacher or aide. He might complete a project on the Midwest to show what he has learned. He could pick one of the subheadings from the book for his topic: *Weather in the Midwest, Midwest Crops, Employment in the Midwest.*

Students with PDD become easily overwhelmed. A worksheet packet with three pages is too long for Patrick. Choose only the page with the most important information for him to complete.

Score Rationale

This response includes some appropriate modifications and accommodations for Patrick. Recorded textbooks can be helpful, but the use of additional strategies should be included. Also, choosing to simply eliminate two of the worksheets could cut valuable information. A more careful assessment of what to leave in the written work should be made. The worksheet may need to be rewritten to include the most critical information from all three of the pages.

Sample Response C
Score: 1

Patrick's reading level makes it impossible for him to use the fourth grade textbook. He can stay in the inclusion class to hear the lessons, but he should not be required to complete the same written work.

Purchase an activity book from a teacher supply store on the same topic. Try to find reproducible worksheets that match the topics of the lessons. Cross out the ones that do not apply.

Score Rationale

This response does not include enough explanation of material and assignment modifications or accommodations. In addition, choosing a book from the teacher supply store to use in place of the school's curriculum can create further gaps in Patrick's skills and knowledge as compared to his peers in the general education curriculum.

Sample Response D
Score: 0

Patrick could also use a second grade book from the same publisher for Social Studies. If he cannot read the fourth grade material, he is not ready to understand the concepts in the fourth grade classroom.

Score Rationale

Using the second grade book from the same publisher will not give Patrick the same information that his fourth grade peers are receiving. Although his reading skills are lower than his peers, that is not necessarily a reflection on his ability to understand the fourth grade concepts. Refer to Response A for a thorough explanation of accommodations that could be made for Patrick.

References

Adams, G. L. (2000) *Comprehensive Test of Adaptive Behavior—Revised.* Seattle, WA: Educational Achievement Systems.

Ager, C. L. & Cole, C. L. (1991). A Review of Cognitive-behavioral Interventions for Children and Adolescents with Behavioral Disorders. *Behavioral Disorders, 16* (4), 260-275.

Allsopp, D., Kyger, M. M., & Lovin, L. H. (2007). *Teaching Mathematics Meaningfully: Solutions for reaching struggling learners.* Baltimore, MD: Brookes Publ.

American Association on Intellectual and Developmental Disabilities. (2010). *Intellectual Disability: Definition, classification, and systems of supports* (11th ed.). Washington, DC: American Association on Intellectual and Developmental Disabilities.

Balla, D. A., Cicchetti, D. V., & Sparrow, S. S. (2005). *Vineland Adaptive Behavior Scales II.* Circle Pines, MN: American Guidance Service.

Banks, J. A., & McGee Banks, C. A. (1993). *Multicultural Education* (2nd ed.). Boston: Allyn and Bacon.

Baratta-Lorton, M. (1978) *Mathematics Their Way.* Menlo Park, CA: Addison-Wesley.

Barrett, T. C. (1968). What is Reading? Some current concepts. In H. M. Robinson (ed.) *Innovation and Change in Reading Instruction: The sixteenth handbook of the National Society for the Study of Education.* Chicago: The University of Chicago Press.

Bley, N. S. & Thornton, C. A. (2001). *Teaching Mathematics to Students with Disabilities* (4th ed.). Austin, TX: Pro-ed.

Bloom, B. S. (1956). Taxonomy of Educational Objectives, Handbook I: The cognitive domain. New York: David McKay Co. Inc.

Brodesky, Amy R., et al. (2004). Planning Strategies for Students with Special Needs: A professional development activity. *Teaching Children Mathematics, 11,* 146-54.

Brown, R. (1973). *A First Language: The early stages.* London: George Allen & Unwin Ltd.

Bruininks, R. H., et al. (1996) *Scales of independent Behavior—Revised.* Chicago: Riverside Publishing.

Caine, R. N., et al. (2005). *12 Brain/Mind Learning Principles in Action: The fieldbook for making connections, teaching, and the human brain.* Thousand Oaks, CA: Corwin Press.

Cartwright, G. P., Cartwright, C. A., & Ward, M. E. (1984). *Educating Special Learners* (2nd ed.). Belmont, CA: Wadsworth.

Clark, G. M. (1994). Is a Functional Curriculum Approach Compatible with an Inclusive Education Model? *Teaching Exceptional Children*, 26 (2), 36-39.

Coles, G. S. (1989). Excerpts from the Learning Mystique: A critical look at disabilities. *Journal of Learning Disabilities,* 22 (5), 267-278.

Council for Exceptional Children. (2003). *What Every Special Educator Must Know: The ethics, standards, and guidelines for special educators.* Arlington, VA: Council for Exceptional Children.

Craig, E., & Craig, L. (1990). *Reading in the Content Areas.* Videocassette & manual series. Northbrook, IL: Hubbard Scientific Company.

Cummins, J. (1994). The Acquisition of English as a Second Language. In K. Spangenberg-Urbschat & Robert Pritchard, *Kids Come in all Languages.* Newark, DE: International Reading Association.

Cummins, J. (1999). *BICS and CALP: Clarifying the distinction.* ERIC Document 438551.

Deno, E. (1970). Special Education as Developmental Capital. *Exceptional Children,* 37 (3), 229-237.

Drummond, R.J. (2000). *Appraisal Procedures for Counselors and Helping Professionals.* (4th ed.). Englewood Cliffs, NJ: Merrill/Prentice Hall.

Duke, N. K., Bennett-Armistead, V. S., & Roberts, E. M. (2002). Incorporating Information Text in the Primary Grades. In C. Roller (ed.), *Comprehensive Reading Instruction across Grade Levels* (pp. 40-54). Newark, DE: International Reading Association.

ERIC Clearinghouse on Disabilities and Gifted Education. (1993). *Including Students with Disabilities in General Education Classrooms.* ERIC digest #E521. Reston, VA: ERIC Clearinghouse on Disabilities and Gifted Education. ERIC Document 358677.

Diagnostic and Statistical Manual of Mental Disorders: DSM-IV-TR (4th ed.). Washington, DC: American Psychiatric Association.

Ekwall, E. E., & Shanker, J. L. (1983). *Diagnosis and Remediation of the Disabled Reader* (2nd ed.). Boston: Allyn and Bacon.

Espinosa, L. M. (1995). *Hispanic Parent Involvement in Early Childhood Programs.* Urbana, IL: ERIC Clearinghouse on Elementary and Early Childhood Education, University of Illinois. ERIC Document 382412.

Flippo, R. F. (2002). *Reading Assessment and Instruction: A qualitative approach to diagnosis.* Portsmouth, NH: Heinemann.

Fuchs, D., & Deno, S. L. (1992). Effects of Curriculum within Curriculum-based Measurement. *Exceptional Children 58,* 232-242.

Fuchs, D., & Fuchs, L. S. (1989). Effects of Examiner Familiarity on Black, Caucasian, and Hispanic Children: A meta-analysis. *Exceptional Children, 55,* 303-308.

Gardner, H. (1999). *Intelligence Reframed: Multiple intelligences for the 21st century.* New York: Basic Books.

Gleason, J. B. (1993). *The Development of Language* (3rd ed.). New York: Macmillan Publishing.

Goddard, H. H. (1912). *The Kallikak family: A study in the heredity of feeblemindedness.* New York: The Macmillan Company.

Hallahan, D. P. & Kauffman, J. M. (1994). *Exceptional Children: Introduction to special education* (6th ed.). Boston: Allyn and Bacon.

Halpern, A. S.; Benz, M. R., & Lindstrom, L. (1991). *A Systems Change Approach to Improving Secondary Special Education and Transition Programs at the Local Community Level.* Eugene: University of Oregon.

Harrison, P. L. & Oakland, T. (2003). *Adaptive Behavior Assessment System.* San Antonio, TX: Psychological Corporation.

Hatfield, M. M., Edwards, N. T., Bitter, G. G., & Morrow, J. (2005). *Mathematics Methods for Elementary and Middle School Teachers* (5th ed.). New York: Wiley.

Henley, M., Ramsey,R. S., & Algozzine, B. (1993). *Characteristics of and Strategies for Teaching Students with Mild Disabilities.* Boston: Allyn and Bacon.

International Reading Association. (1997). *The Role of Phonics in Reading Instruction: A positional statement of the International Reading Association.* Newark, DE: International Reading Association.

International Reading Association. (1981). *Resolution on Misuse of Grade Equivalents.* Newark, DE: International Reading Association.

Ireton, H., & Ireton, H. (1992). *Child Development Inventory.* Minneapolis, MN: Behavior Science Systems.

Johnson, D. W. (1972) *Reaching Out: Interpersonal effectiveness and self-actualization.* Englewood Cliffs, NJ: Prentice-Hall.

Johnson, D. W. (1978) *Human Relations and Your Career: A guide to interpersonal skills.* Englewood Cliffs, NJ: Prentice-Hall.

Johnson, D. W., & Johnson, R. T. (1990). Social Skills for Successful Group Work. *Educational Leadership, 47* (4), 29-33.

Johnson, S. W., & Morasky, R. L. (1977) *Learning Disabilities* (2nd ed.). Boston: Allyn and Bacon.

Katsiyannis, A. and Maag, J. (1997). Ensuring Appropriate Education: Emerging remedies, litigation, compensation, and other legal considerations. *Exceptional Children, 63,* 451-462.

Kirk, S. A., & Gallagher, J. J. (1986). *Educating Exceptional Children* (5th ed.). Boston: Houghton Mifflin.

Lambie, R. A. (1980). A Systematic Approach for Changing Materials, Instruction, and Assignments to Meet Individual Needs. *Focus on Exceptional Children, 13* (1), 1-12.

Lavoie, R. (2005). *Social Skill Autopsies: A strategy to promote and develop social competencies.* Retrieved from *http://www.ldonline.org/article/Social_Skill_Autopsies%3A_A_Strategy_to_Promote_and_Develop_Social_Competencies.*

Lund, N. J., & Duchan, J. F. (1988). *Assessing Children's Language in Naturalist Contexts.* Englewood Cliffs, NJ: Prentice Hall.

Male, M. (1994) *Technology for Inclusion: Meeting the special needs of all children.* (2nd ed.). Boston: Allyn and Bacon.

Mannix, D. (1993). *Social Skills for Special Children.* West Nyack, NY: The Center for Applied Research in Education.

Marston, D. B. (1989) A Curriculum-based Measurement Approach to Assessing Academic Performance: What it is and why do it. In M. Shinn (ed.). *Curriculum-Based Measurement: Assessing Special Children.* New York: Guilford Press.

Mastropieri, M. A. & Scruggs, T. E. (2000). *The Inclusive Classroom: Strategies for effective instruction.* Upper Saddle River, NJ: Merrill-Prentice Hall.

McGinnis, E., Goldstein, A. P. (1990). *Skill Streaming in Early Childhood: Teaching prosocial skills to the preschool and kindergarten child.* Champaign, IL: Research Press.

Mercer, C. D. (1987). *Students with Learning Disabilities* (3rd ed.). Merrill Publishing.

Mercer, C. D., & Mercer, A. R. (1985). *Teaching Children with Learning Problems* (2nd ed.). Columbus, OH: Charles E. Merrill.

Morsink, C. V., Thomas, C. C., & Correa, V. L. (1991). *Interactive Teaming, Consultation and Collaboration in Special Programs.* New York: MacMillan.

National Association of Special Education Teachers. (December 2006). *Collaboration between General and Special Education: Making it Work.* NASET Special Educator e-Journal. Retrieved March 26, 2010 from *http://www.naset.org/2401.0.html.*

National Association of Special Education Teachers. (2008). *Characteristics of Children with Learning Disabilities.* LD Report, 3. Retrieved August 17, 2010 from *http://www.naset.org/2555.0.html.* Full text available only to NASET members.

National Council of Teachers of Mathematics. (2005). *Principles and Standards for School Mathematics.* Reston, VA: National Council of Teachers of Mathematics.

National Reading Panel. *Teaching Children to Read: An evidence-based assessment of the scientific research literature on reading and its implications for reading instruction: Reports of the subgroups.* ERIC Document 444127.

Newcomer, P. L. (1993). *Understanding and Teaching Emotionally Disturbed Children and Adolescents.* Austin, TX: Pro-Ed.

Notari-Syverson, A., & Losardo, A. (2001). *Alternative Approaches to Assessing Young Dhildren.* Baltimore: Paul H. Brookes Publishing Co.

Phillips, V., & Mccullough, L. (1990). Consultation-based Programming: Instituting the Collaborative Work Ethic. *Exceptional Children, 56* (4), 291-304.

Pierangelo, R., & Giuliani, G. A. (2007). *EDM: The Educator's Diagnostic Manual of Disabilities and Disorders.* San Francisco, CA: Jossey-Bass.

Polloway, E. A., Patton, J. R., Payne, J. S., & Payne, R. A. (1989). *Strategies for Teaching Learners with Special Needs* (4th ed.). Columbus, OH: Merrill Publishing.

Reid, D. K. (1988). *Teaching the Learning Disabled: A Cognitive Developmental Approach.* Boston: Allyn & Bacon.

Roberts, P., & Kellough, R. D. (1991). *A Resource Guide for Elementary School Teaching: Planning for Competence*. New York: Macmillan.

Robinson, G. A., Patton, J. R., Polloway, E. A., & Sargent, L. R. (eds.). (1989). *Best Practices in Mental Disabilities*. Renton, VA: The Division on Mental Retardation of the Council for Exceptional Children.

Salend, S. J. & Lutz, J. G. (1984). Mainstreaming or Mainlining: A Competency Based Approach to Mainstreaming. *Journal of learning disabilities, 17* (1), 27-29.

Salvia, J. & Ysseldyke, J. E. (1995). *Assessment* (6th ed.). Boston: Houghton Mifflin.

Schloss, P. J., & Sedlak, R. A. (1986). *Instructional Methods for Students with Learning and Behavior Problems*. Boston: Allyn and Bacon.

Schloss, P. J., Harriman, N., & Pfiefer, K. (1985). Application of a sequential prompt reduction technique to the independent composition performance of behaviorally disordered youth. *Behavioral Disorders, 11,* 17-23.

Séguin, E.-C., & Séguin, E.-O. (1866). *Idiocy and its Treatment by the Physiological Method*. New York: W. Wood.

Shannon, G. (1994). *More Stories to Solve: Fifteen folktales from around the world*. New York: Beech Tree Paperback Books.

Smith, D. D., & Luckasson, R. (1992). *Introduction to Special Education: Teaching in an Age of Challenge*. Boston: Allyn and Bacon.

Tomlinson, Carol A. (1995). *How to Differentiate Instruction in Mixed-Ability Classrooms*. Alexandria, VA: Association for Supervision and Curriculum Development.

Torgesen, J. K., & Wagner, R. K. (1998). Alternative Diagnostic Approaches for Specific Developmental Reading Disabilities. *Learning Disabilities Research and Practice, 13,* 4, 220-32.

U. S. Department of Education. (1993). *To assure the free appropriate public education of all children with disabilities: Fifteenth annual report to Congress on the Implementation of the Individuals with Disabilities Education Act*. Washington, D. C.

U. S. Department of Education. (1998). *Early Warning, Timely Response: A guide to safe schools*. Washington, DC: U. S. Dept. of Education.

U. S. Office of Special Education and Rehabilitative Services. (1985-). *Annual report to Congress on the implementation of the Education of the Handicapped Act*. Washington, D. C.: U. S. Dept. of Education, U. S. Office of Special Education and Rehabilitative Services.

Warger, Cynthia. *Helping students with disabilities participate in standards-based mathematics curriculum*. Arlington, VA: Eric Clearinghouse on Disabilities and Gifted Education, 2002. ERIC Document 468579.

Watson, J. B. & Rayner, R. (1920). Conditioned Emotional Reactions. *Journal of Experimental Psychology, 3,* 1, 1-14.

Resources

Autism Society of America
7910 Woodmont Avenue, Suite 300
Bethesda, MD 20814
www.autism-society.org Tel: (800) 328-8476
Open to all who support the mission of ASA. Mission: To increase public awareness about autism and the day-to-day issues faced by individuals with autism, their families, and the professionals with whom they interact. The Society and its chapters share a common mission of providing information and education, supporting research, and advocating for programs and services for the autism community.

Brain Injury Association of America
8201 Greensboro Drive, Suite 611
McLean, VA 22102
http://www.biausa.org Tel: (703) 761-0750
Open to all: Provides information, education, and support to assist the 5.3 million Americans currently living with traumatic brain injury and their families.

Child and Adolescent Bipolar Association (CABF)
1187 Wilmette Ave. P.M.B. #331
Wilmette, IL 60091
http://www.bpkids.org
Physicians, scientific researchers, and allied professionals (therapists, social workers, educators, attorneys, and others) who provide services to children and adolescents with bipolar disorder or do research on the topic: Educates families, professionals, and the public about pediatric bipolar disorder; connects families with resources and support; advocates for and empowers affected families; and supports research on pediatric bipolar disorder and its cure.

Children and Adults with Attention Deficit/Hyperactive Disorder (CHADD)
8181 Professional Place, Suite 150
Landover, MD 20785
www.chadd.org Tel: (301) 306-7070/Fax: (301) 306-7090
Email: national@chadd.org
Open to all: Provides resources and encouragement to parents, educators, and professionals on a grassroots level through CHADD chapters.

Council for Exceptional Children
1110 N. Glebe Road, Suite 300
Arlington, VA 22201
www.cec.sped.org Tel: (888) 232-7733/TTY: (866) 915-5000/Fax: (703) 264-9494
Teachers, administrators, teacher educators, and related service personnel. Mission: Advocate for services for disabled and gifted individuals. It is a professional organization that addresses service, training, and research relative to exceptional persons. CEC has many divisions available at the same location, including: Children with Behavioral Disorders, Educational Diagnostic Services, Administrators of Special Education, Children with Communication Disorders, Division for Early Childhood, Physically Handicapped, Visually Handicapped, Career Development, and Mental Retardation.

Epilepsy Foundation of America
8301 Professional Place
Landover, MD 20785
www.epilepsyfoundation.org Tel: (800) 332-1000
A non-membership organization: Works to ensure that people with seizures are able to participate in all life experiences; and to prevent, control, and cure epilepsy through research, education, advocacy, and services.

Family Center on Technology and Disability (FCTD)
1825 Connecticut Avenue, NW, 7th Floor
Washington, DC 20009
http://www.fctd.info Tel: (202) 884-8068/Fax: (202) 884-8441
Email: fctd@aed.org
Non member association: A resource designed to support organizations and programs that work with families of children and youth with disabilities.

Hands and Voices
P.O. Box 371926
Denver, CO 80237
www.handsandvoices.org Tel: (866) 422-0422
Email:parentadvocate@handsandvoices.org
Families, professionals, other organizations, pre-service students, and deaf and hard of hearing adults who are all working towards ensuring successful outcomes for children who are deaf and hard of hearing: Supporting families and their children who are deaf or hard of hearing, as well as the professionals who serve them.

The International Dyslexia Association
Chester Building, Suite 382
8600 LaSalle Road
Baltimore, MD 21286
http://www.interdys.org Tel: (410) 296-0232/Fax: (410) 321-5069
Anyone interested in IDA and its mission can become a member: Provides information and referral services, research, advocacy, and direct services to professionals in the field of learning disabilities.

Learning Disabilities Association of America
4156 Library Road
Pittsburgh, PA 15234
http://www.ldanatl.org Tel: (412) 341-1515/Fax: (412) 344-0224
Anyone interested in LDA and its mission can become a member: Provides cutting-edge information on learning disabilities, practical solutions, and a comprehensive network of resources. Provides support to people with learning disabilities, their families, teachers, and other professionals.

National Association of the Deaf (NAD)
8630 Fenton Street, Suite 820
Silver Spring, MD 20910-3819
http://nad.org Tel: (301) 587-1788/TTY: (301) 587-1789/Fax: (301) 587-1791
Email: NADinfo@nad.org

Anyone interested in NAD and its mission can become a member: To promote, protect, and preserve the rights and quality of life of deaf and hard of hearing individuals in the United States of America.

The National Association of Special Education Teachers
1201 Pennsylvania Avenue, NW, Suite 300
Washington, DC 20004
Tel: (800) 754-4421/Fax: (800) 424-0371
Email: contactus@naset.org
Special education teachers: To render all possible support and assistance to professionals who teach children with special needs. To promote standards of excellence and innovation in special education research, practice, and policy in order to foster exceptional teaching for exceptional children.

National Mental Health Information Center
P.O. Box 42557
Washington, DC 20015
http://www.mentalhealth.samhsa.gov Tel: (800) 789-2647
Government Agency: Developed for users of mental health services and their families, the general public, policy makers, providers, and the media.

National Dissemination Center for Children with Disabilities (NIHCY)
P.O. Box 1492
Washington, DC 20013
Tel: (800) 695-0285/Fax: (202) 884-8441
Email: nichcy@aed.org
Non membership association. A central source of information on:
- disabilities in infants, toddlers, children, and youth
- IDEA, which is the law authorizing special education
- No Child Left Behind (as it relates to children with disabilities)
- research-based information on effective educational practices

Office of Special Education and Rehabilitative Services
US Department of Education
http://www.ed.gov/about/offices/list/osers/index.html
Government resource: Committed to improving results and outcomes for people with disabilities of all ages.

Wrights Law
http://wrightslaw.com
Email: webmaster@wrightslaw.com
Non membership organization: Parents, educators, advocates, and attorneys come to Wrights Law for accurate, reliable information about special education law, education law, and advocacy for children with disabilities.

TASH (Formerly The Association for Persons with Severe Handicaps)
29 W. Susquehanna Ave., Suite 210
Baltimore, MD 21204
www.tash.org Tel: (410) 828-8274/Fax: (410) 828-6706

Anyone interested in TASH and its mission can become a member. Mission: To create change and build capacity so that all people, no matter their perceived level of disability, are included in all aspects of society.

American Psychological Association
750 First Street, NE
Washington, DC 20002-4242
www.apa.org Tel: (800) 374-2721 or (202) 336-5500/TTY: (202) 336-6123
Psychologists and professors of Psychology: A scientific and professional society working to improve mental health services and to advocate for legislation and programs that will promote mental health, facilitate research, and professional development.

Association for Children and Adults with Learning Disabilities
4156 Library Road
Pittsburgh, PA 15234
http://www.acldonline.org
Parents of children with learning disabilities and interested professionals: Advancing the education and general well-being of children with adequate intelligence who have learning disabilities arising from perceptual, conceptual, or subtle coordinative problems, sometimes accompanied by behavior difficulties.

The Arc of the United States (Formerly the National Association of Retarded Citizens)
1010 Wayne Avenue
Suite 650
Silver Springs, MD 20910
www.thearc.org Tel: (301) 565-3842/Fax: (301) 565-3843
Parents, professionals, and others interested in individuals with mental retardation: Works on local, state, and national levels to promote treatment, research, public understanding, and legislation for persons with mental retardation; provides counseling for parents of students with mental retardation.